BERNARD BROGAN

THE HILL

BERNARD BROGAN

THE HILL

WITH KIERAN SHANNON

Reach Sport

www.reachsport.com

This book is dedicated to Donagh and Keadán,

My only wish is for your happiness.

Hold your dreams close, chase them with an endless passion and know that with hard work, belief, grit and determination you'll get there.

Reach Sport

www.reachsport.com

Written with Kieran Shannon.

Paperback edition published in 2021.
Hardback edition first published in 2020 by Reach Sport,
5 St Paul's Square, Liverpool, L3 9SJ.

www.reachsport.com
@reach_sport

Reach Sport is a part of Reach plc.
One Canada Square, Canary Wharf, London, E15 5AP.

With thanks to Gill Hess Ltd.

Hardback ISBN: 9781910335956
Paperback ISBN: 9781914197062
Ebook ISBN: 9781911613145

Photographic acknowledgements:
Bernard Brogan personal collection, Sportsfile, Inpho, Tony Woolliscroft.

Printed and bound by CPI Group (UK) Ltd,
Croydon, CR0 4YY.

Contents

Acknowledgements

I'D like to take this chance to thank some of the amazing people I have in my life. Firstly I'd like to start with Mam and Dad who provided such a loving and supportive home life for us, for backing us in everything we do and always being there when we need them most. Also my brothers Alan and Paul: Alan who inspired us and always led the way in such a humble and understated way; Paul who is the glue of the family, hard on the outside and soft in the middle, always making time for his family and showing us what really matters.

To Keira: my wife, for your love, care and friendship ever since we were kids and for the amazing family we are so lucky to have now. I am forever grateful for your support and patience to allow me to fulfil my dreams. To my brother-in-law Colin for his warmth of friendship and his guidance and care of the twins; Liz and Martin without whom we would be lost, especially during the Covid period, selfless and caring. You have always welcomed me as part of your family.

To my good pals and contributors to the book: Ross McConnell, Declan Lally, Paul Flynn, Éamon Fennell, David Whelan. And to my pals at home who have been by my side all along my amazing journey: Cush, Jude, McQuaid, O'Reilly, Moro, Vinny, Dayla, Quigley, Mo, cousin William and my good pal McCann who is no longer with us and his constant advice to 'Go for the Gap'.

To the teams in Legacy and PepTalk for giving me purpose every day and your support; to Alan Clancy for bringing me on an exciting journey into the pub business and continuing to teach me the ropes.

To my cousins the Curries who have hosted the family BBQ in Phibsborough. Since Alan started in 2002 it has connected our wider family like no other through our love of GAA and allowed the family to share in the special times together. To all the Brogans for their support and passion for Dublin GAA, and my family from Kerry and Mayo who always had our back even if they didn't always want the Blues to win.

To Jim, Pat and Pillar for giving me the chance to live my dream, for your guidance, the life lessons and values you taught me. Also the Dublin county board for continued support to allow the team to be the best they can be. All the individuals on the management and medical teams I was lucky enough to soldier with over the years: you are the unsung heroes of the journey who made every session a joy to be involved with.

To Kieran Shannon for writing the book with me and investing so much of yourself and expertise into this project. I will be forever grateful to you and have made a friend for life. To your wife Ann Marie and children Aimee and Andrew for sharing their dad and husband with me for so long. To Tommy Conlon for his craftsmanship in reviewing the manuscript; Harry Casey for his keen eye; Roy Gilfoyle, our copy editor, for being such a pro and gent; Paul Dove and Reach Sport for their support and providing the platform for the book; Simon Hess of Gill Hess for making the book happen and teaming us all up together; and to Declan Heeney, also of Gill Hess, for his promotion and support on the ground.

To Plunkett's for developing my love for the game and portraying the values I hold dear and doing it the right way. The lads, the craic and the bond fuelled my ambition and I look forward to more in years to come.

To the Hill and Dublin fans everywhere for the energy and love you have given me over the years and for sticking with the team through thick and thin, rain, hail or snow.

And finally to the players over the last fifteen years: for me it was all about the friendships and bonds we built, the memories we made which live in my heart forever.

'All in'.

1

Innisfails

February 8, 2018

EVERY YEAR UNDER JIM THIS IS WHERE IT STARTS. And for me, after tonight, maybe where it all ends.

Innisfails wouldn't be one of those illustrious names normally associated with Dublin GAA, hidden away in the junior ranks on the fringes of the city, out in that no-man's land between the airport and the concrete sprawl. Their grounds would hardly be the most glamorous either.

For team meetings we retreat to the small, old clubhouse. Punters could still be finishing their pints and playing pool while Jim and the management are setting up the projector in a side room. Sometimes we've even all squeezed into that bar area and held the meeting there, with lads sitting up on the pool table as Jim has gone through the game plan for the next day.

In the dressing rooms we use plug-in electric heaters to generate some warmth. A nail hammered into a plank of wood qualifies as your clothes hook. The concrete walls sport the club colours of green and black but it's been some time since they last got a coat of paint. The club's junior team train on the pitch next to us, and as they usually finish up before us, sometimes there's no hot water left by the time we hit the showers. As for the pitch, its sand base means it has been among the most durable in the county at this time of the season but in recent years it's been peppered with rabbit holes, prompting the club to surround it with a meshed wired fence.

For Jim though, it's ideal. The place has lights, the pitch is never waterlogged, and the club are always welcoming, from its officers to the lads on the junior team who we have some banter with on our way in. After the league final we'll return to the relative comfort of DCU and the Bunker in St Clare's, but when there's a real chill to the wind and rain, when frost fringes the grass, when you've to blow into your hands and dance on your toes and huddle up close to shield yourself from the elements, out here in Balgriffin is our base, our home.

It's been good to us, it's been good for us. We've won four national leagues out here with hopefully more to come, and we've gone on to win four All Irelands as well, including the last three. Our main challengers may already be meeting up and training away in their county grounds or custom-made centres of excellence but at this time of the year Jim wants our training environment to be more Rocky Balboa than Ivan Drago. So this is where we pull sleighs, hoist rocks, chop wood. This is our Siberia.

As someone with a couple of young businesses, I'm big into looking up how to develop talent and the right culture, and the Jim Gavin that I know – although how much I or any of the lads really know Jim Gavin is open to question – would also be into reading up on all that in books by the likes of Daniel Coyle, Rasmus Ankersen, James Kerr. A few years ago Jim even established a team library in the Bunker, putting up a shelf in the dressing room full of books on leadership. *Extreme Ownership*, by a couple of US Navy Seals, I found particularly powerful, and I suspect from how he reacted to our only championship defeat on his beat, Jim read it too. We still have an active book club, only now it extends to podcasts, with Kevin McManamon, Jonny Cooper and Michael Darragh Macauley regularly making recommendations. And what you learn from material like this is that often the grittier and grimmer a place is, the better. A kid in a Premier League academy might subliminally think he's already arrived, rocking up into a state-of-the-art training facility in a taxi or sports car, only for you never to hear of him. Comfort can lead to complacency.

Jim doesn't allow or tolerate that. Think you're a big man, being called up to train with the Dubs and can now swan around the plush Gibson Hotel the day of a match in Croker? Think you've done everything with your All Stars and your All Irelands, coming off another team holiday in the sun? Innisfails never fails to keep you grounded. By keeping it simple, spartan, it keeps us humble, hungry.

Driving in here this Thursday night, just past the austere gates of Balgriffin Cemetery, I'm ravenous, chomping. There was no team holiday for me this past winter, I passed on it, mainly because I was passed over for a starting spot all through the 2017 championship. I got no game time at all in the All Ireland semi-final dismantling of Tyrone and only the last ten minutes of another one-point final win over Mayo. So while the rest of the lads were in South Africa, on the piss and on safari, taking in the splendour of Cape Town and the Garden Route just like myself and Keira did on our honeymoon twelve months earlier, I was at home: pumping and sweating it out in an altitude chamber in Castleknock and kicking a bag full of balls out in Westmanstown.

I wanted that head-start because I seemed to be always playing catch-up last season. We had a Christmas wedding, a fantastic day down in Kilkenny, and though I kept ticking over in the gym on the honeymoon and was back training with the group by early February, it wasn't like I could walk straight back onto a team like ours. I'd to wait until our sixth league game for my first start, when I kicked three points from play against Roscommon. Then in our last round-robin game, I came off the bench at halftime up in Clones to grab a goal before Jack McCaffrey pounced for another in injury time to extend our unbeaten run to a record thirty-six games. I got the start the following week in the league final against Kerry but when three consecutive balls were kicked in over my head, it was as if Jim decided I was no longer a starter.

I tried everything to change his mind but I couldn't. I was flying in training the month leading into our opening championship game against Carlow below in Portlaoise, but Jim saw it as a chance to try a couple of young lads. Neither Con O'Callaghan nor Niall Scully had started in that one-point league final loss to Kerry, but both were promoted to the starting fifteen for the Carlow game while I was relegated to the bench. And fair play to the two lads, they grasped their chance and never let go of the jersey. I came on alright shortly after halftime that evening to kick a couple of points and the same again the following day against Westmeath but that wasn't long enough of a runway for me to properly take off for the year.

I thought things might change with the Leinster final when I came on against Kildare after Dean Rock was black-carded and kicked five points from play. But I was again left out of the starting fifteen for the All Ireland quarter-final against Monaghan, and I found out the same way as everyone else, in the circle before the start of training on the Thursday night.

I was annoyed about that. Normally Jim would take aside a player who had started the previous day or a senior player who'd have reason to think he might be on. He'd afforded me that courtesy before the 2016 All Ireland final replay when I was dropped for the first time ever in championship but he hadn't extended it to me in 2017.

I brought it up with him when we met at my request before Christmas in the Westin Hotel, just off O'Connell Bridge and around the corner from where he works with the Irish Aviation Authority. I needed to know before I committed for another year: Did he want me back? Did he see a space for me? And he needed to know why I wasn't happy with some aspects of 2017, like that episode before the Monaghan game.

'Jim, I felt disrespected. I come on and kick five points in the Leinster final, and you don't think to tell me in advance that I'm not starting the next day?'

I haven't challenged Jim like that before but I felt I owed it to myself to speak my mind. And I also think sometimes Jim likes for you to have a hard conversation with him, that it shows that you're still passionate and not passive about all this.

Looking back, there were times over the years when I probably could have pushed back at managers more. Under Paul 'Pillar' Caffrey, I had to wait until the third game of my third summer on the panel for a championship start, and the match just prior to it for even my first appearance off the bench. I was twenty-three by then. In years like 2005, and especially 2006, I sat and watched more senior players being favoured ahead of me when I felt I was going better than them in training; Pillar's regime was the opposite of Jim's that way. I tried to stick to the old formula of just letting my football do the talking, thinking that should have been enough. But maybe I'd have been better off asking him what more I needed to do to get game-time. It would have put the ball back in his court and let him know I wasn't happy with just being there.

In the Westin, I told Jim, 'I think I've still got a lot to add. I feel fit, I feel strong, I feel like I can offer something different than forwards who are there. But you have to give me the same opportunity as you'd give a young lad who's just come in. Con O'Callaghan plays well in training and he gets to start the next day. But that doesn't happen with me because you've seen me for ten years, so you think, "Yeah, he's moving well but sure I know what he can do; I'll only need him for twenty minutes in this game." If I'm playing as well as anyone in training, you have to play me. And if I'm not playing well in the match, then take me off! But you can't have one rule for a young lad and another rule for an older guy. That's ageism!'

I laughed saying that last bit, prompting Jim to smile too. Fair point, he nodded.

With those couple of businesses of my own, I sometimes try to see things from the viewpoints of others, such as one of my employees, or a leader like Jim. Everything he does is with the team's best interests at heart; you can't dispute that or his record. But when you're the head of a group of people, you can't always spot what the person on the ground does. So that meeting in the Westin was a chance to relay how things looked from my perspective.

'All I'm asking is that if I come back, you give me as fair a chance as you'd give a Brian Howard or Niall Scully or a Collie Basquel. Whoever's going best in training, then they're the man for the team.'

And to Jim's credit, that's the approach he has taken with me so far this year. He's going on how I'm moving in training and he now has a better understanding of how I view things. That I feel that I play my best football when I'm playing more football, right from the start of the league straight through to the summer, building momentum, building confidence. The other week he told me with a grin that when he picked me to start in our opening league game, against Kildare in Croker, he initially got some grief from Declan Darcy, his long-serving selector: Why the hell are we playing Bernard at this time of year? We should be minding him! He'd to explain to Declan then about the grief I'd given him in the Westin.

I went well in that Kildare game. Showed real intent, real desire. I was annoyed I didn't stick my own goal chance away – I always preach to keep it low yet I struck it too high – but I set up both our goals, quickly flicking the ball off to Dean Rock and then to Brian Fenton as they each made a dash towards goal.

It's something I've tried to bring into my game the past twelve months – to be more of a provider and link more of the play. I thought I was doing it a good bit in training last year, opening up gaps and putting teammates through on goal, but I didn't seem to get much credit for it. But when you do it in actual games, it's more noticed. It's videoed, reviewed, dissected, by management and pundits.

A few days after the Kildare game, I came across my old teacher in St Declan's and partner in crime, Senan Connell, on eir Sport with another, more recently-retired comrade, Denis Bastick, and they did a segment highlighting my role in our two goals and how my game has evolved.

And it has evolved. I've realised that I need to bring something different to my game and to our forward unit. Rather than just looking to burn my man and kick it over the bar, like in the clip they showed of me going on the outside of Marc Ó Sé to point off my left in the 2013 All Ireland semi-final, there can be more value in showing a bit of guile and unlocking the defence with a pass to a runner coming off you and creating a goal chance.

BERNARD BROGAN

A big word for me now is 'scanning'. Scanning what's around you, even – especially – when you don't have the ball. Seeing past the thing that's right in front of you, like the snooker player planning a few shots ahead, or the quarterback surveying his options before the ball is snapped.

Jason Sherlock, our forwards coach, was excellent at that towards the end of his playing career. Before he ever got a ball, before he even made a run, he could anticipate not just the defender that would be coming towards him but in the corner of his eye spot a potential runner to play the ball over the top to and put through on goal. In some of the psychology I've read up on, they talk about different quadrants of attention: on the X axis you have broad and narrow, on the Y axis, external and internal. Where I'm trying to spend more time is in the broad-external space.

In the Kildare game, Niall Scully played a ball in from the wing towards me in the D. Earlier in my career, my 'attentional style', as they call it, might have been too narrow and even too internal. I wouldn't have had a quick look either side of me, I'd have only been concerned with the relationship between myself and the ball and little else, or maybe carried on an inner dialogue about the possible consequences of getting on that ball or not. But the other night just before Niall put the ball onto his foot, I'd a quick scan around and spotted that Brian Fenton out on the 45 was coming like a train straight down the middle. So instead of trying to catch the ball over-head and then see what play to make, I just ran out and cushioned the ball down to him so he didn't have to break stride before firing it into the net.

It was something similar with Dean's goal sixty seconds earlier. I fell to my knees after breaking down a ball. I could have just grabbed it and tried to get up and kick it over the bar myself, but with that greater sense of awareness, I was able to spot Dean on the burst so I just palm-scooped the ball to him as it bounced.

I'm trying to be more of a fulcrum for the forward line, especially against mass defences. Back at the start of the decade when we were playing the likes of Cork in the big games, football was bliss: my man two yards behind me and forty yards of grass in front for the lads to plop the ball into and for me to then swivel or shimmy and kick it over the bar. Now I'm lucky if I get even a couple of yards of space. But I can still be that pivot inside. Because once I win that ball played over the defensive wall, it forces every defender to turn their heads. They all have to switch their attention towards the ball and onto me, which means they've lost track and sight of the men they were supposed to be directly marking. They're scrambling whereas we've been scanning and next thing we've runners coming from everywhere and I'm putting one of them through on goal – pop, bang.

Tyrone last week would have been a nice game to try that out some more but I was left out for that one as Jim wanted to rotate the forwards and give Paul Mannion and Kevin McManamon their first starts of the year. But just now tonight as we've come out onto the pitch Jim has a quiet word with me.

I'm back in the starting line-up for Saturday night's game against Donegal in Croker. Even better, I'm on the frees as it's Dean's turn to drop out of the starting rotation.

I'm buzzing after hearing that. I haven't taken the frees for Dublin since the day Donegal ambushed us in the 2014 All Ireland semi-final; being entrusted with them again is another little boost for the confidence. Even though it's a light session tonight, just two days out from a game, I'm jumping out of my skin, feeling sharp, mad for ball.

Just before we wrap it up for the night, we go into a four-corners shooting drill; just how a forward likes to finish up heading into a game at the weekend, striking a few balls over the bar. The field is alive with the sound of shouts – Here, Fento! – and the thud of ball meeting boot.

And then it happens.

I shuffle out from my corner as Mannion pings a ball from the 45 for me to run out to and fetch overhead. But as my eyes track its flight and I leap, the ball suddenly becomes a blur, lost in the blazing low floodlights. I shift my upper body, trying to regain sight of the ball, but it skims off my fingertips. And then I come crashing down to earth. My legs aren't aligned from having to adjust in mid-air and my left knee rolls from all the weight heaved onto it.

I pound my fist against the turf and let out a roar that pierces the night air. I've felt this sensation before. Fourteen years ago, while in a heap on Parnells' old pitch in Collinstown, clutching my right cruciate. Jesus, let it not be that again.

Our team doctor, Diarmuid Smith, dashes on and helps me to my feet but I'm able to gingerly make my own way off the field.

As I hobble through the door to the dressing room, I'm met by Paul Flynn, one of my closest friends on the panel.

What happened to you?

I grimace. 'Twisted my knee.'

Paul says what most friends say in a situation like this – Ah, I'm sure you'll be grand, don't worry about it – but later he'll admit to me that my pale face told him something else: Shit, he's after doing something bad here. Normally I make light of a knock. Last week I dislocated my finger blocking Kevin Mc in training (he's so much his own man, he insists even his nickname is Mc, not the customary Mac) and while I was racing through the same door, I passed

Diarmuid Connolly. When Dermo shouted back, asking what was wrong, I smilingly held up the baby finger hanging off me. I'm not smiling now about the knee.

And so, Paul stays back with me, waiting for Dr Smith and Kieran 'Dicey' O'Reilly, one of our physios, to come in and examine the knee.

Dicey pulls it, checking the roll on the outside and inside. I actually don't feel much pain, probably because all the heightened adrenaline is overriding and sedating it. And so, at first, Dicey thinks I've only tweaked the knee. But he wasn't on the pitch when it happened. He didn't see the way I landed or how I instantly reacted. He's working off limited information.

'I definitely felt a roll of something,' I tell him. 'Can we get a scan first thing tomorrow?' Initially Dr Smith doubts it. But then he gets out his phone and within minutes we have a slot for 1.30 tomorrow in the Santry Sports Clinic.

I don't stick around long after that. Darren Daly, one of the most solid citizens of the panel, tells me I'm better off heading away before everyone comes in and asks about the knee. So I skip having a shower and limp upstairs to grab a quick bite, only to end up scraping most of the meal into the bin – my appetite is gone.

On the way out to the car, I meet Jim.

You still okay for Saturday?

I do a Flynner on it: brave face, positive spin. 'Ah yeah, absolutely. Just a scare, I'd say. I get worried when my knee is involved but I'm sure it'll be good for Saturday. Can't wait for it.'

I'm trying to convince myself as much as him. But it has happened before where I've gone for a scan and it has turned out to be nothing. And I'm desperate to play on Saturday night. Make another big statement.

Well, get yourself looked after, he says. Best of luck with it.

'Will do. Cheers.'

But once I get into the car, fear devours hope and I feel like breaking down crying, only I hold off because I want to call Keira first. I don't want to alarm her. She's pregnant.

When I tell her about the knee, she's her usual upbeat self. I'm sure it will be fine, she says. And when I get home, she already has the big bag of ice ready, wrapped in a tablecloth. I put the leg up on the couch, then the ice on the knee, then something on the TV.

But I can't even tell you what we're watching. All I see, staring at that screen, is the abyss, that it's already the closing credits.

The End.

2

War Gaming

SOMETIMES I FEEL LIKE I'M BEING BURIED ALIVE here.

Friday lunchtime at the pristine white Santry Sports Clinic and I think me and the staff here know each other too well at this stage. As I hobble up to the desk on my crutches, Jamie recognises me. I've scanned you before!

'Yeah,' I smile, taking the form she hands me, 'I've been in here a little too often.'

My ankles alone must have been scanned five or six times. There wouldn't be much ligaments left on either of them at this point, with the left one especially still feeling tender.

I had keyhole surgery in early 2012 on this same left knee that's troubling me now and had it scanned again last summer when it felt a bit wobbly but was ultimately fine.

With the club already knocked out, I didn't kick another ball for six months after the 2013 All Ireland final and those two goals against Mayo because my two groins were suffering from osteitis pubis; again, they were scanned here, though I'd eventually undergo the knife in Harley Street in London, the same place the celebs go to get their nose jobs and fake boobs.

Not every injury requires a scan, like when my nose was broken again last year after Paul Flynn opened me up with his head in a tackling drill (it's still a bit bent, come to think of it: where's that number for Harley Street again?). But, in most cases, Santry is my first port of call. For broken fingers. Knees. Ankles. Groins. Shoulders.

Shoulders for me are probably the worst kind of scan. You've to go in head first and as you disappear through that tubed archway, it's as if you're being buried alive. More than once in there I've thought of Una Thurman in that coffin in Kill Bill II, punching her way through the lid and up out of the grave. Get me out of here!

But now I'm so accustomed to the drill, I no longer get squeamish; and anyway, today I've only to go in feet first and up to my hips. I can nearly set my clock to it; three and half minutes in and the almost deafening techno-beat gives way to a different cadence, more like the cackle of an old internet dial-up. So I just lie back, put on my earphones and some Michael Jackson to dilute the droning noise, and count the dots on the ceiling while trying to remain perfectly still.

After twenty minutes it's all done. Before I head out the main entrance, Jamie gives me a disc of the scan, for the record, even though I wouldn't have a clue what I'd be looking at. But she would, and whatever way she looks at me, I suspect she knows something but can't say. But after that momentary pause, she says she'll get that scan across ASAP, and further disguises any hint of alarm with a smile and a best of luck.

I head straight back to work, where I already was first thing this morning. It's a big day for us in PepTalk, one of the two businesses I've founded with my cousin James. We've had this strategy day red-circled for a while. We're just after launching in the UK: in fact yesterday began in London for me before I caught a flight to be back for the session in Innisfails.

As well as our four founders – me, James, HR guru Michelle Fogarty and my old mentor David Clancy – also in the room are our top tech guys Anthony O'Callaghan and Karl Tapley, and our head of client relations, Ailís McSweeney, the former international sprinter who is married to Bryan Cullen, our lead S&C and high performance manager with Dublin.

We're looking at ways of devising as user-friendly a platform and app as possible for our clients. Take a firm like MJ Hudson who'd have been at our lunch in London the night before last. They have a workforce of over five hundred people. Traditionally, a wellbeing company like ours would take maybe fifty or a hundred of them at a time into a room and give a talk about the various resilience skills they could use. But that's a very sporadic, limited and passive form of interaction. With this gamified app we're developing, all five hundred of those employees can track their wellbeing daily. They can take part in fun challenges, share photos and we have pretty cool on-demand content from both local and international experts. We want it to be fun and practical and as engaging as possible.

There are great ideas and a tangible energy firing around the room but a little over an hour after I've come back from Santry, I have to step – or rather limp – out. It's Dicey on the phone.

I gaze out the window at the Liffey meandering through Lucan, still holding out for good news, bracing myself for bad.

Unfortunately, Berno, he says, your concern last night was justified.

According to the technical term in the report he's got back from Santry, I've suffered a 'partial if not complete rupture of the anterior cruciate ligament'.

I actually give a small laugh at first. 'Partial?!' Does that mean it mightn't be that bad? But no. It means I've done my cruciate.

I hobble back into the meeting room and straight away James can tell by me what the diagnosis is. He's done his own cruciate three times. In fact, just the other night at the launch in London, the two of us were talking to Eamon Devlin, an impressive Tyrone man who is the managing partner of MJ Hudson Law, and we took him through the remarkably dodgy family history of the Brogan knee. My dad twisted his in his first season with the Dubs, back in '74, keeping him out of that September's seminal All Ireland breakthrough win; even when he'd get back to win a couple of All Irelands on the field, he'd have to walk sideways up the stairs after matches. My youngest brother Paul, like James, a panellist in our generation's watershed All Ireland triumph of 2011, has also done his cruciate three times. Our cousin Aisling, who has played camogie with Dublin, did her cruciate playing with our club, St Oliver Plunkett's. My father's only sister, Anne, has a son, David who has done it twice, while my uncles Ollie, Aidan and Kevin have been similarly plagued. Even Keira, almost by osmosis or association, has been afflicted by the condition, twice doing her cruciate playing basketball. And now I've done a cruciate for the second time. Christ.

James and Dave tell me to head home. We've covered enough here for one day. And now I have some other appointments to make and people I need to consult with.

THE following morning I'm back out in Santry and maybe out of obligation to the bond his brother Kevin and my father would share from playing with the Dubs back in the seventies, Dr Ray Moran has kindly come in on his day off to talk to me and Keira about my options.

I'm already quite familiar with both of them – surgery or rehab – having talked to both our physios, Dicey and James Allen; and to teammates who've had the same injury – Mick Macauley and Eoghan O'Gara; and by text to other county players – like Colm Cooper and Henry Shefflin. But none of them are surgeons. Ray is, one of the best in the world.

I've been over and back on this the last twenty-four hours. Surgery seems the more sensible, safer option, the same one I chose back in 2004 when the right knee went. But there's something intriguing and alluring about the alternative which the likes of Kieran McGeeney took to return as early as possible to the field: forgo having an operation and instead compensate for the damaged cruciate by growing and strengthening the muscles around the knee through intense rehab. Surgery means a longer lay-off but less risk of breaking down again; rehab involves a quicker return but a higher risk of breaking down again. So the question is: is the rehab option worth the risk?

Eoghan O'Gara tried rehab. Didn't work. James tried it with his second cruciate. Didn't work. When I asked them what they'd go for had they to do it all over again, they both said in a flash they'd go for surgery. Then when I was talking to Michael Darragh, he said I absolutely should do the rehab! It worked for him!

What does Ray think? The stereotype of surgeons is that they just cut you open and ask questions later, but not Ray. He says that over the last twenty years in his job he's been humbled and amazed by the human body. And some of that has come from having seen athletes back performing within a couple of months of doing their cruciate.

I get energy from how candid and open-minded he is but just as Keira and I are walking out, I ask, 'But if I put a gun to your head, which would you say?'

I'd get the operation, he says. Gun to the head. But it's marginal.

BERNARD BROGAN

THE whole country knows about the injury now. Jim didn't mention anything to the media after the lads beat Donegal in Croker last Saturday night, but word filtered out the day before last and now every paper and sports bulletin has had something about it and speculated about my future. At thirty-four in April, is my career over? Can I get back?

Typical Jim, he's already looking at controlling the controllables and planning the various scenarios, or, as he likes to call such an activity, war-gaming. So here at a coffee desk in the lobby of the Clayton Airport Hotel, he has his iPad out and this spreadsheet up with all our likely dates, games and opponents in 2018 colour-coded. I shuffle in beside him so I can see it too and then I start our war game.

'Okay, so either way I'm out for the rest of the league and the club month of April. Say I do rehab the knee and am back training with the group in May. You're probably not going to play me in the first round anyway there – May 27; I'll still be too far behind the other lads. You still probably won't risk me the game after that either – June 10. Leinster final – June 24 – I've another couple of weeks under my belt, you might throw me on for the last ten, fifteen minutes to see how I'm going, otherwise you're not going to trust me in the Super 8s against whoever wins Ulster, or a Mayo or Galway. That's just the reality, there's no point saying otherwise. Five years ago it might have been enough for me to say I was feeling good and for you to put me straight in, but that's not the case anymore. So, either way, I'm not going to be of any major benefit to you until the August bank holiday weekend.'

I go on. About how if I had to bet my house on it, I reckon I'll break down again if I skip having surgery. I'm not a freak of nature like Michael Darragh, I'm not using him as a data point. I've genetically bad knees. My game is all about explosiveness – short, sharp turns: very severe on the ankles and knees. Rehab the knee and I might be fine running in a straight line. But when I'm out there against Mick Fitzsimons on a warm summer's evening in St Clare's, or I have a Keith Higgins breathing down my neck in Croke Park, and I'm trying to shake them off or blow right past them; in the heat of that battle, can the knee take it or does it break down again? And even if it does withstand it, I'll still have been half-afraid that it won't. I'll be tentative, and at this level tentative won't do. The psychology as well as the physiology of it all has to be factored in.

I ask Jim to be straight with me. 'When will I be of value to you?'

He points to that bank holiday weekend in August. The third to the fifth. Game Three of the Super 8s. There, that's when I need you. The way this new format and these Super 8s work, it's a panel game now. After the first two games of the Super 8s, there's a two-week break before the third game, and then, just a week's turnaround for the All Ireland semi-final. Players will need to be rotated and rested. And if you're going to feature at all in an All Ireland semi-final or final, realistically you'll have to have featured in that third Super 8s game.

'Okay,' I say. 'Well, if that's the case, then that's my target.'

It's basically five and a half months away. The average return time for someone with this injury is six months. I know that's the timeline Jack McCaffrey is working towards at the moment, but with Christmas in the middle of it, I doubt he was rehabbing every day. Back in 2004 I made it back after surgery in five months. Fergus McFadden returned to play for Leinster in four and a half months. It's achievable. It's possible. We both rise to our feet, rather buoyed by the chat. I now have a timeframe, a target, and he has a picture in his head of me playing in that third Super 8s game too.

Before we part ways, he tells me to check in with Enda King, the head of performance rehabilitation in Santry: get as much information as I can before making any final decision. So I talk to Enda and that seals it for me. Out of all the people he's come across who bypassed having an operation, only sixteen to twenty percent of them didn't break down again. Nowhere near a high enough success rate for me.

My mind is more at ease now. The rehab would always have been a squeeze. And for what? If I'm going to play meaningful game-time for this team, I need to be at the best of my best, at least as electric as I felt against Kildare the other week. Rehabbing the knee just to get to level par isn't good enough.

I'm also taking a longer view. I want to be back at my best for the club this autumn. It's the one medal that has eluded me, a county title, and I know people who question the Brogans, and me in particular, for that missing line on the CV. Doesn't matter that we made it through to three finals and were within a kick of a ball of winning them all: we didn't get over the line. And the consensus out there now is that with our age profile, our window to win is shut. But I'm an optimist by nature and I still see a chink of light for us there.

I have an eye to 2019 too. I war-gamed it with Jim as well. Say we win this year's All Ireland. Although as a group we don't tend to talk about how many successive titles or games we've won, the reality is that it would put us within one of an unprecedented five All Irelands in a row. Being part of that journey to try to achieve history would be hard to resist – if he'd have me back. Whereas if I were to now skip on having the op and go straight for rehab, realistically I'd be in no space to go again next year. It would just be asking too much of the knee, with being another year older, for it not to break down again.

I've had several pangs of anxiety in recent days as the thought has struck me: Jesus, I might never play for Dublin again. And when I ask myself why is it I'm afraid, why it is I don't want it to be over; why is it I'm meeting James Allen first thing tomorrow morning to help minimise the swelling of the knee so that it's in the best possible shape it can be ahead of next week's op; why is it I'm willing to sign up to the hardship and the grind that goes with trying to come back from this; it keeps coming back to four things – the lads and the journey, the jersey and the Hill.

Winning All Irelands is great, but I guarantee you, even if we hadn't won any, we'd be like the Mayo boys, trucking on, because there's nothing else we'd rather be at and no one else we'd rather be with. It's the pints together after a championship game, the buzz after winning a league game down the country in the shit and the rain; dogging it out some night in the icy rain in Innisfails or some morning in the snow out in Clontarf, and the deep, unspoken, collective satisfaction afterwards.

I've made friends for life on this journey: the likes of Paul Flynn and Michael Darragh Macauley who are still on board, and the likes of Declan Lally and Éamon Fennell who stepped off a good few years ago now. Michael Darragh and myself were only talking about it the other day, how there should nearly still be a WhatsApp group for every year, that every one of our soldiers through the years should in some way remain part of the band of brothers.

There is a group alright for the boys of 2011: a lot of that crew are retired now and also it was such a watershed win for the county, it will always be frozen in time: we'll always have that bond and those reunions to mark what we did when we were young men thirty or forty years ago. But otherwise, the only other Dubs WhatsApp is for the boys currently training away in Innisfails. If you came in after

2011 but are gone now by 2018, there's no WhatsApp group for you.

Take a lad like Kevin O'Brien, who came along in 2013 and broke forward from corner back to feed me the pass for my first point in that year's epic semi-final against Kerry. He was central to that score, that win, that All Ireland, and was hugely popular within the group for his toughness on the field and good humour off it. But then injuries, not unlike the one I've just suffered, meant he dropped off the panel a few years ago, and now the two of us are no longer in the same WhatsApp group. I'm no longer in any WhatsApp group with Tomás Brady either. A Ciarán Kilkenny is no longer in the same WhatsApp group as a Denis Bastick. I don't want to leave our WhatsApp group. I'm not ready yet to say goodbye to the lads.

And I don't want to hand back that jersey. Not yet. It means too much to me. I remember when I dislocated my shoulder for the first time, after coming on in a trial game for the Dublin U16s; though I never played underage for Dublin, at least not until the 21s, I had plenty of trials. Mick Bohan would have been the manager of those 16s and we were playing Meath in Parnell Park. I contested this high ball with their goalkeeper and he ended up landing on my shoulder. I was carted off onto an ambulance and then to hospital, my shoulder feeling every bump along the way before they knocked me out with the anaesthetic. When I woke up, they wanted to cut the jersey off to manipulate the shoulder, but I insisted that no, they couldn't. My father had worn the Dublin jersey. My brother Alan was now playing in one with the county minors. This was mine, even if it was just a No.23. And so, with great difficulty for her and with great discomfort for me, the nurse had to navigate and slip it off over my head.

Months later, when my arm was still in a sling and I'd long been discarded from the panel, one of Mick's selectors rang the house, asking for the jersey back. Mam nearly jumped down the phone and strangled your man. Almost ten years later when Mick was coaching me with DCU, she still hadn't forgotten or forgiven that episode, confronting him one day on the side of a pitch in St Clare's. The cheek of you! Not one of youse rang to see how he was, after he was carried off in an ambulance, and then ye ring to see if ye can have the jersey back?!

I can still tell you where that jersey is. When I'd finally establish myself on the senior county team, I'd gift it to my close friend, Vinny Tyrrell, who I won a junior schools soccer All Ireland with in St Declan's and who went on to captain the Irish U18s and play in America. Every September Vinny comes back from New York and delights in telling the story of the retro Arnott's No.23 jersey he wears to the All Ireland.

All I want is to wear a Dublin jersey again. To run out in blue and stand to face the flag and the Hill and then play in front of it, whether it's for just another minute or another ten games or whatever else this knee has left in it.

As a kid the Hill was a dream of mine; to score a goal into it was as much an ambition as playing for Dublin itself. I grew up on old video clips and stories of my father bearing down on goal and Paudie O'Mahony of Kerry at the height of the 1977 All Ireland semi-final and him sending the Hill into delirium with one of the most famous goals in football history. Twenty-five years later my brother Alan in his debut year would score into the same end against Kildare in the Leinster final, the first Dublin had won in seven years and the first day the new Croke Park was pushed to its 82,500 capacity; he still has a framed picture of himself blowing kisses to the Hill after that goal, a present Pillar Caffrey and his wife Yvonne thoughtfully knew he'd treasure. So five years after that again when I'd score a goal myself into the Hill in a Leinster final playing for Pillar, slipping it past Laois's Fergal Byron, I was overcome. I was so ecstatic, racing to salute the Hill and seeing it salute me back, my legs actually buckled while trying to run back out to wing forward where I was positioned that year. Our physio John Murphy had to sprint in to enquire if I was okay. 'Jesus, John,' I said to him, 'I just had to lie down! I'm after burning myself out here!'

I've since scored another twenty championship goals for Dublin, more than anyone else ever has, according to the record books, and it never gets old. Especially scoring into the Hill.

I stood on that sacred terrace as a kid with my dad, then later on with my friends and our few cans of cider we'd have sneaked in. When Ciarán Whelan powered a left-foot rocket to the roof of the Armagh net in the 2002 All Ireland semi-final, we were among the blue wave that heaved and surged forward, giddy and merry in our teenage rebelliousness, loving being part of this great communal joy. 'COME… ON… YOU…BOYS IN BLUE, COME ON YOU BOYS IN BLUE…!'

Even when I became a boy in blue myself in the summer of 2005 after being called in by Pillar, I'd still go into the Hill with the lads anytime – which was most of the time – I wasn't on the matchday panel. When Mossy Quinn kicked the 45 to win that year's Leinster final, it was as if he was aiming it right towards me and I had willed it over the bar. Seconds later when the whistle went, a gang of us bolted onto the field, seeking out Alan, and ended up in a photo in a paper the next day.

I obviously no longer go there with the lads: Cormac Cushion, Stephen McQuaid, Stephen O'Reilly, my cousin Joey Brogan, Ross McConnell. But I still make sure they're sorted for tickets for any game and sometimes those tickets are for the Hill: Stephen O'Reilly still goes there for every game. The same with some CEOs and serious businessmen I deal with. Conor Brennan, a friend who runs one of the country's biggest insurance companies, Arachas, wouldn't think of going into a corporate box whenever the Dubs are playing – it has to be the Hill. It's the universality of it. On the Hill, just like in our dressing room, everyone is equal, everyone is a Dub. Doesn't matter what your club, colour or creed is, if you're a chief executive, chef or cleaner. This is your tribe, your place, where you can revel in some one-liner from an ould fella from Whitehall or an old dear from Cabra as much as a score from any of us lucky enough to be on the field.

I'd love one new memory of the Hill, or even better, to create one more for it. Of all the privileges and thrills that go with playing for Dublin, my favourite is turning to face Hill 16 and the flag as the Artane Boys strike up *Amhrán na bhFiann*. Because at that moment I'm on the verge of playing football, the thing I enjoy more than anything else; it's when I have the most football ahead of me. Fifteen minutes into a game and grains of sand are already pouring through the pinched centre of the hour glass. By halftime there's as much sand in the lower bulb as there is in the upper one. But when we're standing for the national anthem, the hour glass has yet to be turned over. It's all still ahead of us!

For me that time and place is heaven: when I'm about to play the game I love, alongside my buddies, competing in the most amazing coliseum, with the most celebrated terrace and support in Irish sport willing us on. In that moment I'm not really following the words of the anthem. I'm not imagining the boys manning the bearna bhaoil or the roar of cannon fire. I'm picturing getting out in front of my man, winning the ball, swivelling, shooting, scoring. I'm like a kid at the frontroom door on Christmas morning. Let me at it! Let me tear into it! Where's my ball?! Just give me that ball, give me that ball, give me that ball!

Give me that feeling one more time.

3

Blue Blood

OPERATION DAY BUT IT HELPS KNOWING I'M not alone. Driving me into the Santry Clinic this morning is my dad, with Mam behind in the back. And as I wait in admissions, they wait as well.

They know what goes with a day like this. Dad inherited as well as passed on those dodgy Brogan knees while Mam has been a nurse or carer all her working life.

They met actually when he was barely a year back from twisting his knee and she was a student nurse: Dad, a Dub working in Kerry; Mam, a Kerry woman training in Dublin. It's part of the folklore of the Dublin-Kerry rivalry now, not least because of the identity of their matchmaker. Shortly after Dad as an engineer was stationed to the small harbour town of Tarbert to help with the new turbines they were installing in the power station, he befriended a local teacher: Jimmy Deenihan, corner back on the young Kerry team which had famously shocked the Dublin side which Da had played for the previous September.

The rivalry between the two teams was already on its way to becoming the fiercest and most magnificent in the history of Gaelic football, but Jimmy and Dad found they shared something else too:

an intense love of athletics and personal fitness. Together that winter and spring of '75-76, they'd power through the sand dunes of Ballybunion, and up the hill behind Jimmy's school in Tarbert, and time each other as they'd do the fitness circuit they'd set up in a local gym. After one of those midweek runs along the dunes, with the fresh ocean breeze cooling their sweat, Jimmy mentioned that his club, Finuge, were having a dance as part of the Easter carnival. And that was where Bernard Brogan was introduced to Jimmy's longstanding friend, Maria Keane-Stack from neighbouring Listowel, who was back home for the weekend.

Dad would get to know Maria and Listowel so well, he'd come to call Jimmy 'Dan Paddy Andy' after the matchmaker renowned in the writings of the town's resident literary genius, John B Keane. More importantly, Da can still call Jimmy a good friend; over forty years on and they still chat regularly on the phone and meet up a few times a year.

In September 1976 Dad played midfield on the Dublin team that turned the tables on Kerry and Jimmy Deenihan in the All Ireland final. My uncle Jim was a sub for Dublin that day, just like he was in '74 and '77, and after the game he swapped jerseys with Kerry's supersub, Seán Walsh, dad of Tommy. That night Dad and Jim and a certain guest of honour hit a Plunkett's pub, the Breffni, on the Navan Road. And there Maria Keane-Stack was slipped into Seánie Walsh's jersey and paraded around the pub on Dad's and Jim's shoulders.

That would have been Mam. That's still Mam: so vivacious with a word for everyone and everyone having only love for her. She'd have another episode with a Kerry player's attire, or lack thereof. In 2010 after a Saturday night International Rules match in Limerick, myself, Tadhg Kennelly, Tommy Walsh and David Moran, all of us sons of fathers who played in those All Irelands in the seventies, retreated to Listowel. We popped into the Mermaids nightclub before a lock-in in John B's pub next door. At some stage while our generous host Billy Keane, the late John B's son, was entertaining us into the early hours, David fell asleep at the counter, much to the amusement of Tadhg and Tommy who left him there. Being the good Samaritan, I threw his arm over my shoulder, somehow dragged him down the street to my mam's house, and slipped him into bed. The following morning while I was still out for the count, he got up and was walking around in his boxers in this unfamiliar house when my mother walked in. And that's when a mortified David uttered the famous words: Please tell me you're Mrs Brogan! When I eventually surfaced, I found the two of them in the kitchen, having breakfast, getting on like a house on fire.

Mam would attribute much of her personable manner to her own mammy. Kathleen Connolly was born on the Falls Road in west Belfast. She lost her father when he fell from a height working in the Harland and Wolff shipyard, causing his children to be separated and minded by different relatives in Ireland and England. Granny was sent to an aunt in Listowel where she'd become immersed in the local scene, in particular the arts. She loved her sing-songs and her theatre, especially anything her neighbour John B wrote, and interacting with the punters that would frequent the small family shop where she worked and lived.

My grandad Jamesie was more reserved, but he had a gentle, kind nature, farming and providing for his family of two boys and three girls: Stephen, Jim, Mam herself, Gráinne and Fiona. As kids we loved going down there during the summer, jumping around on hay bales and helping Stephen and our cousin Neil bring in and milk the cows. We'd play football with the local kids in the lane behind

William Street, kicking the ball off the back of John B's pub and the children's clothes store that Johnny Sexton's indomitable granny, Brenda, still runs. It felt like home from home, the way they adopted us city slickers as if we were their own. In 2013, only months after I'd kicked four points from play in a massive semi-final win over Kerry, the people of Listowel still kindly invited me to turn on the town's Christmas lights. The fact that 1500 people turned up was a measure of the standing that the Keane-Stacks were held in – and my father as well. Because that's another lasting image I have from those magical eternal summers in Listowel: watching friendly strangers come up to my father on the street, shake his hand and want to talk about those old Kerry-Dublin games. Even at the time I was struck by it: the grace and good humour he showed them, the regard they had for him, and consequently the pride I felt in him. I was still too young to appreciate for myself what my father had done, only that he must have done something good, something special.

And I suppose subconsciously it planted a seed: that I wanted to do something special myself when I grew up.

AT 10.15am I get the word to head up to my room so I say goodbye to Mam and Da. 'Sure I'll see ye later on.' I'm shown to my bed and soon I'm watching Netflix. I'm taking this hospital stay as a window to binge on *Manhunt: Unabomber*, based on the true story of how the FBI tried to track down this bomber through the use of forensic linguistics.

At about half-three in the afternoon, I get the call for the op. I head down with my pillow to this freezing, sterile room, wearing nothing but my boxers and this gown they've given me. Dr Ray Moran comes in, his usual pleasant, assuring self. I'm well warmed up, he cracks, this is my eighth today! The one just prior to me was

Josh van der Flier, the Leinster and Irish rugby player. I'm his final one for the day.

'Good,' I smile. 'Go gentle on this one, Ray. I need to be back for the summer, remember.'

The anaesthetist enters. We shoot the breeze between questions about any allergies I might have. It's a small world: turns out his sister is married to our team physio, James Allen. Well, I say, between yiz all I'll definitely be back playing this year so.

It's nearly time. I actually love this part, when they start to give the ten-nine count and you know you're about to pass out, but almost for the craic, you try to fight it.

'Five…' Still awake! 'Four…' Still… And then your eyes close, the lights go out and you just slip awaaayyyyy….

DAD'S people also came from passionate football country, in their case, Mayo. But like so many others from there, they had to leave to find work. And so Jim Brogan from Foxford and Bridget Gilvarry from Ballymachola, a blink-and-you'll-miss-it place between Crossmolina and Killala, met in a ballroom on Parnell Square.

Granny was a very unassuming, traditional woman, constantly offering you another slice of cake or top-up of tea. Grandad was a Garda, initially by accident. Apparently he just tagged along with his friend Tom Langan, the great full forward who would play on the last Mayo side to win the All-Ireland and made the GAA team of the millennium. It was Tom who wanted to join the guards, but Jim then decided that as he was only fishing and working in the local Foxford Woollen Mills, he might as well fill in an application form too. He'd go on to be superintendent in Cabra, Blanchardstown and Castleknock, and to this day I meet people who worked under him and talk so fondly about him. Cathal Jackson, who runs and owns

Copper Face Jacks, raves about what a fantastic copper and under-standing boss James Brogan was. He knew every one of his men and women by name, carrying around a little notebook with him so if he ever came across them on the beat, he could ask how were they and how all the family were doing. Long after he'd retired, we'd go along with him to the shopping centre and could get stuck there for a couple of hours from him wanting to stop and chat to every tooth-paste or mince-pie promotional rep.

And yet, as sociable as he was, he never drank and rarely went out. Dad says part of it had to do with money; that once the third or fourth kid arrived in their modest house near the Cabra Gate at the Phoenix Park, they had very little left to spend it on.

They ended up having nine children: eight boys and my aunt Anne. All of them high achievers, all thankfully still alive, and, as it has worked out, all living in Dublin. Uncle Jim, the eldest, is a trained barrister and a qualified town planner who now runs his own planning consultancy. Ollie has been CEO of ESB Interna-tional. Stephen manages his own international tech company along with his cousin, Ambrose. Benny runs Brogan's, the popular old-style bar on Dame Street which he part-owns with my dad, and also builds and owns other properties. Francis works for the land registry. Kevin, a strong, fresh-looking man into his boxing and kickboxing, was the one kid in the family who preferred wearing a blue collar than a white one; a highly-skilled carpenter who built his own house, he now works as a fireman and as an ambulance driver. The young-est then, Aidan, has worked as a CEO for multinational companies before recently teaming up with Stephen and Ambrose in their tech company. Yet they'll all say the biggest brain of the lot belongs to my godmother, Anne, a wiz at maths which she teaches in a community school in Tallaght.

Dad was the engineer – and the athlete. He won Leinster medals for running, a Tailteann Games inter-provincial schools medal for the high jump and played underage international basketball for Ireland; St Declan's, where he and all his brothers and sons went to school, used to be a real basketball nursery. He also played minor hurling for Dublin. But when it came to the big ball, he'd have to wait a good while before any county selectors would stoop to coming out to a junior club such as Plunkett's were at the time. And when they eventually did, he wasn't that bothered.

Playing football for Dublin was not something he had aspired to. While he and his brothers would go to games in Croke Park where Granddad Jim would be on duty and lift them over the stiles, he never equated Dublin GAA with great historic days. The All Ireland win in '63 made no impression on him – his dad, his people, were from the country – and the decade that followed did little to change his indifference. Before Kevin Heffernan, the standout player of that '63 team, came out to Plunkett's' old ground in the autumn of 1973 as the new Dublin manager to see him play, Dublin had won only four championship games over the previous eight seasons. Dad wouldn't have gone to see any of their games. So when Heffo watched him play, on a tip-off from a local referee called Senan Connell – father of the well-known Dublin player of the same name – and asked if he'd come out to train, Dad told them thanks but he hadn't the time or the interest: he was in his final year in UCD so was focusing on his studies.

A few weeks later though Heffernan and selector Donal Colfer were back out in Plunkett's' old ground in Kinvara Avenue, again inviting him to join the group who were doing some circuit training out of a school hall in Finglas. His brother Jim, a tenacious back, was asked to come along as well. So, with each other for company, they both signed up, unaware that it wasn't so much a team they had enlisted with as a movement.

The setting of Da's competitive debut for the Dubs couldn't have been less glamorous: a league game in Nowlan Park, Kilkenny, on a cold, rainy December afternoon. It was the famous day Paddy Cullen and the lads rocked up thinking a decent enough crowd had turned up to see them play the home team, only for the stands to empty once the curtain raiser, a local minor hurling final, was over. For the three men and a dog that did stay on, they'd have caught John McCarthy, James's dad, bagging four goals and in the closing minutes, my da jogging on as Dublin's last sub.

Wouldn't you know it, he twisted his knee shortly after that but made it back for the opening round of the championship to be picked at full forward against Wexford. A small crowd was in Croke Park that day, and most of them were only there to see the second game, a league final replay between Kerry and Roscommon. Apparently some supporters of those counties openly mocked the fare on offer on the undercard, particularly Dublin's struggles from frees. But that was the same day when Heffo, driving home and grumbling about all the missed frees his side had kicked, heard a seven-year-old voice pipe up over his left shoulder: My da brings me to all Vincent's games and Jimmy Keaveney never misses a free. And so, prompted by that observation from little Terry Jennings, the son of a friend of the family, Heffo put in a call to his Vincent's clubmate.

Jimmy had retired two years earlier from county football at the age of twenty-seven, having failed to get back to even a Leinster final after winning one in his debut season. He'd watched the Wexford game from the Hill, the furthest thing on his mind being that he'd be running out in blue again the following Sunday. But he was. At full forward. Instead of Dad. Jimmy must have been almost three stone heavier and three inches smaller than Dad but it paid off: Dublin beat Louth in Navan with Jimmy kicking six points.

A fortnight later the two of them would play key roles in one of the most pivotal games in Dublin football history: a Leinster quarter-final against Offaly. At the time Offaly were going for a fourth Leinster title in a row and had won two of the previous three All Irelands. No one gave Dublin a prayer, including the Dublin public: my uncle Jim remembers there being only about eight hundred supporters in the entire Cusack Stand. Yet Dublin won, thanks to five points from Jimmy, my dad coming on as a roving corner forward to win some crucial ball, and an injury-time point from Leslie Deegan. With that, everything changed. Everything opened up.

There was one downside to that day. In the closing minutes Dad twisted his other knee, ruling him out for the rest of the summer. But when they beat Galway in the final that September, two days before his twenty-first birthday, Dad and Uncle Jim were on the Hogan Stand steps with Seán Doherty and Sam Maguire, looking down on an ocean of blue. A soccer town that only months earlier had largely looked down upon the GAA as a sport for boggers was now revelling in having its own Keegan in Keaveney, its own Shankly in Heffo and its own Kop in the Hill.

It's hard for younger Dubs, even me, to comprehend now. That Dublin once went eight years without even contesting a Leinster final. That before county chairman Jimmy Gray appointed Heffo as manager, there had never been one man over a team, but a five-man committee, handpicked by the county board. That even in that summer of '74, a player like Gay O'Driscoll would have booked and gone on his holidays, so slim was the prospect of Dublin playing into July – and that the same day he got back, he'd play a game for his club that morning and come on in a Leinster semi-final that afternoon. That Dublin had to win five games to win Leinster because seven teams were seeded ahead of them and they'd to win two pre-liminary games to even make the provincial quarter-finals. That there were no TV cameras to capture their shock All Ireland semi-final win over Cork because RTE sent their only outside broadcast unit to the RDS Horse Show, considering it the bigger event.

Then again, it would probably have been even more difficult to believe if someone had said at the start of 1974 that Dublin would win the All Ireland, play in the following five finals as well, and transform Gaelic football into the biggest and most glamorous sport in the country.

It's a huge source of pride, and inspiration, for me that Dad was part of that revolution, featuring in '74 and then starting in each of those five subsequent finals, all at midfield alongside the legendary Brian Mullins. I love everything about that team. How they out-worked the competition to become the fittest team the GAA had known. How they brought a rare cerebral approach to the game and outthought the opposition, with their lengthy team meetings in the Room in Parnell Park, devising strategies like Bobby Doyle and Tony Hanahoe roaming outfield to leave space upfront and their markers baffled. How successful they all went on to be in their careers: doctors, surgeons, economists, entrepreneurs, engineers. How they became a brotherhood. How they're still a brotherhood.

As a kid, I could see – feel – that bond, tagging along with Dad when he was managing Plunkett's, and the big greeting we'd both get whenever he'd bump into an old comrade at their club's grounds.

When Pat Gilroy had Caroline Currid in as our performance coach, we were all gathered in a circle for one of her sessions when she posed the question: Why are you here? Why are you giving up close to forty hours of your week to play intercounty football? It was a simple but powerful question – often you get so wrapped up in *what* you're doing and *how* to go about it, you lose sight of *why* you're doing it. Caroline, from studying organisations and human behaviour, understood that when people express and identify their why, it can establish a shared meaningful purpose and an environment of openness and collaboration.

I was one of the first to volunteer my why. I said I wanted to be part of a special group, like my father was. To achieve the things they did on and off the field, to have the bond they still had decades later. I've had a couple of lads who were in the room that day mention how they found that session with Caroline something of a watershed, how she got us to open up to one another and how I helped get that ball rolling, talking of how much Da and his team meant to me.

Jim Gavin is very mindful that we stand on the shoulders of giants. In his first season over us, he brought the boys of '63 in so we could meet them and present them with a gift. We then had a lovely bite to eat and chat with them. And what position did you play? And would ye go for pints after? In some small way making that link with the team that won the All Ireland fifty years earlier helped us go on and win the All Ireland of 2013.

And he particularly taps into the legacy of the sides my father played on, and the sides that Dean Rock's and Jack McCaffrey's and James McCarthy's played on too. He'll bring in Ronan Conway, from the same SOAR foundation that Kevin Mc works with, as a "team connection coach" to do something similar to what Caroline did and further cement our sense of trust, belonging and purpose. And Ronan will put together this amazing video. You might remember that old Ryan Giggs Reebok ad – through CGI they had him playing one-twos with former United greats like Law, Charlton and Best before he curled the ball into the far top corner. Well, Ronan makes one like that for us, with lads from the seventies combining with lads from our team, as if we're on the one team – because in many ways we are.

Jim has put other packages like that together through the years to underline that connection. And often in those clips, Dad will pop up. Loping through the middle and taking that swiped handpass from Tony Hanahoe to fire home that drilling-for-oil goal against Kerry. Or taking a pass on the edge of the Offaly square and with the outside of his boot scored the goal to win the Leinster final of '79 at the death. *'And there was fourteen on, fourteen was off, Jimmy on the sideline, havin' a gawk... Anton O'Toole's pass, I never will forget, Bernard Brogan kicked a bomber, it landed in the net...'*

All through those glory years of the 1970s, work could take Dad anywhere. There was that year in Tarbert; another year down in Cork, training with Nemo Rangers and Dolphin rugby club; six months in London where he fell in with Hitchin rugby club. The summer of '77, he listened to the Leinster final on the wireless from France, where he was testing a rig which would operate in the Kinsale gas field. So when he was back for the All Ireland semi-final and came on to score that goal, Michael O'Hehir couldn't resist – the man who had been helping drill for oil was now drilling for goals.

In March 1980 something entirely different took Dad abroad. It's surreal to think of now but in those days there was a television show called *The Superstars* in which athletes from different sports competed against each other in a range of events to see who was the best all-rounder – a kind of decathlon, only with bikes, basketballs and rowing boats thrown in as well. Pat Spillane won the first Irish edition, famously winning himself a place at the world finals – and a farmer's tan – in the Bahamas. Then Da won it the second year, beating the likes of future world champions Stephen Roche and Barry McGuigan the year before they each turned pro.

The prize for winning out in Belfield was again a flight out to the Bahamas with Jimmy Magee. For the 100-yard dash you had on the starting line three American football stars – future NFL MVP Joe Theismann, then reigning Heisman Trophy winner Charles White, and former rookie of the year and Superbowl champ, Russ Francis. Also waiting for that gun to fire was the serial British and European Superstars champion Brian Jacks and the world Superstars champion Brian Budd. And yet Dad outsprinted them all to win the 100-yard dash. By the end of the two days, Dad had finished just three points out of third place, right bang in the middle of an eleven-man field. Not bad going, considering everyone else was either a pro or an Olympian.

Dad continued to be a feature of the *Irish Superstars* for some time. The year after the Bahamas, he'd win the 100m, 800m and soccer events in the Irish final, only to finish overall runner-up to the canoeist and chin-ups machine Declan Burns. Even now people talk to me about how they remember my da from watching him climb 25-feet obstacle walls one minute and do ten-pin bowling the next.

Dad's last *Superstars* would have had a certain poignancy for him. It was down in Kerry in August 1983, only days after the Dubs and the Hill famously went on tour down to Cork and ransacked the locals in an All Ireland semi-final replay. Dad still wasn't even thirty then but had been cast aside two years earlier; as he'd half-joke to us, when all the old lads moved on or were moved along in pretty much one fell swoop, he was moved along with them! The following month when the side fell over the line with twelve men against Galway, two other rookies from '74, Anton and Mullins, were still there, but not Da.

They'd ask him back a few months later and he'd answer the call, even though Mam was pregnant with me and Alan was about to turn two. Their first league game back after the Christmas, they put him in at full forward, where he had started out ten years earlier. He was supposedly motoring well that day before being creased going for a ball by one of the opposing backs.

He was carried off unconscious and brought to Blanchardstown Hospital where they took good care of him. When he was leaving, he gave a nurse the Dublin jersey he had been wearing upon admission. It turned out to be his last. Heffo and his selectors never rang him again. The only word he ever heard was from a county board official a little while later looking for that jersey back.

That hurt Dad for some time but it wouldn't end his love affair with Dublin GAA. When Uncle Jim was a selector to Pat O'Neill, Dad would act as their eye in the sky – I'll always remember Jim sneaking myself and Alan into the dressing room after the All Ireland in '95 and seeing Keith Barr bounce the Sam Maguire off the ground and catching it again.

And eventually Dad came to see the funny side of Jerseygate. One Sunday he was walking out of Croker with Alan on his shoulders when a man approached him. Dad assumed it was going to be another yarn about where they were for the drilling-for-oil goal. But no, this was about where his last No.14 jersey was. That stranger was the proud owner of it, having received it as a present from the nurse before she had moved to Australia. Well, smiled Dad, the county board are looking for it.

That last game for Dad happened to be against Kildare. In the league. First game back after Christmas. In Croke Park. With him at full forward, his back to the Hill, kicking a point and laying on scores for others in a seven-point win. Almost precisely the same as my game the other week. Hopefully there's no omen in that. I suppose that's why I'm here in Santry. That unlike Dad after such a fine career, I hopefully get to choose how I go out. And that maybe once more a Bernard Brogan kicks another bomber into the net.

THE day after the operation I get the all-clear to head home.

Dad collects me but on our way back we pop into Philly McMahon's BeDo7 gym in Finglas. Among the many things Philly has on the go is the distribution rights to Bluetens, an electronic muscle stimulator that he's kindly gifted me to help with my recovery.

He comes out with the kit, has a big welcome for Da and we chat for a bit.

So you're back at it! he smiles before we head off.

'Yeah,' I grin. 'Back on the road!'

And that's the line I give to all the lads when they text, asking how the op went: Back on the road! I know this path back to recovery is going to be tough and often lonely. Already I can see the ship with Captain Gavin at the helm powering on without me and it's a humbling feeling. Something that has been such an important part of your life and that maybe you once were an important part of, now views you as irrelevant, miniscule, if it even bothers to take a quick look back to the shore – which it won't. But that's all the more reason I've to remain positive in any interaction with the lads. In radiating energy, I find I get even more back.

I suppose that's always been my natural disposition. Declan Lally talks about the evening years ago he called up to the house to collect Alan for training and found me pucking a ball against the wall. Earlier that day I'd learned that I hadn't made the Dublin minor football panel. Instead of feeling sorry for myself and playing the victim, I was already out playing hurling. 'I didn't make the football,'

I apparently told him, 'but I'm going to see now if I can make the hurling.' And I did, even if I would remain rooted to the bench for our two-point first-round loss to Kilkenny.

I had a similar outlook two years later when I did my first cruciate, trying to throw a shimmy playing against Parnells out in their old grounds by the airport. Almost right away I saw it as both a challenge and an opportunity. Barry Cahill had been out the year before with the same injury and gave me a chart of the various milestones he and others like Trevor Giles had hit along their way back, so I chased down their times.

All the way up when I was trying and failing to make Dublin underage squads, the message I kept getting was that I was too small and too weak. But then my last year at minor I had a growth spurt and then in that timeout with the cruciate, I hit the gym. Every day. Either I'd be in Total Fitness in Castleknock or out in the back shed which Dad and I had converted into a little weights room. At the time how you played and prepared for football was being determined by the northern teams, especially Armagh. And if I was going to win contested ball kicked into the full-forward line against the likes of the McNultys and Francie Bellew, and ride supporting tackles from the likes of Kieran McGeeney, I was going to have to strengthen up. The day of that injury out in Collinstown, I was just a skinny nine-stone nineteen-year-old rake. I came back a muscular, ten-and-a-half-stone senior footballer.

And I was a more accurate one too, off my left foot. I'd go down to the club pitch with Ross McConnell or on my own and kick ball after ball with my 'weaker' peg, as I couldn't kick with my right. And from that I'd come to probably strike the ball better with my left than with my right; what was once 'weaker' became a strength.

Sometimes I think if I didn't do my cruciate that time, I wouldn't have gone on to be the player I became. I mightn't have played for Dublin at all. I needed and used that timeout to really go after things I otherwise wouldn't have made the time for.

And so that's how I'm looking at this. Where and how can I get better? I'll be able to pound it out now in the gym for eight weeks. By the time I'm back on the field with the lads in three months' time I'm going to be in unreal nick. I'm going to be diet perfect; already I've been on to our team nutritionist Daniel Davey and ordered a pack of fish oils that should help me build muscle, burn fat and recover faster. I might do some boxing like I did after my first cruciate; the skipping and the intensity of the training out in the Arbour Hill club really helped strengthen my knee and improve my stamina. I'm going to be more agile because I'll be able to do a lot more footwork. Although I won't play a game for months, there are little wins I can have everywhere I look.

Already I'm chalking them up. A few days ago I met up with James Allen to check if the swelling on the knee had receded enough for the op to go ahead. Already he could see how well I was following his protocols: Jesus, your knee is in some shape given what happened ten days ago!

He called into the hospital last night after the operation. In a few days' time we'll meet up in his gym and put in place our plan. All in the hope and the belief that it's going to help at the back end of this. That come the summer and I have to be at it in a training game and then Croke Park, I'm there – I'm there because of all the little things I've done in dreary old February.

So how am I after the op?

Back on the road. Mad for road.

4

Beating Hearts

ANOTHER TRIP TO ANOTHER HOSPITAL – MY life seems to be revolving around them these days – only this visit doesn't revolve around me. Today it's Keira that is the centre of attention.

In truth, in private, her pregnancy has been the centre of our world for the last six months. My knee and my hopes of playing with Dublin again, for all I go on about them, have been secondary compared to how much we yearn for reassuring news on a day like this.

We're here in the Rotunda. An initial scan has told us there are two hearts beating, not just one. And while another scan two weeks ago gave us cause for cautious optimism that both will be fine, we haven't told anyone that we're expecting twins. Because we can't say we're having twins. It's all still too uncertain.

I've known Keira since we were eleven. She lived just across the road. We first kissed when we were thirteen. We kind of went out after that during first year of school but sure we were babies ourselves and it soon petered out back to being just friends.

But we were best friends. In our mid-teens we'd talk every evening on the phone. We had the drill down to a tee: at 8.30 on the button her house landline would ring and then for the next three-quarters

54

of an hour she'd be in her parents' room, giggling and chatting away. Her parents didn't know who it was that was calling until they went through an itemised bill and recognised it was the one number ringing the whole time.

Every Sunday night during our Leaving Cert year, we'd amble together around the estate, Laurel Lodge, and up by Mount Sackville, to a spot where we'd look out over the valley and the Liffey. We'd be talking about virtually everything but skirting around one thing: I was mad about her! She was sociable, popular, but independent. She was sporty, swimming for Leinster and playing basketball for Loreto College in town. And she was bright, pretty, kind, witty, ambitious.

She'd tell me about her dreams and aspirations, how she didn't see herself staying in Ireland – she was going to travel and work abroad. And while I admired that and told her that was great, inside a part of me was dying: But I'm going to be staying here, playing with the Dubs!

Eventually I plucked up the courage to tell her how I felt. It was on one of our Sunday night study-break walks, up near our spot overlooking the Liffey. 'Keira, will you go out with me?'

Well, she was pretty emphatic with her answer. No!

I wanted a hole to open up and swallow me right there. Instead I had to walk home along with her for a good fifteen minutes, dragging my tail between my legs, inwardly berating myself for not having at least the sense to have asked her closer to home and preserved some degree of dignity in case I was rebuffed: What are you like, Berno, thinking it would work out like it does in the movies? You flippin' eejit, ya!

We finally arrived back in the estate. We said our awkward goodbyes, I gave her a hug and a kiss on the cheek, then started walking back towards my parents' house. After a few yards, I stopped, turned around and watched her walking back towards her home.

But then she stopped and turned around as well.

We didn't necessarily live happily ever after. We were together all through college – where it was first-class honours for her in every course but not quite the same for me – and for a little while after she started work, but we began to get tetchy with one another a bit too often. I was still in DCU, doing yet another postgrad and trying to win another Sigerson, and in becoming more obsessed with my football, probably became a bit more self-centred as well. So we broke up when we were both twenty-four.

Deep down though I still had a feeling that we'd get back together. That she was still The One. She went on to take in some of the rest of the world like she'd talked about on those walks around the park, travelling China and Australia, but even when she was far away, she was never far from my thoughts. Whenever her birthday would come round – December 22 was ingrained in my brain – I'd drop her a text: Hope you're well.

I know she didn't appreciate those texts, not least because she'd never reply, but during that time she'd show in her own way that she still cared too. In the spring of 2011 Grandad Jim Brogan passed away. Keira still showed up to pay her respects for a man and a family she had so much time for. And I remember thinking at the time: Keira Doyle is still a class act.

When we broke up we came to a sort of divorce settlement: certain parts of town were hers and out of bounds for me, and vice-versa. I was more than happy with how the dice had rolled for me in our private little game of Monopoly, the Dublin edition. While she had got Leeson Street, Harcourt Street was mine! Which meant I'd seized the most prized property in all the city – Copper Face Jacks!

Fast-forward to December 22, 2012. As it was the last Saturday before Christmas, my best friend and Dublin and Plunkett's team-mate Ross McConnell, myself and a few other lads from home were heading out for a few drinks, but before we did, I sent the annual text. Happy birthday, Keira. Hope you and your family are well.

It didn't drop. At least not right away. She was up in Johnnie Fox's in the Wicklow mountains with a gang of girls and there was no phone coverage. But on their way into town on the bus, the message landed. Again, I heard nothing back, but it might just have been the trigger for her to agree with the girls that they should head to Coppers. She mightn't have been there in almost five years but where else at this time of the night were fifteen of them all going to get in, and in the off-chance the ex was there, well, was he really going to object with the special night that was in it?

And, of course, I didn't. When Ross told me that he had just bumped into her, I took my time before approaching her in her seat by the bar. I asked since it was her birthday if I could buy her and her friends a drink and she didn't object. That was progress: she was back talking to me! After the Christmas, I dropped her another text, wondering if she was on for meeting for a coffee over the next while. This time I got a reply, and even better, a yes. So we met one lunch-time for some tapas on Fade Street for what was meant to be a brief catch-up and we ended up chatting til the early hours.

So here we are, twenty years on from that first kiss and five years on from those tapas and that boy and that girl find ourselves in this scan room in the Rotunda.

We were here this past autumn of 2017. The ultrasound showed a healthy heartbeat about eight weeks old. And, of course, we were delighted. Then Keira detected a hesitancy from the midwife. Well, actually, she said, there seems to be a second heartbeat here.

Keira and myself were ecstatic. I actually started laughing. We had only been talking about twins on the way into hospital that morning!

But the midwife was subdued.

Then she said it: that heartbeat is really weak.

And with that, our own hearts sank.

It was explained to us that the second foetus was most likely dying, a vanishing twin. So the way I interpreted that was we were going to have a baby but we were also likely going to lose one. On one hand we had cause to be happy – Keira was pregnant – but on the other we were obviously devastated.

I tried to stay strong and supportive for Keira, and in time I became more positive as well. Ahead of the following scan I said to her more than once, 'I actually have a hunch this [second] one is a little fighter. I think we'll be fine.'

Fourteen weeks into the pregnancy, we went for that second scan. It was the same midwife. Only this time, her demeanour was far more positive. The second baby had grown and its heartrate was strong! The vanishing twin had somehow refused to disappear! Incredible!

It still isn't out of the woods though. With twins it can get troublesome if there's a significant size difference between the two. So that's why we're here today. We know now they're two little boys but we're looking for more reassurance that they'll be two healthy little boys.

And we get it. The second heart is beating stronger again. Great news.

In truth, it's doubtful if Keira will be able to relax at any point in this pregnancy until the two of them are here safe and sound. But she's a warrior. I think that second little fella takes after her. On top of having to deal with the stress of the pregnancy and working full-time, she's recently taken on helping others with their stresses and concerns. As well as coaching the Dublin seniors, Jason Sherlock is managing the Dublin minors, and he's co-opted Keira onto his backroom team as a liaison for the players and their parents. If lads are struggling with their school or sporting workload, if they're feeling pressure from home, they can chat to her in confidence and she'll help them as well as filter appropriately back to management what they need to know.

It's a great call by Jayo to create such a role and have Keira as the one to fill it. She's played sport herself, she knows from knowing me all these years what goes with being involved in a county setup, and she has great emotional intelligence. Jayo's lucky to have her.

And I know I'm even luckier.

5

The Little Wins

A TUESDAY MORNING AND AT 07.15, PRECISELY quarter of an hour after I hit the snooze option, the phone alarm goes off again. It's time to wake up – but not quite yet get up.

I've to remain here on my bed for another ten minutes. This is where my exercise regimen commences: every day – straight away.

I push back the bedclothes and start with a few straight leg raises. With my back flat on the mattress and bending my right, non-operative, knee, I tighten my left quad, then slowly begin to rise the left leg, keeping it fully extended until it's the height of the opposite knee, making sure I'm getting a bit of a burn on. I hold it there at forty-five degrees for about ten seconds, then slowly lower it down as far as I can go. Then repeat – twenty-nine times. James Allen always says, Motion is Lotion, and these few sets of ten help regain the motion in that knee.

Some mornings waking up, it can feel particularly sore, and a little voice tells you not to bother. But then another voice overrides it. No, do it! Stick to it! So I do, because I know that afterwards I always feel a million times better for the exercise, for that discipline.

That doesn't mean the results are always better. It's exactly a month now since the operation and I'm finding it's just like it was with the first cruciate; you can have a great day and then a week later the knee is worse than it was. Recovery with something like this is never linear.

But this morning, when I do eventually get out of bed and put my feet on the floor, I'm able to walk to the shower freely, without a limp. A small rush of serotonin courses through me. Yes! Most of last week I was limping heavily. So this is a little victory here.

The same leg felt stiff yesterday. Myself and Keira were out looking at prams for twins so I was walking around on it a good bit. But after we got back I went into the front room and spent the next two hours rehabbing the knee.

It's almost a semi-laboratory, quasi-treatment room, the way I have it set up at the moment. The sofa obviously doubles up as a physio couch, so yesterday evening I plopped onto it, turned on the telly and began icing the knee for half an hour, observing the RICE (Rest, Ice, Compression, Elevation) protocol James and Dicey have drawn up for me. I used the Game Ready therapy compression system they've lent me as well. Basically it's this ice machine which pumps water and air through a connector hose to a strap wrapped around my knee, helping to reduce the swelling and pain and increase the blood flow around it.

Even before the cruciate, I had just invested a grand on NormaTec, another dynamic compressed device that's linked up to a strap around your leg to help accelerate recovery between training and games. And there's that Bluetens system which Philly McMahon gifted me, so last night I again hooked up its electrodes to my quads to help strengthen them when otherwise they could waste away.

Then I got up to get more ice for the Game Ready machine and the process began again.

It's tedious. And like the leg raises three times a day either in bed or on the couch, and the other exercises I've to do, it's repetitive. But it's necessary. And it's working, as a little win like this morning's shows.

I've been breaking it all down into seven-day goals which I write in a little journal I'm keeping. Where do I want to be this time next week?

Two weeks ago I was still on crutches. Ten days ago I started back driving. Last Tuesday the seven-day goal I set for myself was to be able to walk without a limp for a full day. I ticked that box over the weekend, even if I still felt a bit stiff, so now that I'm walking freely this morning, it confirms for me that I'm ready for another significant step. Tonight for the first time I'm going to be back around the place with the Dubs.

The night I came out of Santry after the op, Jonny Cooper sent me a text: Be around as much as you can. I appreciated the gesture and the sentiment, and last week I sent in a little video and message to the group WhatsApp of me and a few of the other injured lads doing a weights session together with James. But I haven't yet been in with the whole group. To me there was no point being out in Innisfails last week, limping about the place, while the lads were prepping to play Galway in Salthill, or hobbling around at one of the midweek collective gym sessions out in St Clare's in DCU.

When the group see me I don't want to show any semblance of weakness. I want to walk in tonight with a bounce, nod 'How ye lads?' and bang out a few weights, radiating positivity, energy, strength.

I like the gym; I'd be like my brother Paul that way but the opposite of Alan, possibly because a talent like his didn't need it to make Dublin teams, whereas I did. I've struggled alright out on the track or the field when it comes to endurance runs but coming back from that first cruciate, the gym became a refuge and it has remained one. I've never been the biggest, but for most of my career I've been in the top five in the group when it's come to testing speed, power and strength. And that's where I want to stay, or at least get back to soon.

So in the evening I leave work in Lucan and head out Glasnevin way to DCU's St Clare's Sports Campus. There are essentially two ends to St Clare's. At the bottom, tucked away up a small red-bricked entrance just off Griffith Avenue, there's the Bunker, attached to St Clare's nursing home, a grand grey-stoned old building which has been there since early Victorian times. The Bunker has been our base for ten seasons now, ever since Pat Gilroy identified it and had it renovated within months of becoming county manager. Its interior is plain, bare, functional. The main room doubles up as a meeting room and canteen with an adjoining kitchenette; that's where we'll analyse video ahead of upcoming championship games. Then beyond that that there's a decent-sized dressing room, with a warren of smaller rooms running off it, like the physio room and the management's room where Jim might call you in to give you some bad news or some specific instructions concerning the next day out. That then leads out to the bottom pitch, secluded from public view. As a package the Bunker is ideal for our purposes. Come the summer it is our little hub, war room, sanctuary.

At the top end then, which you enter coming off the Ballymun Road, just before the Glasnevin tennis club, is the main DCU Sports Campus. Its main building is almost the complete opposite of the Bunker: slick, modern, state-of-the-art, having been built from scratch only in 2013, to go with a full-size floodlit artificial GAA pitch.

Upstairs there's a carpeted meeting room with every conference chair featuring a folding side table to help conscientious players take notes. Downstairs there's a canteen and a fully-stocked gym.

It's mostly the domain of the hurlers and the ladies footballers. This is where they usually eat and war game, with the all-blue stairway walls decorated with images and mottos acknowledging the Dublin hurling tradition and the one they're trying to create. But a couple of times we've had a meeting here and it's where we have nearly all our collective gym sessions, only we split into two groups, an early evening slot and a later one.

I stride in through the glass door and right away I see friendly, familiar faces everywhere. Mannion. Butsy. Dean. Bryan Cullen, supervising it all. Howiya, what's the story?! Good to see you back. Even better to be back.

The tunes are on, thumping. The clank of weights, the sound of graft, surrounds me. Lads dropping squats, pinging weights, slotting back in bench presses, slapping on more plates.

I'm feeding off it, buzzing. With the ever-dependable James Allen keeping an eye on me, I start out on a leg-press machine, something that doesn't put strain on the cruciate, just some power into the quads. I start off gentle, with 20kg, then 40, 60, on one leg. By the end I'm pushing 100kg. It always seems to happen that way; whenever I'm working out with other lads, I tend to exert myself that extra ten, twenty percent more than I would on my own. There's a science to that; a few years ago one of the backroom told us it's called the social facilitation effect: studies have shown that the mere presence of others, especially those doing a similar task, improves your effort and performance.

It's certainly in effect in St Clare's tonight. The energy, encouragement, is infectious. Lads gravitate over to teammates on the verge of personal bests, urging them on. This evening Jonny Cooper is doing pull-ups with 40kg of weight swinging between his legs, chained to a belt around his waist.

More than anyone on the panel, Jonny is the ultimate Process Ninja. He's another guy who had his share of rejection and set-backs earlier in his career; he couldn't make a championship match-day squad in Pat Gilroy's time. But the rocky road hardened him, improved him. His personal motto is Be Unrivalled – in his prep and his effort. The last few years I don't think there's anyone in foot-ball who can match his mindset and application. And this Tuesday evening in March, he's pushing himself like he's chasing down Paul Geaney or Andy Moran in Croke Park in September. His eyes are popping out of his head, the veins in his neck bulging, his teeth gritted, as he again manages to pull his chin over that bar.

We're all gathered around him, willing him on. C'mon, c'mon, c'mon! And another one! That's it! And again!

And when he does complete that third set, it's as if we all did.

There might be no cup, no crowd, but it's nights like these and little wins like that which lead to them.

6

Big Brother

IT'S STRANGE NOT SEEING ALAN OUT THERE.

April in the new GAA calendar means club month now, so after seeing off Galway in the league final, every Dublin player is back where it all started. This evening out in Garristown, in a field overlooked by a dreary, overcast sky and surrounded by still-leafless trees, St Oliver Plunkett Eoghan Ruadh are playing Raheny. And while our opponents have Brian Fenton in his prime and Brian Howard approaching his, for the first time this century Plunkett's won't have a son of Bernard and Maria Brogan starting in championship.

We're all still here. I'm *maor uisce* for the night. Paul is over with Mam and Dad on the far side, having dropped down to junior this year where the demands aren't as taxing on his battered legs. And then in the dugout is Alan. There could be a half-hour in him yet where he'll join our cousins Darragh and James in the fray, but with himself and Lydia now having a third kid, he's found it increasingly hard to commit, as well as shake off all the aching bones.

For as long as I can remember, Alan has been out there – starting, starring, shining a light for me to follow.

At school he was the standout player on Declan's teams that cleaned up all around them; when I came along a few years later we didn't win a dicky bird. Games often bypassed me at corner forward; Alan consistently dominated them, roaming all over the field, racking up big scores. I never made a Dublin football team before U21; Alan never failed to make one, all the way from the first-ever Dublin U15 development squad up to captaining the county to its first-ever U21 All Ireland. Through all that time his progress compared to mine never demotivated me. It inspired me.

If I didn't have the vision of following him, I would likely have given up somewhere along the way after those setbacks. I was a better hurler than a footballer but to hurl senior with the county was never the goal or the dream – consciously or subconsciously, it was to play football with the Dubs like Dad and Alan. Watching him break forward from wing back to score a brilliant goal in the 1999 All Ireland minor semi-final against Down and burst onto the senior team in 2002, I thought to myself, That's what I want, that's where I want to be. I saw the respect people had for him and the joy he was bringing to the family, now that it had another Brogan in blue for us all to follow. There was no element of jealousy to it. Whenever people introduced me as Alan's brother, I actually felt proud, not irritated.

Declan Lally still slags me about it, but in my early years in college out in Maynooth where he and Alan already were, I didn't just wear the adidas boots Alan was endorsing at the time, I made a point of parading the custom-designed ones that visibly had the name 'Brogan' intricately stitched onto them! I wasn't even making the Sigerson starting fifteen at the time, with talents like Alan, Lally, Alan Dillon, Ross Munnelly, Colm Parkinson, Rory Kavanagh and Barry Cahill all playing from midfield up, yet still I swanned around in those Brogan boots! But then, all I wanted was to literally follow in Alan's footsteps. He had gone to Maynooth so I went to May-nooth. He had picked finance so I picked finance.

It was the same when we were kids. I was that starry-eyed, nerdish younger brother who just wanted to tag along with my cool dude older brother. When we were on holiday in Marbella, we'd go down in the evening to the camp disco where there was a little bar. I think the legal age over there to drink was sixteen, so Alan was able to buy a can of San Miguel beer. The first evening he gave me a sip from it, even though I was only fourteen. I thought it was the coolest thing of all time: kicking back, soaking up the rays and the tunes, having a beer with my big bro. We were the men! The next day then he didn't offer me a sip. And I didn't ask. I was too in awe of him and too afraid he might say no.

Not long after that, my thirst for drink landed both of us in hot water; although we were literally altar boys in primary school, we didn't stay altar boys forever. On Friday evenings myself and a few mates would go to the local youth club, and then in the park might share a six-pack of Scrumpy Jack that a pal of Alan's was able to get for us.

This particular night we were hanging around in the park while Alan was across the road by the green with his pals when he got a call: Get up here! Bernard's twisted! After my second can, I was falling about the place, blood dripping down my face; I had braces back then and had managed to get my lip caught, only to free it and cut myself. So Alan was there, a little merry himself: What am I going to do with this fella? How am I going to get him past Mam and Dad?

First he cleaned me up; then he managed to get me as far as outside the house. Right, hopefully Mam and Dad are in the front room, so we'll go round the side, tip-toe in the back, heads down, bolt straight to our rooms, and if anyone asks, just say we're calling it an early night.

No such luck. We had taken only a few furtive steps in through the side entrance when we heard a shout. Mam and Dad were still out the back garden with a few friends.

Where are ye slinking away off to?!

Of course we tried to breeze it off with a big well-howayiz-all! But Dad could read us a mile off.

Right, let me smell yer breath!

I thought I was being very smart, blowing out through my nostrils, but again, I was fooling no one.

Bernard, if you blow your nose once more, I'm going to bleedin' clatter ya!

Then he made us both walk the line and touch our nose with our index finger, as if we were a couple of American spring-break students that had been pulled over to the side of the road.

We were busted. Dad would be a mild-mannered man, not one to raise his voice or lose his anger, but he did with us that time. The next day he was talking about moving house. He even brought us out for a drive around the mountains for what seemed like hours, the inference being we could be stuck out there for the rest of our days; I was in bits at the back, somehow staving off the urge to puke. For the rest of that year, we were grounded. Even when I was across the road, kicking ball on the green with Ross McConnell and some buddies, I had to report back home in person every half-hour to Mam or Dad.

Apart from that saga though, Alan was little bother to the parents. And little seemed a bother to Alan. Everything seemed to come easy to him. Except when it came to his speech.

Growing up, he had a strong stammer. He could barely complete a sentence. I'd be there when he'd be in company, whispering under my breath, *Come on, please let him get it out*, but invariably he wouldn't. And yet I didn't see him get down about it; he was popular in school, so rarely got any grief, and when he did, he was able to dust it off. He didn't like it alright when a teacher might ask him to read something out, but he liked when he'd be taken out of class for Dad to bring him to see another speech and language therapist.

They finally struck gold when he was about twelve or thirteen in this hypnotist over in Stillorgan called Bernard Stein. He gave Alan this relaxation tape which he listened to most nights, helping him control his breathing. I'd sometimes lie beside him, take one of his ear buds, and we'd close our eyes, picturing and listening to the dolphins and waves. When I hear him now in the media, speaking so well, I sometimes think back to those nights listening to Dr Stein's old cassette tape.

JUST as Dad coming up didn't have any aspirations of playing for Dublin, he didn't have any of us playing for them either. He never sat down and thought, Right, we're going to do A, B and C so the lads can play for Dublin. All he and Mam wanted was to encourage us to try out whatever we wanted and support us while we tried those things out. And that was probably the secret to all three of us playing for Dublin.

Paul played golf on underage Leinster squads, going up against a fella from Ulster called Rory McIlroy. Alan was a fine soccer player. And I tried everything. I was on for anything. Jumping on it, climbing up it, swinging off it – I was completely hyperactive. I still have a scar on my forehead from crashing into a fire-escape door handle in the gym in Declan's while Dad was taking the Plunkett's senior team. All that blood didn't deter me. And it didn't deter Dad. Shortly after that we were holidaying in Mont Saint-Michel. Mam popped off to the shop, Dad dared me to climb the sheer wall in front of us. When Mam arrived back, she nearly died, seeing me twenty feet above her.

For a while we took out a family membership at Castleknock tennis club so we all played a bit, though I seemed to lose interest shortly after my cousin James beat me 6-0, 6-0! We all ran for the parish in the community games; I came third in Dublin in both the 110m hurdles and 200m sprint but found it nerve-wracking lining up on the blocks. After I turned fourteen, I realised I needed a team to fall back on, I was done with individual sport. I didn't play much competitive basketball in secondary school but still signed up for any midterm or summer camp put on by the likes of Kelvin Troy and Lennie McMillian in St Vincent's; those Americans had a great magnetism about them and I always found there were things they showed us that I could try out in the Gaelic. Mam and Dad were happy for us to go to every camp going, even a hockey one out in Mount Sackville where I can still remember us running around, laughing, playing Bulldog. For them it was just about making friends and having fun.

If I had a third sport along with the football and hurling, it was soccer. I played with Castleknock Celtic and in school with Declan's; not surprisingly, I was a striker. I even made a representative Dublin team when I was about twelve, playing alongside my clubmate Paul Keegan who later signed for Leeds and went on to win leagues with Drogheda and Bohemians.

But much of our sport was simply informal – free play. We lived on the green and the road, playing rounders, Manhunt, football and hurling All Irelands, World Cups, Wimbledon. Ross McConnell still walks by the green to get the train and is saddened to see it almost always deserted. Kids now are indoors, on their phones or Xbox, and whatever sport they play is nearly all structured, organised by adults. Back in our time on the green, there were no adults, no cones, no whistles – just a ball, maybe a racket or a hurley, four jumpers and our imaginations.

The more I read and listen to some of the material recommended within our Dublin dressing room, the more I realise I had almost the ideal upbringing in sport – partly because not everything went ideally at the time, and largely because of how Dad and Mam nurtured and supported us.

A big term now in talent development is "physical literacy", or "fundamental movements": coordination, agility, balance – running, hopping, dodging, jumping, landing. Before learning any skills specific to a particular sport, it helps to have those foundations in place. Without even knowing of those terms, Dad and Mam gave us the freedom and opportunity to acquire them. They'd take us to the gymnastics club and the swimming pool in Coolmine Community School. Sometimes Dad brought us to a track out in Lucan to give us a few pointers on how to run properly – high knees, swing the elbows, breathe right into your belly. When he was player-manager with Plunkett's he would bring along these lights and a generator and put them on the wall so that on winter nights the lads could run along the side of the pitch; Alan and myself would tag along and join in the stampede. A lot of the time he just let us roam, explore.

Lally still talks about the time the DCU Sigerson team were on a training camp in Portugal and an American football was being thrown around the pool. I made some acrobatic leap back and caught it with one hand and whoever was next to him said, How does he do that? Lally put it down to natural athletic ability. But I attribute a lot of it and something like the first goal in the 2013 All Ireland against Mayo – flicking the ball over my head with my left hand, having jumped off my "wrong" foot – to some of my one-handed catches playing rounders on the green and how I used to somersault about the place as a kid.

The research also shows that allowing us to try out a range of sports helped us to play for as long and as well as we have at football. Kids who specialise early in a sport might gain an advantage in the short term but they're more susceptible in the long run to suffering mental and physical burnout – they just get sick of the same thing.

And they miss out on acquiring "transferable skills". A lot of the soccer and basketball I played as a kid has stood well to me in Croke Park. I developed a real goalscorer's mentality from soccer, even though I ultimately loved Gaelic and kicking points even more. With my pace I used to look for that ball over the top, a bit like the one Niall Corkery brilliantly bombed into me for the goal at the start of the 2010 All Ireland semi-final against Cork. The 2015 Leinster semi-final against Kildare: my first goal that day came from just striking the ball off the ground with my left foot (the one where I ended up smashing the ball off Dermo's head as he was already behind the goalline!). If I hadn't played soccer, I probably wouldn't have had that shot in my locker and would have opted to pick the ball up and got tied up instead.

Or take that year's All Ireland semi-final replay against Mayo. Midway through the second half we were a goal behind when Fenton blazed a ball across the goalmouth. Instinctively, I stuck my left foot out: game level and game on again. 'A poacher's finish' is how Darragh Maloney described it in his commentary and that's what it was. Not so much straight from the training ground in the Bunker as the soccer ground out in Castleknock Celtic or the green across the road.

From the kickout then, the basketball told. The lads out the field won the restart, Ciarán Kilkenny played the ball in to me and then I just took on Ger Cafferkey. Fake to the outside, then rip the ball over to my other side, drive left baseline-endline, before spotting Philly McMahon with my peripheral vision making a cut to the goal and then popping the pass for him to palm to the net.

It was something similar with a point I kicked in the drawn game. Shortly after Kevin Mc got our second goal, I transferred the ball from my right hand onto my left foot with a crossover dribble I'd have tried out and honed from those camps in Vincent's with Lennie and Kelvin. That was the same year Jayo first came in as our forwards coach and we did some preseason sessions with DCU Mercy coach, Mark Ingle. Both of them came from basketball backgrounds and a lot of the principles of that sport were absorbed into our attacking play that season – spacing, cutting through, screening down – and the fact a good few of us had played it when we were younger helped accelerate that process.

In recent years Dr Áine MacNamara has spoken at numerous conferences at my alma mater of DCU alongside current and former members of the Dublin management like Jayo, Bryan Cullen and Dr Niall Moyna. She and a couple of colleagues recently had a paper published called *Superchamps, Champs and Almosts: Important Differences and Commonalities on the Rocky Road*, where they interviewed fifty-four active or recently-retired UK and European athletes. And it's a fascinating insight into talent development and talent pathways.

The "Superchamps" had won at least five medals at the Olympic-world championship level, or, if they were from soccer or rugby, more than fifty international caps. The "Champs" had been among the top forty in the world or played at the Premier League level, without ever winning more than one world medal or four international caps. The "Almosts" then had all won multiple international underage medals or caps but none at senior and hadn't operated at a level higher than second-tier professional football or rugby.

One of the biggest findings – and ironies – was that often the eventual Almosts were Superchamps at underage and the eventual Superchamps were Almosts at underage. Contrary to what people tend to think, development, like success, is rarely linear. It's far more circuitous and bumpy than that; as the subtitle of the paper suggests, it's a rocky road. For every Alan Brogan, Ciarán Kilkenny and Con O'Callaghan who excel all the way up, there is a minor "reject" like a Bernard Brogan, Brian Fenton and Michael Fitzsimons – and a hundred eventual Almosts that made those U16 and minor teams ahead of us.

The study confirms what I've long thought: how much it helps to have supportive – but not pushy – parents when it comes to sport. Playing with Plunkett's teams all the way up, there would have been twenty-plus other kids there but most of them wouldn't have had any parent watching on. Mam and Dad took the view that young kids like to see their parents there – which they were right about, at least in our case. It was the same with Ross McConnell and his parents, Kevin and Irene. It's not a coincidence that of that crop, we were the ones that went on to play with Dublin and we're the ones still playing with the club.

On the other extreme then to the parents of those other Plunkett's kids, the Almosts' parents were very hands on – quite often, excessively so – leaving their sons and daughters retrospectively bemoaning the barrage of sideline instructions and the inquests in the car home. Personally, I didn't come across much of that behaviour on the sidelines of Dublin when I was growing up, but I know Dad in particular made a conscious decision that he wasn't going to be the stereotypical sports dad, trying to joystick coach his kids. Unknown to themselves, he and Mam took an approach similar to that of the Superchamps' parents in Dr MacNamara's study, being 'quietly present' and offering 'positive facilitation and gentle encouragement'. Mam made a point of serving the Sunday roast on a Monday so we were all out the door in time for our games at the weekend. She also ran the club kit shop with Joan Fagan and Betty Mullen, while Dad was very active in the club, serving as club chairman and senior team manager for a number of years. But when it came to our actual teams, they took a back seat. One year alright Dad managed a team of Paul's because they were stuck, the same reason he helped out as a "selector" with one of Alan's soccer teams, carrying the bag of balls and water. But otherwise he preferred to let us and our coaches off. He knew we were in good hands with mentors like Eddie Byrne, Brendan Hayden, Tony Hayden and my uncle Ollie with the club, and Senan Connell, John Caffrey and Brian Avery in Declan's.

The study's biggest finding though was how the Almosts and, to a lesser extent, the Champs struggled to deal with challenges and setbacks when they eventually encountered them. The path had been so smooth and easy for them for so much of the way, they didn't know how to cope when they inevitably hit a couple of speed bumps.

According to the research, they never quite had the same commitment levels as the eventual Superchamps. They might have loved their sport but they seemed more concerned with looking better than getting better, their status rather than their craft and game.

Almosts spoke about how they had been 'coasting', taking things for granted. They loved the games but practice was 'just a chore'. They avoided the bits they were 'shit at'. 'I felt no pressure,' one said, 'and agreed when everyone told me "You're a natural."'

The Champs also tended to neglect any skill gaps. One of them, a soccer player, told Dr MacNamara's research team, 'Rather than staying on at training and thinking, "Right, I'm going to really focus on my crossing", I did no extra work.'

That wasn't the case with the Superchamps. One of them, from a combat sport, spoke about how for them it was all about getting better, "perfecting this combination", "building my armoury". And that's how it was for us. We were bit by bit building our armoury.

Again, Dad helped, providing that 'optimum balance of challenge and support' that Dr MacNamara recommends. He wasn't directive in how we played, not least because we were different players to him, but he did encourage us to develop both feet. He'd challenge us to kick ten frees in a row when we'd be over on the green. And I remember when I was about seventeen, he took me down to the field in Plunkett's for a kicking session and suggested I study the kicking style of Gareth 'Nesty' Smith, a player in the club who went on to play a bit with Dublin and then Cavan. Nesty had – and still has – this beautiful way of striking through the ball, almost like a model golf swing. Dad felt there was something in it for me, and there was; I started to kick the ball higher, truer, better.

He would occasionally drop little suggestions and tips like that. When he took us out to the track in Lucan, he showed us how to breathe properly while running; when people get tired, he'd learned from taking a yoga class, they have a tendency to lean over and take shallow breaths – don't pant, take proper deep ones, 'right into your belly'. It was in keeping with what Dr MacNamara and other psychologists recommend how a sports parent should help their child – encourage them to be less concerned about perks and prizes and instead focus on how they can get better and have fun.

The study found that it wasn't so much about what kind of setback or challenge you encountered as how you interpreted and responded to that setback or challenge. A similar incident – illness with glandular fever – was reported as high impact by four Almosts but rated low by two Superchamps. Deselection from a team seemed to derail Almosts and demotivate Champions, but the Superchamps viewed such setbacks as 'catalysts for development rather than roadblocks'. They had 'an almost fanatical reaction to challenge, both proactively and in reaction to mishaps'.

The first representative team I went for was a north Dublin U14 panel. Ross McConnell made it but I didn't. I was a bit jealous that I didn't get on their trip to London but I didn't get too down about it; at the time someone like Ross was just another level to me. And as Ross has pointed out to me since, most of the lads sent to those trials by their clubs were either centre backs or midfielders. They were nearly all big, powerful lads, strong on the ball, with a lot of the play going through them. There wouldn't have been as much store put on a slight, skilful lad at corner forward who might get only five touches a game but could kick off either foot. At least I had got a vote of confidence from my club to even be put forward.

In hindsight, the experience of a "failure" like that served me well. Maybe if I had made that team at a time I was winning community game medals in athletics I could have started to fall into the Almosts' trap of thinking I was "a natural", something I'd hear later in my career, only I'd remind anyone who said it that it took me until I was twenty-five to look like a natural with Dublin! An early bump like that prepared me for the long and rocky road to Dublin and the top.

Likewise when I didn't make the U16s or the minors – they all helped mould me into one of those resilient "take the knocks but keep going" athletes that Dr MacNamara contends any talent system should want to generate. I never didn't believe.

The first cruciate during my middle U21 year wasn't going to derail me either; if anything it gave me 'a different mental capacity' like one of the Superchamps spoke about when bouncing back from their serious injury. I had my Dad to lift me back up and help convert the back shed into a gym so I could rehab there. And of course he was a living example himself of someone who came back from their own knee injury to play for Dublin.

And I also had the shining light of Alan guiding me. Interestingly, the study found siblings played a significant role for the Superchamps. 'It was when my older brother became professional, that opened the door in my mind that it was possible,' one of them said. And that's how it was in my mind when Alan became a Dub. *It's possible.*

BEING his brother opened other doors. I'd say it helped get that scholarship to Maynooth under Willie Hughes in the autumn of 2002, and another one in DCU three years later. Declan Lally had a meeting with Declan Brennan, the director of the DCU academy, to talk about going there and mentioned in passing that 'Alan Brogan's brother' was a handy player. I sometimes wonder if they thought they had recruited Alan himself! Our first game was a challenge match against Monaghan out in Ballymun and when Niall Moyna was naming the team in the dressing room, he prompted an outbreak of laughter when declaring that our number fifteen for the evening was Alan Brogan!

I just had to live with it. Before I came along, Alan had to contend with being "Bernard Brogan's son" and he carried it lightly, looking at the upside of it while differentiating himself as a player. So that's what I did.

I knew I wasn't a replica of Alan. He could run and solo twenty yards past three or four players. I was a different athlete with a different skillset – more of a gunslinger. So that's what I focused on. I realised I hadn't the engine or sheer energy of Alan but that I could be more accurate and deadly in front of goal than him. It's something I still tell younger players today: yes, work on skill gaps in your game, but the real marginal gains are made by strengthening your strengths.

My first year in Maynooth I didn't make the Sigerson starting fifteen. I also have some memory of being taken off at halftime in some match or other after kicking four wides. There was the odd murmur that "that Brogan fella" was "too greedy". But that went with being a striker and as that year progressed, I was regularly kicking seven or eight scores a game. We won that Kildare U21 championship and I brought that form with me back to Plunkett's.

It caught the attention of the Dublin U21 management team. Lally at the time was playing with St Brigid's alongside Declan Darcy, who was in his first year involved as a selector, along with another just-retired Dublin player called Jim Gavin; between them they took most of that team's training while Tommy Lyons was doubling up as senior and U21 manager. One night that summer of '03, Darcy told Lally and Barry Cahill, both of whom were in with the 21s, that after being at a Plunkett's game he felt 'that Bernard Brogan fella is better than the brother!'

I got the call up to the 21s sometime after they had won Leinster and was on the bench for the All Ireland semi-final and final. I didn't get on but just being around it, seeing Alan lift the cup after they beat Tyrone in Navan and going back with him to the club that night with the silverware, gave me a taste of what it was like to be a Dub. I was immediately addicted. Doing my cruciate the following year was no impediment to getting back wearing that blue. By 2005 I was starting with Maynooth in the Sigerson and winning a Leinster U21 championship and after we lost the All Ireland semi-final to Down, I was brought in to the senior panel for the summer.

With that a whole other rocky road would open up. Trying to make the bench, come off the bench, get a start, keep my place, win the big one. And, especially in the early years, just trying to carve out my own identity within the dressing room. To be more than just "Alan's brother".

There was definitely that syndrome during Pillar's time. There was nothing malicious about it, just some good-natured slagging from some of the lads, but it definitely drove me on, to prove I was a fine player in my own right and there on merit. Did being Alan's brother hurt me? When I finally broke onto the team, it was in the half-forward line, more Alan's natural habitat than mine. Dad reckons it probably cost Dublin the All Ireland that year having me as a mini-Alan out there; that we needed a pure gunslinger in the full-forward line in that 2007 semi-final against Kerry whereas having me out on the wing was like trying to fit a square peg into a round hole.

But maybe if I wasn't his younger brother I mightn't have even been on the team by then. I don't know if I'd have been called up to the senior panel in '05 straight from the 21s if I had been anyone else. But the management probably calculated: Alan's obviously one of our key men, and there's a glimmer of something there with the younger brother. Let's nurture it. Let's bring him in.

AT halftime this evening out in Garristown, our manager Paul Curran puts Alan on; we're five down to Raheny and need a bit of guile to try and break the fourteen men they're getting behind the ball.

A few minutes later, Lally comes on as well, another star man of the 2003 Dublin U21 team but who is thirty-six now, just back from injury. And while the lads fight back gamely, with Ross still a pow-erhouse around midfield, we then concede another silly goal – the story of our lives in Plunkett's, the nearly men.

We're raging against the dying of the light. Between lads being injured or regraded or retiring, we're down ten of the team we had two years ago. We have a young lad called Seán Bugler who is magic and should play for Dublin, he just needs more confidence, but though he kicks five points from play, Raheny just have too much power and legs for us.

We troop back sombrely to the dressing room. I'm only pulling out of the grounds when I get the customary call: it's Dad. After every Dublin game when I check my phone, there'll always be a missed call from him. I usually wait until I'm on the team bus to give him a quick ring back. And you can tell that he has it all in his head, what he wants to say. Jesus, you played great out there!

'God, I don't know, Da! I only scored a point. I wasn't that good.'

No, you laid off three scores too. You won a couple of frees. And you made a great decoy run for Dermo's point there before halftime. You were looking for that shot alright, you just probably struck it too high, but…

Little things I'd have noticed but thought no one else had.

This evening the chat is more subdued. The goals killed us. 'Ah, desperate.' We could have pushed up man-to-man earlier on their kickout. 'Probably could have, yeah.' But still there's some cause for hope. Alan moved quite well, he could start the next day. 'Lally too.' Bugler's class, isn't he?

And then he mentions that he's taking Alan's eldest lad, Jamie, out to the running track tomorrow, just like he brought us all those years ago. I can picture it already. Take a deep breath there, Jamie – right into your belly!

Some other Brogan traditions will continue this summer. After every championship game Dublin play in Croker, Dad and his brothers and some of their children and spouses and grandchildren will gather on Jones's Road outside the premium section of the Hogan Stand. They'll have a quick post-mortem there and then most of them will move on to a house in Connaught Street. And there, in the shadow of Dalymount Park, they'll have a barbecue with the rest of the clan in the backyard of the house that now belongs to Paula and Helen Currie, daughters of my grand-aunt Dolie, Granny Brogan's sister.

Now that he's finished up, Alan sometimes pops in there, though most of the time he'll meet up with a few old teammates for a few pints instead. But Jamie always goes along there now with his granny and granddad, revelling in the raft of burgers and mingling with three generations of Brogans and hearing all their stories about his da.

It's a ritual that will run as long as I'm still involved, and maybe even outlive my own time in blue. But we're all mindful that it began when Alan broke onto the Dublin team in the eternally sunny summer of 2002.

A few months after Alan's dream farewell point in the 2015 All Ireland final in the rain – playing a one-two with his little brother, then kicking the insurance score with the left foot he had honed from Dad's gentle but constant urging – the whole clan gathered in Celbridge Manor hotel for our annual get-together. It's another lovely little family tradition now, something which began after Grandad Jim passed away and we were no longer all meeting in the old house. His son and namesake, Uncle Jim, has kind of assumed the role of family patriarch and that Christmas he paid a lovely tribute to Alan, his own godson.

On behalf of the family, he said, thank you for the memories, and thanks for giving us a reason to meet up as a family at all those matches in Croker and those barbecues in the Curries'.

I had more reason than anyone else to raise a glass to Alan that night. Only for him, I wouldn't have been where I was in Croker either.

7

The Apprenticeship

B ETWEEN WORK AND EVERYTHING ELSE, I DRIVE
to training by myself nowadays but in the early years it was
more of a team activity – and what a team we had.

Our car was the St Declan's alumni car – Alan, myself, Lally and
Barry Cahill, and then at the wheel, the master of ceremonies and
the main act, Senan Connell.

Senan always drove. He had a sponsored car to show off. Only
this was when GAA commercial gigs were still in their infancy and
Dublin football was in the Inbetweeners years. You weren't going
around in a lovely Skoda Kodiaq that MSL Motors kindly provide
me with these days. Instead Senan had to do with a little washing
machine on wheels, a green Polo. Yet every evening we squashed in
without complaint. We weren't carpooling to save petrol. We were
carpooling to have the craic.

From the moment we got into that car to the moment we got out,
we barely stopped laughing, hearing Senan go on about various
nights out and old football war stories.

But a few people didn't find our mobile comedy club all that
amusing: Pillar Caffrey and his management team. When our car
pulled into the grounds of St David's, Artane, it was as if they could

hear a circus clown horn. After a while, they let it be known that they'd had enough of the five clowns tumbling out of that Polo breaking our sides laughing. Stephen 'Ski' Wade was one of Pillar's selectors, a fiercely respected figure within the group who had a real hard edge about him. He and Pillar told Lally that he should travel on his own to training. If he was going to be challenging the likes of Senan and Alan for their place, he couldn't be laughing with them all the way out to training. We were expending too much energy before training had even started. Our heads weren't tuned in for the session ahead.

Lally got the message and knuckled down even harder – but he still commuted to training in Senan's car. And I suppose that's how it was in the Pillar years. While the management impressed upon us that football was something to be taken very seriously, we took the craic very seriously too.

IN the public memory that era might be remembered for earnest things such as the Blue Book and the pre-match march to the Hill, but those of us who were there will remember something like the Vengabus even more.

The same summer of 2005 that I first joined the panel, a group of lads would meet up the day after a championship match for a round of golf in Hollystown where Ciarán Barry always looked after us well. Back then Wexford were formidable opponents; they had reached that year's Division One league final and Matty Forde was the reigning GPA Player of the Year. So when our team beat them thanks to a late Jayo goal in front of 80,000, the lads were feeling particular buoyant; after two demoralising seasons, they were back in a Leinster final.

I joined them for that round of Monday golf, but as they retreated to the nineteenth hole, I headed off; I was wrecked from Coppers the night before and was working the following morning fitting alarms for my da's friend, Brendan Sweeney, who always landed me a summer job all through college. But then at about eleven o'clock that Monday night, I was fast asleep when Johnny Magee came rumbling up the parents' stairs and barging through my bedroom door and lifted me straight out of bed: Here, you're coming with us! Much to my embarrassment and Johnny's, I was in the nip so I pleaded with him to at least let me put on some clothes. He granted me that request – But hurry up! – so I threw on a pair of boxers, tracksuit bottoms, a tee-shirt, a pair of runners, no socks, and then it was out the door and onto the bus outside to find half the Dublin panel there.

It turned out that back in Hollystown, Jayo and Ciarán Whelan had come up with the idea of asking Shay Wade, a big Dubs fan who drove the Declan's school bus, to bring it over and then they'd go all around Dublin rounding up the rest of the panel. And so, with a few crates of beer on board, that's what they did, going from Castleknock to Rialto, in their own free disco. When the Vengabus was coming, no one was safe and nothing was sacred. At Ray Cosgrove's, about eight of us piled in, snatching not just Ray but his 2002 All Star. When Whelo and myself hauled Barry Cahill downstairs in his pyjamas, Whelo put his arse through the bannisters, breaking them in the process. When Coman Goggins was ambushed, his mother came out furiously waving a tea towel trying to bat us off. Conal Keaney's dad nearly took the head off Johnny Magee, thinking he was a burglar.

By about 1am, we had rounded up just about everyone, including the owner of Coppers, Cathal Jackson, so what better way to round off the night than to head in to his spot? And so in we all trooped, hitting the dance floor in our tracksuit bottoms, Aussie Rules tops and pyjamas.

I ended up crashing in Nesty Smith's because his gaff was just across the road from a fella who worked with me. And that morning I reported to work in the same tracksuit bottoms, tee-shirt and runners that Johnny Magee had kindly allowed me to throw on. It was one of those escapades that everyone will have their own memory of but none of us will ever forget.

It showed the camaraderie Pillar had engendered because only six months earlier he had inherited hardly the most harmonious crew. While younger players like Alan would have had great time for Tommy Lyons for giving them their head, some senior players had been seriously disgruntled by his methods. But now instead of trying to ape how the Clare hurlers had won All Irelands in the nineties and how Mick O'Dwyer had won a couple of Leinster titles in the early noughties, Pillar was studying how Tyrone and Armagh and the Cork hurlers were winning at that time. For years the lads had slavishly ran laps around the barracks in Rathmines and the racetrack in Leopardstown. Now everything was shorter, sharper, more scientific under Paul Clarke, who was linking in with Dr Niall Moyna in DCU and one of his recent sports science graduates, Daniel Tobin.

Ski was coaching the backs. Kieran Duff took the forwards. Gary Matthews was in as one of the first specialist goalkeeping coaches in the country. Brian Talty, as well as being a selector, worked with the midfielders. All of them were excellent. With Clarkey and Daniel on the training ground dovetailing with them so well, we felt any night we trained, there couldn't have been a better session anywhere else in the country.

Then you had Ray Boyne doing stats, giving us some performance targets to go after; Dave Billings looking after logistics as well as continuing as a selector; a proper medical team, and various different people brought in to help with the mindset. Once a week we each had to collect our personal batch of twenty-four bottles of Powerade and water to ensure we were hydrating optimally. We started using ice baths to help with our recovery. After games in Croker we'd use the pool in DCU for the same purposes. There wasn't a tree Pillar didn't rip up trying to improve us.

There were constant team meetings where Pillar broke us into groups to get us to discuss the previous game and the upcoming one. Looking back, it was a huge educational process, a real project in change management. Sometimes though that meant the delivery could be a bit forced.

One summer when I wasn't next to near getting onto the pitch, we were broken into pairs and had to call each other the week of a big match to talk about how they were going in training and games; a kind of affirmation and review exercise, I suppose.

I was paired with Ciarán Whelan, probably our best player at the time. Even in training the energy and intensity he brought was immense. One night he tackled me and it was like going into a car wash – I couldn't get out. I was like a punching bag to him – dush, dush, dush, dush! – and he was throwing me around like a rag doll. In the end I fell onto my knees just to get away from him. Whelo was just a man mountain, someone I was almost in awe of.

I was bricking myself calling him. What was he going to learn from me?! And what would he want to say about me, someone nowhere near seeing the action in the big game he was getting ready for? This guy wouldn't want to talk to me!

We made a stab at it anyway.

'Well, Ciarán, how's things? How's the body after last night?'

Yeah, feeling good, Bernard, thanks. Yourself?

Whelo couldn't have been more polite. But what was I supposed to say to him?! 'You're going well, Ciarán!' 'Great catch last night!' 'Keep it up!'

It was the same when I was paired with Paddy Christie, one of the best full backs Dublin have ever had, a real quiet character who preferred to keep the head down and himself to himself the week of a game. 'Hi, Paddy, yeah, I was marking you there the other night and you're moving well, you got a great tackle in on me...' I didn't know what to be saying!

It was just one of those exercises that a team looking to go to the next level will try and hope someone gets value from. I wouldn't have been aware that for a long time the Dublin dressing room wasn't a particularly welcoming environment for young players; maybe Pillar saw an exercise like that as another way to chip away at that and create a new culture. Lally found he learned loads from his chats with Collie Moran. And in the end I was thrilled to get to talk to the likes of Paddy and Whelo. But I'd love to know now what the two of them made of it all and what value they got from what a young Bernard Brogan had to say to them.

It was disappointing that after Pillar stepped down, the existence of the Blue Book and some of its contents were leaked into the public domain. It left everyone open to ridicule when actually it had a lot of merit – every team trying to make a breakthrough tries these quirky, left-of-centre things, and if they do manage to get over the line, suddenly they're these great pioneers. Pillar was very friendly with Kieran McGeeney from coaching him in Na Fianna; one winter there was even talk around our dressing room that McGeeney was going to join us as he was living in Dublin and supposedly not seeing eye-to-eye with the Armagh management. It didn't materialise but from their conversations Pillar learned Armagh had put together a sort of training journal, sprinkled with motivational quotes, as had the England rugby team which had won the 2003 World Cup. So Pillar took that template and gave it a bit of a Dublin twist.

Like other things we tried around that time, the rollout could be a bit stilted. We were supposed to read certain passages before we trained and we'd be checked up on it, a bit like a kid being asked if they've said their prayers or done their homework. Sometimes in the dressing room before training we had to pair up and recite – or mumble, as often happened – a speech from General Patton that I had also come across in a Jonny Wilkinson book. *'You can't let others be responsible for getting you started. You must be a self-starter...'* But for the most part I thought it had its merits. It helped you get tuned in before you went out training; whatever smiles still left from Senan's car would be wiped off you there and then. As a whole the Blue Book made you more mindful of your preparation. Things the current Dublin team take for granted now were first introduced to us in that book.

There was also a rationale behind the march to the Hill. It was actually Jayo, now such an integral part of Jim's management team with its distaste for any sideshows, who floated the idea to Pillar; by the end of 2004, he felt there was a disconnect between the supporters and the team and it was a way to renew the bond.

I certainly was all in on it. I threw myself into everything we did. Because all those "inches", as was the term en vogue at the time, were adding up to mould us into this unit, this army hell-bent on victory. If you spot me in any old photos or footage of the famous mill by the Hill before the 2006 All Ireland semi-final against Mayo, you can tell by my eyes how immersed I was in our collective mindset. We were on a war footing because once that ball was thrown in, for us it was war.

There was just one problem. I wasn't on the field for that throw-in and I still wasn't on it when the final whistle went. If you look back at that defeat to Mayo which ended our 2006 season, or the equally-explosive Battle of Omagh which began it, I'm there on the margins, standing shoulder-to-shoulder with my band of brothers for the national anthem above in Tyrone, or holding onto Mark Vaughan's jersey as he's trying to hold back Whelo, raging at Mayo's temerity to warm up in front of the Hill. But I felt like I was the one being held back.

I look at the Pillar years, especially the second season, with a mixture of fondness and frustration.

In 2005 I wasn't ready. I was still only a year back from doing my first cruciate and in all honesty, I was just glad to be there, mixing with these legends I had watched as a schoolboy. That summer Pillar rotated lads at the rear end of his thirty-eight man panel and brought along a different couple for every match day; I made it onto the bench for the first-round game against Longford, along with Jonny Cooper's brother Niall, and had no complaints when it proved to be my only day trip of that campaign. A year later though I wasn't as easily pleased.

I made almost every matchday twenty-six that championship of 2006 but never got on the field. Outside of fifteen minutes against Monaghan and two minutes of injury-time against Kerry, I didn't feature in the league either.

There was a term the management had in those years: "apprenticeship". You had to serve your "apprenticeship", do your time, earn your stripes. That concept didn't sit well with me. It still doesn't. It stifles the self-belief of a young lad when he instead should feel empowered: this is whatever you want to make it, try and make it yours – doesn't matter if this is day one for you or year ten.

To me that was the missing piece in Pillar's time. Under Pat Gilroy, everyone felt they had a chance of getting in, just as no one felt their place was safe, as I learned at the start of 2010. Jim Gavin took over a team that had already won an All Ireland yet by the league final of his first season we had five newcomers on the starting fifteen – plus Dean Rock and Shane Carthy coming off the bench. On top of that Ciarán Kilkenny started every game in that subsequent 2013 championship, having been thrown in at just nineteen years old for the All Ireland semi-final against Mayo the previous year by Pat. After the 2017 league he parachuted Con O'Callaghan and Niall Scully straight into the championship starting fifteen. Brian Howard also got some game-time and has now nailed down a starting spot in this year's league. Another kid from last year's U21 All Ireland winning team, Eoin Murchan, has come on for half an hour in each of our last three games, including the league final against Galway. He's small but he's dynamite and because he's been going well in training, Jim is giving him his chance.

Pillar was much more hesitant about giving a lad a shot. I know young fellas now are more physically developed from being exposed earlier to proper strength and conditioning, but it's still all relative to the competition. The Mayo team that beat us in 2006 had four U21s on the field. The Kerry team that beat us in 2007 had three. In 2002 Tommy Lyons took a chance on starting Alan, Clucko, Barry Cahill and Paul Casey. I'd say Tommy would have given me my shot earlier; he had been quick to call me up to the U21s and even after I did my cruciate he ensured I had access to the senior medical team. The only U21 to feature for us in the All Ireland series in Pillar's time was Mark Vaughan coming off the bench. He got one start in Leinster in 2005 but the only other championship debutant that year was Stephen O'Shaughnessy. In 2006 the only two were Kevin

Bonner and Niall O'Shea from St Jude's – and Niall never saw the field again after starting the first round against Longford.

With Pillar there was a set number of players that he trusted. The joke among lads was that he picked his championship team eating his Christmas dinner. Even the subs, you could set your clock by who they were and when they were going to come in. While Pat – and Jim now – would usually have a third or fourth fella in by around the fifty-fifth minute mark, Pillar in 2006 was only putting his second sub in around then; the third fella on average was only coming on with six minutes to go.

The worst part wasn't even that you weren't getting a game – it was feeling you were never going to get a game. David "Dotsy" O'Callaghan went on to have a fine inter-county hurling career but he was a lovely footballer as well. That summer of 2006, I used to get great energy from how well the two of us combined in the full-forward line in A-versus-B games. But then when I saw that he still couldn't get into the starting fifteen after he was regularly burning top defenders like Paul Griffin and David Henry, it nearly deflated me as much as not getting on the field myself.

Pillar would make these gestures to acknowledge the importance of the whole panel. He had a lad like Derek Murray, who toiled for years on the panel but only ever got five minutes of championship football, to launch the Blue Book to the whole team. Before a championship match he'd laud the effort of some lad who hadn't made the match-day twenty-six and present them with the starting jersey number they had been targeting; a number eight, say, in the case of a midfielder like Ross McConnell. But after a while it just felt like tokenism. There wasn't a real sense of competition for places that we had in future setups because there wasn't the same sense of opportunity.

Something of a self-fulfilling prophecy was in effect. Because management weren't conveying to lads that we had a realistic chance of playing, we then came to believe that we had no chance. And subconsciously even that we maybe weren't good enough to play. And so, our behaviour and performance only reaffirmed the management's expectations and evaluations of us.

In 2007 I decided that vicious cycle had to be broken somewhere. Where? How? I suppose after reading it so often, that passage from Patton and the Blue Book seeped through. *'You can't let others be responsible for getting you started. You must be a self-starter…'*

IN all the talk there is about what factors have contributed to the rise of Dublin football, one of the most significant is almost always overlooked: the role and influence of Dublin City University – DCU.

I make it that fifteen of the current senior panel have either graduated from there or are still studying there. Our performance manager, Bryan Cullen, wasn't just one of the first appointments any county had made of that nature; over a decade earlier, he became the first top sportsperson that DCU offered a place to on their sports science and health degree course. Our forwards coach, Jayo, also studied there, as a mature student, though he wasn't quite as mature as a former coach of ours, Dr Mickey Whelan. Before me there was Mossy Quinn. And then in my time there, you had Lally, Ross, Paul Casey as well as Clucko. It has been instrumental in the transformation of Dublin football. And it was pivotal in mine.

When I started there in the autumn of 2005, studying a postgrad in accountancy, the college had never won a Sigerson Cup but it was determined to rectify that and shake off its traditional small-college status in both the university and GAA firmament.

The place was stacked with inter-county talent. Playing right in front of Clucko was Kevin Reilly from Meath, a mainstay on multiple International Rules squads. At midfield you had Owen Lennon, who went on to have a fifteen-year career with Monaghan, alongside Ross. And then upfront you had two absolute sharpshooters in Conor Mortimer of Mayo and Seánie Johnston of Cavan. With those two boys in the corners, there was no place for me in the full-forward line; management felt it had a better balance when at fourteen we had either Shane Smyth, a real workhorse from Monaghan, or Liam Moffatt, a huge man who had played a bit with Mayo and won a club All Ireland with Crossmolina.

I was lucky to squeeze into the team at right half forward ahead of Monaghan's Ciarán Hanratty and one of our management, Declan Brennan, told me as much. When he was announcing our team for the first round of the Sigerson against the Garda College shortly after I had kicked five wides in an O'Byrne Cup Shield match, Declan declared in front of everyone that if it had been up to him, I wouldn't be starting.

I'm sure if the rest of the management also had their way I wouldn't have been starting; that year they were hoping to have Dessie Dolan, Ross Munnelly, Shane Ryan and Diarmuid Kinsella from Wexford, but they were ruled ineligible because their courses were only part-time. You might never have heard of me if they had been free to play. We went down to Templemore to play in a quagmire and with me wanting to prove Declan wrong, I kicked two points as we edged a dogfight, 1-6 to 0-8. A few weeks later in the final in Parnell Park against Queen's, I kicked the opening point, running crossfield from the number ten spot to under the main stand and then curling it over with my left foot. After that Mort and Seánie took over but it helped set the tone and by the end we had delivered the college its first Sigerson.

Dublin-Kerry: My dad Bernard and my mam Maria Keane-Stack on their wedding day, May 1979

Family Man: My granda James Brogan, with me, my cousin Philip and my brother Paul

Superstar, SuperDub, SuperDad: Seeing the respect Dad commanded as a Dub inspired me to want to be one too

Play Like A Kid: Alan, me and Paul

Club Is Family: Dad encouraged Alan, Paul and me to try every sport, but playing football for St Oliver Plunkett's has always been particularly special

See You All In Coppers!: Bryan Cullen getting into the habit, captaining DCU to its first Sigerson Cup win in 2006

The Toughest: Kicking seven points off a top defender like Paul Griffin was a personal breakthrough but losing that 2008 county final was galling

Hold Me Back: There were some great memories and drama during Pillar's time like the famous march to the Hill against Mayo in 2006 but I'd be held back until my third season on the panel

Ordinary Decent Criminals: Dermo, Ross, Mossy, Paddy Andrews, me, Éamo, Flynner, Whelo and Alan watching a 2008 D2 league final in Navan after all being suspended. And no, it wasn't for our fashion sense

Boyhood Dream: I've been fortunate enough to score more goals than anyone else in championship for Dublin but the first, in the 2007 Leinster final against Laois, remains probably the sweetest of the lot. As a kid, scoring into the Hill was a dream

Tough Love: Pat Gilroy benched me at the start of 2010 but it would pay off

Red Hot: In 2010 I was on fire all summer and banged in this early goal in the semi-final against Cork. They came back to catch us but we knew we were on to something

The Real MVPs: With Mam and Dad when I won the 2010 Footballer of the Year to go with my first All Star

In The Name Of The Grandfather: The day after our Grandda Jim passed away, Paul, me and Alan combined for a last-minute winning goal against Down in the 2011 league – and we think Grandda played a hand in it too

Stepping Up: I used to practise my kicking religiously, to the point I relished taking pressure frees in Croker

The Times They Are A-Changin': In 2011 we had to go through our old tormentors Tyrone (top), Donegal and Neil McGee (middle) with their System designed to emotionally hijack teams, and a great Kerry side, featuring Marc Ó Sé (right), my toughest opponent. But nothing was stopping us that year

Perfect Day: The 2011 All Ireland final felt like reaching a mountaintop. It was magical to share it with my brothers Paul and Alan (left below) and our old Dublin management team of the late great Dave Billings RIP and Pillar Caffrey (below right)

Blues Brothers: Paul Flynn (above) has been one of the best players and friends I've had the privilege to share a dressing room with. My best pal Ross McConnell (right) has been playing football with me since we were 11. So it was fantastic to share in our 2011 triumph with them, along with our buddies (below, from left to right): Éamon Fennell, Philly McMahon, Flynner, Alan, Ross, James Brogan, me, Declan Lally and Paul

It wasn't so much winning the Sigerson that brought me on as simply the DCU experience itself. The whole place was geared for high performance – in fact it was one of the first places in the country where that term would have been in circulation.

It had the best gym in the country. We had access to the sports science school – physio, S&C expertise, nutrition. We had use of the pool, the spas, the ice baths. As members of the DCU sports academy, we got complimentary meal vouchers and Puma gear. Every pitch we trained on was immaculate. But it was less about the facilities themselves as the people who were using them and those who had the vision to put them in place.

A couple of weeks after we won the Sigerson, Derval O'Rourke won the world indoor 60m hurdles – she was a regular in the gym. So was Kieran McGeeney; just seeing how much he still craved a second All Ireland drove you on all the more to put in the work to win your first. Fionnuala Britton – like Derval, a future Olympian and a medallist at multiple European championships – was there on scholarship as part of the country's leading athletics programme directed by Enda Fitzpatrick. You had Darren Sutherland the boxer on his way to winning bronze in Beijing. Lindsay Peat and Mark Ingle were establishing DCU Mercy as a powerhouse in women's basketball. Shortly after we won the Sigerson, the college put up a banner in the entrance of the sports hall: DCU – Home of Champions. And that's what it became. A home – and a nursery – of champions.

It was testament to the vision of a few good men. First, you had Declan Brennan, the director of the sports academy who drove the movement. His remark to me before that first-round game in Templemore mightn't have been the most tactful but sometimes management involves challenging people; maybe he calculated that I tend to respond well when people put it up to me. Another Monaghan man, Dr Niall Moyna, was the manager of that 2006 Sigerson team. Much of what DCU has become stems from his time lecturing and working in America and his idea of creating the optimum ecosystem for the student-athlete to excel in, on and off the field. And then you had – and still have – Ken Robinson as CEO of DCU Sport, managing all its facilities and envisaging future ones.

I thrived in the environment they created. I made full use of the gym, especially when it was only twenty yards away from where I lived when I went back for a second year to do a masters in business management. Also staying with me that time were Ross, Paddy Keenan from Louth, the Mort and Seánie. Living with the Mort was an education all in itself. It was like hanging out with a Premier League star. He would drive us out to Club 92 in Leopardstown in his Subaru Impreza – quite the upgrade from Senan's little Polo – when we barely had a pot to piss in. Women loved him and he loved the craic and the perks of being a county man. But the biggest thing I learned about him was just how dedicated he was to the art of point-taking. He was out every day with his bag of balls, kicking, usually first thing in the morning.

Sometimes I went along with him to Albert College Park, a spot just off campus with a few goalposts. Parts of our game were very similar: whereas Seánie, with his low centre of gravity, loved to aggressively turn his man and go past him, the Mort was more like me – he loved to come on the loop and bang.

He'd smile and say in that sort of nasal drawl he has: We'll hit a few spinners here, Berno! Watch this spinner here, look!

That's what we called them: "spinners" or "clippers", when you clip the ball and it spins and spins and you know it's on its way over the bar. It's one of the most intrinsic, purest thrills in football, a bit like a golfer making that perfect connection and then following the flight of the ball, knowing it's going to land almost precisely where you intended, or a basketball rolling off a shooter's fingers and it rotates and rotates before the net dances – swish! Spinners gave me and the Mort the same tingling feeling.

More days then I'd go to Albert College Park on my own, or another Mayo man would sometimes accompany me. As well as Mort, there was Moff, as in Liam Moffatt, the big full forward who came on and got that all-crucial goal in Templemore. He was studying physiotherapy at the time and doing a thesis on athletes in the aftermath of serious injury, so as it was still only a couple of years since my first cruciate, he was monitoring my progress. And he's since talked about how just as I honed my body in the gym to minimise the likelihood of breaking down again, I was refining my kicking and freetaking routine there in Albert College Park: five steps back, shoulders aligned to the left post, deep breath, a little bounce of the knees, then right leg over the left jogging into the kick and make a clean strike. I might not yet have been on the frees with either Dublin or the college but I was quietly preparing myself for the day that I would.

I'd ask Moff for his input too: about my kicking, recovery, injury prevention. There were a million different little conversations like that in DCU around that time and even more in the years that followed.

The impact of that culture on the GAA in general and football in particular has been immense. Only once since 2010 has the Sam Maguire Cup been lifted by someone other than a DCU graduate: Kerry's Kieran O'Leary in 2014. The rest of the time it has been either Bryan Cullen, Michael Murphy or Stephen Cluxton.

The whole GAA has benefitted from the DCU culture. The Go

Games model that guarantees kids get more touches and more game-time originated from a study by Mickey Whelan supervised by Niall Moyna. The first few annual GAA coaching conferences were held on campus until they became so big they had to be moved into Croke Park. Dublin GAA has not been the exclusive beneficiary of the DCU influence. But it has been the biggest.

I've caught online presentations that Niall Moyna, Mickey Whelan and Mick Bohan have all made at that coaching conference either this year or last. All of them have worked with us, either in Pat's time or in Jim's. All of them have coached or managed DCU Sigerson teams. And listening to them explain the value of the games-based approach, and the importance of evidence-based coaching, and how to develop better decision-makers and four-limbed players (both feet, both hands), it brought home the deep-level chats they must have had through the years over a cuppa or in the corridor.

In Niall's presentation at the coaching conference he showed a slide with a quote credited to an eighty-seven-year-old Michelangelo: *Ancora Imparo. I'm still learning.* That, Niall said, has been the key to the success and longevity of Mickey Whelan, who is pushing eighty himself.

And to me that's the mindset many of us developed, working with them in DCU, and that's been established as the default setting now of any Dublin player. Ancora Imparo.

IN 2007 Pillar finally gave me my shot. I came off the bench in each of our first three league games and then started the last four. When the championship came round, I didn't feature in the drawn first-round game against Meath, but I came on in injury time of the replay – and just ran around excitedly – and then was picked to start the next day out against Offaly.

Like in the league, I was playing at wing forward. It wasn't my favourite or most natural position; by this stage I had made my way into the DCU full forward line alongside Seánie and Mort, and had won a Dublin club Blue Star at corner forward. But I was hardly complaining.

In that Offaly game I skewed a shot into the Hill under pressure from one of their backs, Conor Evans, who actually later played with us in Plunkett's. I fell to the ground and as I was getting up, he hit me a shoulder that said: Welcome to Croke Park, rookie! And I remember thinking, Exactly! This is what it's all about. This was my idea of an apprenticeship: getting your chance, getting a knock from a Conor Evans, getting back up, learning from the experience and being the better for it the next day.

And I was the better for it the next day. In the Leinster final I scored that goal against Laois into the Hill where I fell in a heap from the excitement of it all, sporting my surfer beads when I had never seen a surfboard in my life. Then in the All Ireland quarter-final, I kicked three first-half points against Derry. Heading into the All Ireland semi-final against Kerry, I was feeling good about myself and our chances.

Then I ran into Tomás Ó Sé. Or rather, I had to run after Tomás Ó Sé. I actually played well enough in the first half: got on quite a lot of ball, won a few frees and shook off Tomás to kick a score into the Hill to help give us a one-point halftime lead. But then Kerry just turned on the afterburners. If it wasn't Tomás bombing past me, it was Killian Young, and a couple of minutes into the second half he blew past me to set up Declan O'Sullivan for the goal that turned the game. Then I had a shot blocked down and Kerry went down-field to score again. They just blitzed us in that third quarter and shortly after Tomás scorched past me, soloing mid-stride to kick a point, I made way for Darren Magee. I was simply out of my depth.

In fairness to the lads, they got back to within a point entering injury time but Kerry were just that bit craftier and managed to work the ball from one wing over to the other for Declan O'Sullivan to curl over the last score of the game. That autumn I'd win my first All Star nomination while Alan won his second All Star award but the Kerry game made me really question whether I was able for the top level. I clearly hadn't the gas to go up and down the field with a Tomás, and when it came to it, I hadn't the belief either. It might have been that deep down I felt I was being played out of position and when the real heat came on, that doubt bubbled back up to the surface. But that only showed how much more work I still had to do on my mindset.

That was as close as we'd get to an All Ireland under Pillar. In 2008 we again felt we had improved as a team, trouncing Wexford by twenty-three points to win a fourth straight Leinster final, but in the All Ireland quarter-final on an awful dark, wet Saturday afternoon, Tyrone ambushed – annihilated – us.

I was only back having torn my hamstring in the Leinster semi-final against Westmeath, and when I did come on after just five minutes, it was for Alan whose own hammer had popped. Everything that could go wrong did go wrong. Pillar's plan had been for me to come on after about twenty minutes for someone like Kevin Bonner who he wanted on for the early physical exchanges but losing our primary playmaker meant that went out the window straightaway. And it threw me a bit. Though I finished with three points from play, they were academic: one of them was a desperate goal attempt that I blazed over the bar. It was one of those games that I never felt in tune with. It always seemed beyond my grasp, I never seemed to have any time.

But again it was just another part of the rocky road and getting accustomed to the rough and tumble of it all in amongst the big boys. It was still essentially only my fifth championship game with Dublin. Like Michelangelo, I was still learning. I learned a lot from that day.

Within three years of that game and Pillar stepping down the same day, we were the ones swatting Tyrone aside in All Ireland quarter-finals. And that September of 2011 when we got over the line and Tomás Ó Sé famously handed Clucko the match ball, as if to say – Here, ye've earned it, ye're up to the mark now – something he couldn't have said about me in 2007, I spotted a familiar face at the end of a cordon under the Hogan Stand.

It was Pillar, on Garda duty.

I made a beeline over to him. Alan noticed him as well, and that Dave Billings, his faithful lieutenant, may he rest in peace, was also nearby. We embraced, and had some photographs taken together, the four of us beaming while I took a loan of Pillar's cap. I'm so glad we have those pics. I'm so glad we had that moment with them. As I said to Pillar at the time, 'A lot of this is your doing. You've been a big part of this journey.'

And he was. He brought us so much of the way. He helped us appreciate that this was more than just a game, that we were playing for a cause greater than ourselves; Pillar bled blue. He helped reconnect that bond between the team and the Hill, established our dominance in Leinster and forged the first link between the senior team and the immense resource that was DCU, creating Dublin's first ever multi-disciplinary backroom team. There's been a lot of talk about how much Pat and Jim improved "the culture" but Pillar did as well.

True, it still had some way to go. One young player, who by 2011 was one of our key men, first drove into training during Pillar's time and a senior player censured him for parking in "his" spot; the same happened again in the dressing room when he placed his gear bag down. That kind of "welcome" and possessiveness wouldn't be tolerated now. Every year Jim shakes up where we all sit and designates who sits where to help everyone know each other and feel comfortable.

But that same player maybe wouldn't have understood the kind of dressing room that Pillar inherited. There's a book out by Neil Cotter this year on Dublin in the Inbetween Years and Keith Barr talks about how in his time his three best friends on the team were Keith Barr, Keith Barr and Keith Barr; it was every man for himself, survival of the fittest, no place for young men. There may still have been some remnants of that by the end of Pillar's time but that's all they were – remnants. He helped turn a once hostile, fractured dressing room into one with real camaraderie.

We were also coached at a time when not every team would have been coached. We had a kickout strategy when most teams just bombed it out. We had certain playing principles, a "process" of sorts, though we didn't use that term back then. Every night we went into the nuances as well as the importance of tackling and blocking. I can still hear Ski Wade's voice ringing in my ears: Block, block, block! Stephen O'Shaughnessy's nickname even went from Shocko to Blocko, he became so adept at it.

In hindsight, we were probably too open in how we were set up at the back to win shootouts against teams with the firepower of Kerry and Tyrone; under Pat, we'd come up with a more collective and defensive setup to prevent a Tyrone picking us off like they did in that deluge in 2008. But in terms of individual defensive coaching, Ski is as good as I've come across. When Pat Gilroy famously challenged me to improve my tackling, one of the people I turned to was Ski. And so more than once in the pitch in St Vincent's secondary school in Glasnevin, Ski took me through where to position my hands, body and feet, just as he did when we met up a couple of times early on in Jim's reign. What I said to Pillar while wearing his cap applied to the likes of Ski as well. Our eventual breakthrough was his doing too.

I know Alan looks back on the Pillar years as fondly as he does his subsequent time under Pat and Jim. I personally can't go that far, because I played a lot more under the two lads, but there's a lot of points Alan makes about Pillar's time that I'd be inclined to agree with. That the top teams that denied Dublin in the noughties were better than the top teams Dublin have been denying these past five or six years. That Pillar wouldn't have had the calibre of Dublin player available to him that the managers who followed him would. During Pillar's time and Pat's first year we had natural midfielders like Ross or Bastick at full back. Paddy Andrews started out as a corner back. They were plugging holes in defence because we didn't yet have a Rory O'Carroll and Mick Fitzsimons.

Upfront, Alan felt he had to force shots that he would later decline when he had the likes of Dermo, Flynner and myself in our prime to lay it off to. But in Pillar's time we weren't quite ready. Alan says that it was only after I kicked seven from play in the 2008 county final with Paul Griffin on me that he realised I was going to become the player that I would.

By then Pillar was gone. But he's never been forgotten.

8

Hill Climbing

UP ON THIS HILL, MY SWEAT DOESN'T DISCRIMINATE between the pines or gravel that it sprinkles.

A week out from the team bus making its way without me for our opening game of the 2018 championship against Wicklow, I'm here on the foothills of the Dublin mountains.

In front of me is James Allen, my guardian angel through this entire rehab. This is his neck of the woods, out Saggart way, and in recent weeks this has become our Saturday morning routine: first, some strength work on my knee in his shed gym before we each grab a mountain bike and head out into the great outdoors and the glorious early summer sunshine.

Soon enough our cycle morphs into a climb. James leads the charge up the ascent while I try to keep pace with him, making sure to get a full extension into the legs.

They need this. They aren't quite ready for the strain of pounding the pitch or even the treadmill, so this motion is some invaluable lotion for them.

My lungs are feeling a bit of a burn too; again, they've been deprived of the kind of cardiovascular work they'd be used to. But I'm actually liking the sensation, the discomfort. It means I'm working, it means I'm human again, and the more I feel it, the more I want to drive on and stay right on James's wheel.

After a while we enter the woodlands. The family of an old team-mate, Blaine Kelly, who was on the panel during Pat Gilroy's time, own some of this land which hosts seasonal experiences like a Santa grotto and an Easter egg hunt, so we've a pass to ride through its pine-peppered pathways and up and down its rat-runs.

At the summit we pause for a bit and take a selfie with our shades on and thumbs up and send it to James McCarthy. The other week he was telling me how he used to cycle up here a couple of years ago coming back from a knee injury, so this pic will ring a bell with him. Then we race back down, and I'm buzzing from the feel of the breeze and the speed and the adrenaline racing through me again. This isn't just a little win. Although we've cycled only about six kilo-metres, it feels like a big one.

It's all the better for being out in the open air. Almost every day I've been in some indoor gym, either James's here in Saggart, or the one in St Clare's with the team, or on my own in the Anatomic gym at the back of my old soccer club Castleknock Celtic, building up my legs one day, then focusing on my upper body strength the next. This week I started a spinning class in an altitude chamber in Blanchardstown, again getting up a good sweat and making the heart and lungs pump.

The most gruelling workouts this past month though have been in the swimming pool in Marian College on Lansdowne Road. You're literally in at the deep end, treading water, and have to really push yourself to keep your head above the surface and keep marching forward, holding your legs and arms straight.

And again there with me in the water is James. The sessions in Marian have triggered memories of running and squatting in the same pool with Mossy Quinn back in 2009 under James's eye. Back then he was also physio to Leinster rugby and he's also worked with the national team but now he's full-time with Dublin GAA. It's a cause very close to his own heart; his father, Norman Allen, was an outstanding dual player in the 1950s, winning Leinster championships in both codes, so it's fitting that this year James is working with both us and the hurlers.

He's very measured but hugely positive. We're doing a leg lift on the machine at the moment, loading the patellar tendon, that ligament which connects the patella bone and the tibia. And he'll say to me: The ligament loves that now. You're going to get massive energy from this. We're progressing nicely. You've loads of time. You're only in week two of a six-week plan here and in a month's time you're going to be back on the pitch.

It's reassuring to hear because at times you have doubts: How in ten weeks' time am I going to be able to run at full tilt, stop, pivot, jump? But I try to not let them linger. If you think negatively, you tend to get negative outcomes. I prefer to think positively, in the belief it increases the likelihood of positive outcomes.

There's science behind that belief. I've reached out to Ann-Marie Kennedy who has worked as our team sport psychologist and who still does a lot of work for us in PepTalk. She's sent me these scripts and notes on how imagery can help accelerate the healing process. So recently I've been closing my eyes and hearing the words of the script: *See the ligaments coming together… Feel them getting tighter, growing together. Your knee is getting stronger…You're getting better…* Whether it's working or not, I'm not sure, but it feels like it is!

I'm well familiar with the powers of visualisation. As a kid I just called it day dreaming. I'd picture myself getting the ball and sticking it into the net at the Hill end, almost programming myself to score the kind of goal that I slipped past Fergal Byron in that 2007 Leinster final.

Early on in my senior career I was getting three or four goal chances a game with the club but my conversion rate was atrocious. The odd one I'd skew or blast into the net but there were too many I was either blazing wide or over the bar or just hitting straight at the keeper. So I went about addressing it, studying and talking to the likes of Mossy Quinn, and practising myself, but also by just lying on my bed and running in my head how I wanted to finish.

I did it all the more in 2013 after making David Clarke a hero in the previous year's All Ireland semi-final. The danger after a miss like that is to constantly play it over and over in your head. And for a while, I did; it spoiled more than one night's sleep that winter. But then I worked it out that it'd be more productive if I started feeding the mind and the body with what I wanted to happen when a situation like that arose again rather than what I *didn't* want to happen. A few games into the 2013 league we were playing Kildare and I gathered a high ball on the half-turn in the left channel down by the Davin End, leaving me a yard inside my man. I then took a hop and slid it below the advancing Shane Connolly with my right foot. Although we already had the game in the bag by then, I allowed myself a little fist pump, a private nod to the imagery work having paid off.

That then became another little film I could run in my head, usually before going to sleep. And in the lead-up to the 2014 All Ireland quarter-final against Monaghan, that goal against Kildare morphed into one I envisaged scoring that upcoming weekend – instead of it being Shane Connolly I was bearing down on, it was now Rory Beggan. The following Saturday evening, that exact scenario presented itself and I slotted it away underneath him. The same again when we played them in last year's (2017) league, the last goal I've scored for Dublin, actually. It's phenomenal how what you picture in your head can play out on the field.

I'll go through numerous ways I might score a goal; goals have that bit of magic about them where they can suck the life out of the other team or breathe life back into yours. So I might picture myself taking on a man, getting past him and opening my foot like Gooch to pass it into the net. Or playing a one-two with one of the lads before firing it into the bottom corner. Or someone bursting through the middle and me just peeling off my man to palm into the empty net for a "team goal" as we call them, like the second goal in the 2013 All Ireland final when Bastick laid it on a plate for me.

But it's kicking points that I live for − or at least play for. I nearly get a greater high from kicking six points from play than scoring 2-2 from play like I did in that 2013 final because it means I've had more sweet connections with the ball. Say I got a ball thirty yards out from goal: I'd prefer to take that shot on from there rather than run into the 21 and clip it over. And there was a stage earlier in my career when I would do exactly that, and had the likes of Mort and Seánie in DCU muttering about how greedy I was − as if they could talk! In later years I mightn't actually do it because it mightn't be the best decision for the team but I literally get a bigger kick from a score like that.

The point off my left on the outside of Marc Ó Sé into the Hill in the 2013 semi-final: I dreamt, imagined, visualised, whatever you want to call it, that score a thousand times. Coming in at a sharp angle and knowing you've to hit it as sweet as a nut or else it won't travel, and then you get that perfect arc on the ball − to me, there's no better feeling.

I actually bring that into my visualisation: that sensation, that thrill. It's not when the umpire has raised the flag, but that fantastic pregnant pause when he's calculating if he'll have to reach for it and I know that he will. To me that's where the actual joy is: when you've pinged that ball just right and you don't even have to look if it's gone over. You just know.

I'M not sure whether it's visualising or dreaming but these days I'm trying to picture in my head how I might slot into our team at some point this summer.

Again, I have occasional moments of doubt: God, is there any point in coming back? Are they fine without me? I was at last month's league final and the lads showed a lot of composure in the end to get over the line.

But I just think we could do with a bit more of a focal point in the attack, someone to win some dirty ball and create or take more goals; since my injury we've played six games and scored only four goals and none in our last three. I mightn't be needed for seventy minutes but I definitely feel there's something there worth fighting for, that there'll be games late on in the summer where I could be needed off the bench.

People are talking about us being this invincible team but more teams are knocking on the door now. Galway look a proper threat, along with the usual suspects, and they're all coming with different challenges. A set starting fifteen won't win an All Ireland nowadays. It takes different skillsets, physiques, personalities to do a job on different days to win it all: an Eoghan O'Gara in one game, a Cormac Costello in another, maybe a Bernard Brogan in another.

So I'm going to keep ticking over with the visualising through the summer. Ann-Marie's notes mention that athletes who practise imagery during layoff from injury return better to competition than those who don't. Just imagining yourself making plays keeps the neural pathways sufficiently oiled and strong so that when you do return and your brain commands the body to execute those plays and movements, everything is fluent, almost as if you were never away.

You can't be on the whole time though. You've to be able to switch off. Earlier in my career I probably over-obsessed about the game. I read Jonny Wilkinson's first book after he'd won the World Cup and I took it as gospel: not just the hours and hours out with the bag of balls but not even allowing himself a Mars bar! I'd look at Alan between training nights going for a meal and a glass of wine with Lydia and meeting up with friends and think: is that going to hurt his performance?! But in retrospect, he had the right balance. I read Wilkinson's second book then and he talked about how he regretted not savouring the journey more.

I've loosened up the last few years. I'll still feel guilty when I eat something like a bag of chips; I love the taste of them but afterwards I can still feel them lodged in my belly and it leaves this guilt lodged in my mind. But I've found the balance. Even if we have a match in a few weeks' time, I might go out with Keira, not for a feed of pints, but simply for a meal with some dessert and a glass of wine or a pint or two. You're doing so much training anyway, the body will spit out anything that shouldn't be there. Just having that meal or watching a film together at home with a glass of wine is as good for the head-space as a training session.

It's healthy to allow some space for just yourself too. Recently I've been dabbling a good bit in spray art of all things. Years ago some DIT students sent myself and Cian Healy a spray kit and canvas to each do a painting to auction in aid of the ISPCC. I thought it was a cool idea so I did it and since the injury I've been out the back garden with my mask, spray paints and stencils, drawing various landscapes with the moon or sun hovering over them.

In hindsight, I was probably pushing myself and the body too much at the start of the year and it might have brought on this injury. The day I collapsed in Innisfails had begun in London. The previous night we'd had a launch. I didn't drink at it, I went to bed early, but I was also up early to catch a flight. With all the preseason training I'd done to go with all we were doing at work, maybe it was inevitable something was going to give.

I'm trying all the more now to get that blend right of football, work, family. Sometimes alright you've to dive into one more than the other but then you've to redress that balance and give more time back to the others. So last month myself and Keira headed away to Marbella for a break, our last hurrah before any babies come along.

Normally on a holiday our car hire is cheap and cheerful but this time I said, you know what, we'll go all out! Keira was waiting outside when she saw this outrageous red Aston Martin convertible pulling around the corner: Jesus, that fecker is after getting this, isn't he?! We had great craic with it: pulling down the hood, taking turns at the wheel, just cruising around in the sunshine, shades on, wind in the hair.

It was only the five days but I came back refreshed. Ready to attack the rehab again. Ready to attack this hill. Seeing myself playing in front of the Hill again.

9

July

THEY'RE HERE. THEY MADE IT. BOTH OF THEM.

While the Gaelic football world is gearing up for the first-ever Super 8s, my whole world right now is the super twins.

On Tuesday morning, July 10, 2018, Keira gave birth to little Donagh and Keadán Brogan in the Rotunda Hospital.

I can hardly describe the joy. And the relief.

As strong as Keira was throughout the pregnancy and as positive as I tried to remain by her side, we were never comfortable until the second of them was in my hands, screaming.

So once he was, I started laughing. 'I can't believe it!' And I still can't. Both of those beating hearts have made it.

On Tuesday morning we went into the theatre. As a man, you can't but feel pretty helpless and useless at that point, but I tried my best. And then, at 10.03am, there was one of them, screaming his little lungs out. Donagh. It was an amazing sight, but it was still only halftime.

I was still on edge. I don't think I've ever been more panicked. Because we still didn't know about the second one. All I kept thinking was: What's the story with the second fella? Is everything alright with him? Is everything alright with Keira?

Then two minutes later there he was too, bawling. So you did make it, you little fighter, you! You both did!

That was as good a moment as I've had in my life. The two lads both wailing at the top of their little lungs in that delivery room; their mother safe and well, and me just laughing to myself: 'I can't believe it!'

I'm even happier for Keira than for myself after the whole stress of this pregnancy.

A few months ago we bought a book on Gaelic names which explained the origins of every name. We soon identified just the one for the little fella that didn't give up. Keadán. *Little warrior*.

For a short while we were going to call his brother Reece after coming across it on an app but it just didn't fit. So we consulted that book of Gaelic names again. And just as it reminded us that Ciara/Keira means "dark-haired girl", Donagh we learned is Irish for "dark-haired warrior".

So that's what we've settled on. Donagh. Dark-haired warrior.

After his mother.

TWO weeks on from the birth of the twins and I'm the first member of the group in Parnell Park and its new bubbledome by the right side of its gates; over the summer our collective gym sessions have switched to here. While I'm waiting for it to be opened up, I start skipping, side to side, when I see someone else arrive: Jim. Perfect. I was planning to have a word with him anyway and remind him of our war game back in February.

I've been back on the field a month now. Ahead of the Leinster final against Laois, Jim mentioned how pleased he was about that. 'It's great to see Bernard Brogan back on the pitch again with us,' he told Dubs TV, 'and that's really positive for the team and for

Bernard. He's doing trojan work behind the scenes, and hopefully we'll still be in the competition when he returns.'

Well, three wins later we're still in that competition and I want to return. The team are already through to the All Ireland semi-finals, having beaten Tyrone by a goal up in Omagh at the weekend and seen off Donegal seven days earlier in Croker. On Sunday week we play Roscommon in our third Super 8s game. The one Jim and I red-circled five months ago in the Clayton Airport Hotel.

'Don't forget about me now, Jim!' I say to him. 'I'm coming good!'

He smiles, says he hasn't forgotten about me, that he's noticed me moving through the gears.

'Look, I'd love just five minutes the next day,' I tell him. 'Two minutes, even. Just to be the fifth or sixth sub and jog on and feel part of it and be back in the mix.

'I don't even want to be on the panel for the semi-final. I know I'm still off what's required there, there are lads better than me for that one. But if you give me some energy now, make me part of the system, then I've a four-week run into the final, I'm fully focused, I'm moving well in training, and the week of the final I could be electric and be good for ten, fifteen minutes to help win the game for us if we get there.'

While I have the floor, I push my case some more. 'I feel you might still need me. I think I can throw that bit of smoke up in the air when it's in the melting pot and give the opposition something to think about. I know the team is obviously strong and we have power everywhere but it's not like there are corner forwards running amok, kicking six points every game.'

I think it's no harm to point that out – without singling anyone out. Our culture is into data, not blame. And the data shows that none of our starting inside forwards have scored more than two points from play in any of our last three games. Although the team's style of play has evolved and we're getting more scores from the likes of Ciarán Kilkenny and Brian Fenton, we still need to be creating and getting more scores inside.

There's a number of ways I can help with that. The most obvious is first and foremost maxing out in how I prepare. I can also fight my corner to get on the pitch, which is what I'm doing here with Jim: as they say, a quiet priest never got a parish. And then there's guiding the other lads, including those who are ahead of me in the pecking order. That's just the culture we have.

Paul Mannion especially is someone I've been looking out for lately. He's a fantastic lad, no airs or graces, bright, pleasant, humble, so I know he's open to some advice. I just feel at the moment he's not running the lines he needs to and that's a big reason why he has only scored a point over the last three games. He's so powerful and quick with loads of football, but I feel he's been wasted. He's not getting on enough ball. He's just sitting out on the wing, watching the ball, waiting for it to be popped back out only for him to then pop it across to someone else. He needs to be less stationary, more dynamic, more of a threat.

The other evening in the Bunker I called him over to a laptop and we went through three or four video clips that had already been coded on Hudl. I showed him one where he was again just standing there outside in the pocket, beyond the 45. 'So can I ask, what are you doing out there?'

I'm just giving an option, he said.

'Well, let a wing back be the one who gives that option. You're our kicker, our left footer, one of the best strikers of the ball we have, so we need you on the end of things. We want you running in behind the back here.'

117

He nods. Actually, yeah. I could have ran in there.

That's probably been my main strength over the years: being able to get to the right place at the right time. It's one thing being able to win a ball that's been kicked in and turn and score, but if the direct ball isn't on, you can do most damage by getting in behind the back.

Say Michael Darragh Macauley is attacking with the ball. I'll run across and come around on the loop and just let him go. If he gets through on goal, brilliant. But nine times out of ten, he'll be turned back with all the traffic so I'm there for him to pop it back to. And because my man has stayed goalside of the ball to stop Mick, I've the room then to just give it a little clip over the bar. I'd say sixty percent of my scores from play over the last six or seven years have been like that. Paul could get more scores that way too.

'Just run across the line, inside the 45,' I tell him. 'Run through the traffic. You'll turn defenders. You'll lose them. Then you can come around on the loop and be that option.'

Paul, to be fair, has done that occasionally this summer so I also make a point of showing him an example from the Leinster championship. 'There. That's you. You don't have to do it all the time, you don't want to be predictable, but you might want to do it a bit more.' Again, the environment we have allows for those kind of interactions. When one of the values you stress is humility, it means you're not above being coached by a teammate, just as you're not above coaching one.

That wouldn't have always been the way in Dublin setups. Several players from Paul's club, Kilmacud Crokes, have spoken about coming into the Dublin dressing room in the late '90s and early noughties, and how they found it a harsh, unwelcoming, guarded environment where it was almost every man for himself.

That culture started to shift during Pillar's time. Mossy Quinn's finishing was something I studied closely and which he was very generous in going through with me before and after training; how he'd pick a spot, open his foot, and with almost the nub of his toe, calmly strike it low with enough pace out of the goalkeeper's reach.

It went to another level under Pat. I remember early in 2011 he asked me to come out to St Clare's one morning because he wanted the two of us to help Paul Flynn with his striking. At the time Paul was going into his fourth season on the panel and was still in and out of the starting lineup, so he'd asked Pat what he had to do to properly nail down his spot. Pat told him he needed to sharpen his kicking. So when the three of us met up, we basically broke it down into three parts.

The first was composure – Pat identified that while it was fine for Paul to be going at a hundred miles per hour trying to win a ball back, he was making the mistake of still going at that rate when taking a shot. He needed to bring it down a notch instead of rushing it.

The next part then was about getting a good strike. The three of us stood there on the front pitch in St Clare's, lifting and pointing at one another's feet, specifying exactly where on the boot the sweet spot was. An onlooker could have wondered if there was something wrong with our footwear or if we were about to launch into some game of hopscotch, but we pressed on anyway. Paul had a tendency to kick with the outside of his boot when the sweet spot is actually that area between the knuckle of your big toe and your ankle.

I told him not to bother at first looking to see where his shot went. To just concern himself with keeping the head down, striking the ball with the sweet spot and then following through. The feel of it was what mattered. If it felt like a good strike, then usually that meant it was a good strike and had gone over the bar.

So that was it: composure, sweet spot, follow through. Even if you didn't catch the ball just right on the sweet spot, it still had a chance if you had the other two blocks in place.

Looking back, it was classic Pat. While he initiated the intervention, he let us take ownership of it through asking questions, or "guided discovery" as they call it. And Bernard, where do you make connection with the ball? Paul, where do you tend to strike the ball? And what does that look like, Bernard? Take it away so.

After that, Paul routinely brought a bag of balls and practised what we spoke about that day, especially around that pocket over on the right wing which he'd make his own. I'd say eighty percent of the shots he practised were from there because that's where he would shoot in games; our conversations would have covered the importance of practice relevance and practice transfer as well. And for the next four years straight he was an All Star, kicking two points a game. There hasn't been a season since that morning in DCU where he hasn't won either an All Ireland or an All Star.

That culture of peer learning and peer coaching is even more pervasive now. Where once it was me helping Flynner with his kicking, now the likes of Niall Scully ask Flynner to take them for a kicking session, just as I'm trying to mentor Mannion here. They might be competing for the same jersey as us, they might have taken that same jersey from us, but still our attitude is to be generous, not guarded. If I help you, I'm helping the team – all of us. Because the team is bigger than all of us. I don't want to get on the field by default. I want to get on the field by getting better while you're trying to get better too.

Kevin McManamon best personifies that mindset. The two finals in 2016 are the only All Irelands he's started in. For all the others he was on the bench. And yet he'll give other lads in the forwards honest feedback which they'll fully accept because they know his motives are totally pure and for the betterment of the team. He'll pass on mental skills he's learned from his own tribulations and from his line of work now as an accredited sport psychologist, just as he'll have the humility to ask a Flynner to help him with his kicking. Because he understands: the better a teammate gets, the better it gets for the team, and the better it gets for him. It might mean him giving up a little bit more game-time, but ultimately he's going to end up playing in more games – and winning more medals. So far it's helped him win five All Ireland finals, all of which he's played in at some point and often turned and decided in our favour. In the end, you're rewarded. Ultimately it's in your own self-interest to be selfless.

The only thing is we're all clamouring to play in this Roscommon game.

Kevin Mc has yet to start a game this summer. Neither has Flynner or Eoghan O'Gara. Cormac Costello came off the bench in the Leinster final and kicked four points from play but just like me after the same fixture last year still can't get back into the first fifteen. Paddy Andrews started all through Leinster but has yet to see the field in the Super 8s.

And I know if I was Mannion or Con, I'd want thirty-five, forty-five minutes the next day to rack up a few scores and really find my groove. When I was an automatic starter and Jim would come to me ahead of a league game where we'd already qualified for the semi-finals, I'd tell him I still wanted to play, that it was an opportunity for me to really drive on.

So that's why I'm talking to him here now in Parnell Park. If I remain that quiet priest, I'll likely have played my last game for Dublin. So I ask him, 'What do you need to see from me?'

I need to see you train fully, he says. In games. In everything. See how you're moving.

Myself and James Allen have been thinking the same way. The knee is strong again. My straight-line speed is where it needs to be. The weekend between the Leinster final and the opening round of the Super 8s, we had a camp down in Kilkenny and I was clocking 8.8 metres per second in a speed test on the side of the pitch in Nowlan Park, faster than most of the group.

I also asked Bernard Dunne while we were both on the sideline to throw on the boxing pads. He's not around much now that he's performance director of Boxing Ireland but it's always good to see him. I used to meet up with him quite a bit when he first came in with Jim as a sort of mentor. Usually it would be in the Deadman's Inn on the old Lucan Road and we'd talk about how I could push on and always strive to be better. Looking back on it now, what he said seems so basic, but it wasn't so obvious or ingrained then. I could be playing well while we were cruising through Leinster but Bernard instilled into us through his sheer intensity, personality, credibility, that we shouldn't measure ourselves by the standards of others but by our own: strive to be *the* standard.

Some of us would also meet up with him for some early-morning boxing sessions out in the parish centre in Palmerstown: myself, Paddy Andrews, Mick Macauley, Flynner, Ciarán Kilkenny, James McCarthy. Mostly it would be ten two-minute sets of padwork, but we could also do a bit of sparring at the end, without hitting the head – you wouldn't want to be paired with James McCarthy, an absolute beast. Bernard is still available if lads reach out to him, so while he was in Kilkenny, it made sense that he put on the pads while I put on the gloves. And again we did a series of those two-minute sets, him calling out the combinations and me throwing punches.

It was a great cardio workout and particularly good for moving the lower body and testing and stabilising the knee.

In every session James Allen has been pushing me that next twenty percent. At that camp in Kilkenny I'd have only been soloing a small ball around to get the leg back accustomed to that motion. Then the week before the two lads were born I was back punting a full-sized O'Neill's. The session after they came along I was back kicking a few balls over the bar.

But the last twenty percent in any recovery is in your head. It's grand running in straight lines, or even going side to side and twisting and turning where everything is all nice and structured. It's when you're in the chaos of a game of, say, backs and forwards, trying to chase people, lose people, turn left and right instinctively, that's the real test. And that's what I need and want. It's time to remove the safety net.

So the next night in our pitch session I stay in for everything, and again on the Thursday. Then on the Sunday, a week out from the Roscommon match, I come in for the last twelve minutes or so of a forty-minute in-house game. I'd like to have got on a bit earlier – and been on someone less tenacious than Mick Fitzsimons – but I do okay, I look lively. Conditions are drizzly but I handle some ball, put in a few tackles, and then get a nice strike off. To be honest, it's one for Hawkeye but when Declan Darcy tells me afterwards that it's good to see me "back kicking scores", that's good enough for me! I just hope Jim and Jayo saw it the same way!

During the week I have to go back into Santry for a six-month recovery test, though they've moved it forward by a fortnight in my case. To help me get the green light there, Keira has told me to go into the spare room where I can get more restful sleep.

Everyone's been so good. The day after the twins were born, the

123

office in Parnell Park rang, checking to see how exactly their names are spelt. The following day two little Dublin jerseys arrived in the post with Keadán on the back of one and Donagh on the back of the other. Funny. There was a time the Dublin county board used to ask Brogans for their jersey back. Now they're posting them out to us. Another small measure of how we do things better now.

For the team's last two games, the boys have been on the couch with me, in their jerseys.

But as cool as that was, Daddy doesn't intend to be with them next Sunday.

I want to be back on that bus. I want back on that field.

10

Back On The Bus

'WHERE AM I MEANT TO GO HERE, LADS?!'
I've made it back onto that bus for Roscommon, but I've been around long enough to know how some dynamics can change while you've been away.

I've always gravitated towards the back of this bus, without ever going as far as the back row itself. That has always been the preserve of the jokers, the craic merchants, the alpha dogs. In the old days Senan would occupy the centre back seat, holding court, with Alan cackling along beside him, and the likes of Kevin Bonnar and Brendan McManamon as well as Jayo chirping in with a wise crack of their own. But then when Pat took over, it was as if the nearer you were to the back of the bus, the closer you were to being thrown off it altogether.

I'd assume a seat on the row second from the end, on the left, close enough to enjoy every line and join in on the chorus when I wanted, without ever having to sing lead vocals.

Sitting alongside me was Éamon Fennell, a gregarious character more inclined to turn around and engage with the row behind him than the one in front. But then when Jim took over, Éamo was another one of the back-of-the-bus boys left sitting in the bus station, so Michael Darragh Macauley shuffled in beside me and has sat in Éamo's seat ever since.

Today he's gesturing for me to shuffle in alongside him.

We kept your spot for you, he grins. Welcome back on board.

Eoghan O'Gara behind us offers a similar greeting, then remarks that the back of the bus has changed a bit this year. And as we pull out of the Gibson Hotel on the north dock of the city, I can see that it has.

Denis Bastick used to sit alongside EOG (which we pronounce as E-Odge) but Denis called it a day over the winter. His seat remains empty.

And right in the centre of the back row is another vacant seat, that which used to be occupied by Diarmuid Connolly. During the league Dermo opted off the panel and is now playing in Boston for the summer. But likewise no one has dared sit in his seat yet. It's barely cold, and who knows, next year he could well be back.

Quite a lot here though remain the same. Just as O'Gara still occupies one corner of the back row, Darren 'Butsy' Daly takes up the other. In front of him then and across from me are Cormac Costello and Paddy Andrews, both of whom the public barely hear a word from but could fill Vicar Street if they wanted with their wit and impersonations.

The further up the bus you go, the younger or more conscientious it seems to get. Usually right in front of Cossie and Paddy are Ciarán Kilkenny and Brian Howard, and Niall Scully and Brian Fenton, though all of them bar Scully have been given today off to rest up for next week's semi-final.

A bit further up from them again then, just before the halfway exit steps, is Paul Flynn. Ever since he and James McCarthy broke on to the starting team back in 2011, they've sat together, just as they're beside each other again today. But while James remains one of the first names Jim puts on the team sheet, this is Flynner's first start of the summer.

It's a big game for a lot of us, especially those of us towards the back here. While Butsy has come on in every game this summer, this is his first start, at centre back. O'Gara hasn't seen a minute's action this summer but he's starting, at full forward. Cossie and Paddy are down to play alongside him, Cossie having yet to start a game this summer and Paddy having yet to play a minute in the Super 8s. Michael Darragh was dropped from the starting fifteen the last day against Tyrone so he's another one out to make a statement from the throw-in.

And then there's me. This is the fixture that drove me on these past six months, helped keep me sane, sometimes drove me mad, motivated me, deflated me, drove me on again.

In fairness to Jim, he invited me to travel with the team for the Leinster final as a nod to my progress, but I said I'd prefer to wait until I was on actual match-day twenty-six. That's how I'd envisaged it: being on the bus, primed to explode onto that field. And now that that day is finally here, I'm feeling a lovely little buzz. The sun is high in the blue sky, and I'm on the bus again to Croker with my mates.

Michael Darragh here beside me – who I just call Mick – is one of those people who just radiates good vibes. In the early years I would put on some headphones heading from the hotel to the game but after a while I didn't bother, preferring just to chat to Mick and the lads around us or share an ear with whatever Mick has banging.

The two of us have a couple of WhatsApp groups on the go. One is the Hair Club, where the two of us and my cousin James try to meet up on Saturday mornings for a coffee in town and go get a haircut while we're at it. Mick and James are good friends from when James was on the panel during Pat's time and both are big musos, so while it can be challenging to get all three of us to meet up at once with Mick the only one of us still young, free and single, he always seems able to secure at least one Brogan to convene a meeting of the Hair Club.

The other one then is the Started from the Bottom group, consisting of myself, Mick and Flynner. It's named after a Drake song that he played to the two of us on his phone at Flynner's wedding last December when the three of us were well on. So for the day that's in it, he hands me one of his earbuds, skips a few tracks on his playlist, presses play.

Started from the bottom, now we're here
Started from the bottom, now my whole team f****n' here

Roscommon learn that the hard way. We may only have five lads starting who also started the last day up in Omagh but the back-of-the-bus brigade are all intent on making the most of their opportunity and maintaining the standards and process Jim demands from any Dublin team. Twelve minutes in and Cossie already has four points on the board, taking a pass from Mick rampaging through the middle. Twenty minutes in, O'Gara wins a ball, pops it to Flynner cutting across the 20-metre line who instantly fires a rocket across his body into the top corner. Ten minutes on again EOG lays off another ball, this time to Mick who powers through and blasts to the net. Trotting in at halftime, we're 2-12 to 0-7 up, with no intention of letting up. The Process must continue, which for Roscommon means so must the pain.

I head into the green-carpeted warm-up room with the other subs. Bryan Cullen takes us through a series of re-activation exercises;

already a couple of lads are coming on, Conor Mullally for Cian O'Sullivan and James McCarthy for Jack McCaffrey; with just six days to an All Ireland semi-final, Jim and the selectors obviously feel Cian and Jack have done enough for today.

Meanwhile, the starters are next door in the dressing room following their halftime protocol. I've been in there enough over the years to know what's going on.

Like most things in this setup, it's very much player-led. Usually a process ninja like Jonny Cooper, regardless of whether we're five down, or eleven up like we are today, will remind everyone to stay quiet and relaxed and just get in their recovery: get your water and fluids on board, any cut or niggle, get it looked after by the medical team, and we'll talk in two minutes; today, with Jonny being cocooned for the next day, it's probably someone like Philly or Butsy setting that tone and temperature.

Then they break into groups. Clucko and the backs form one huddle, usually joined by the midfielders so they can discuss how we're doing on our own kickout. Similarly in the other corner of the room, over where jerseys ten to fifteen would have been all hanging in a row when we entered the dressing room a few hours ago, the forwards congregate and review the first half. What's working? What isn't? Have we leaked too many short kickouts? How is our tackling? How are we setting up defensively? How are we going forward? Are we showing for the ball? What has our conversion rate been like? Do we need to control the ball better?

In each group, some player will be tasked with facilitating the discussion and relaying the three or four key points back to the management once they emerge from their own conclave. Quite regularly through the years when we've filed in through the door, Jim would have told me to take the forwards, then the next day handed the figurative pen to someone else. He rotates it, sharing – growing – the responsibility within the group.

Under Jim there is no Al Pacino or D'Unbelievables, no big drama, no big speeches, no thumping of tables, no raised voices. Instead, after he and his selectors have had their own brief summit, he might ghost over to the forwards and discreetly sit in, catching the tail-end and summary of our discussion, just as Declan Darcy will with the backs. He may be one of the best football brains of recent times, but Jim won't jump in and dictate what happens next; instead he might begin with raising a stat that confirms or challenges what we'd just been saying. The way he sees it, and the way we've come to see it – not least from those leadership books he's left floating around our little library in the Bunker – the more engaged and more empowered we as players are in the process, then the more committed and attuned we will be to enacting the process. The more decisions we participate in off the field, the better decisions we tend to make on the field. He doesn't want us to be mere followers; he wants us to be leaders.

There isn't a doubt what has been my most recurring contribution in that huddle over the years: 'Lads, get the ball in earlier!' Fellas must be sick of me saying it at this stage. Sometimes I've said it to the whole group just before we've gone back out and Dec, Jayo and Jim have said their final words. 'Lads, we're eating them alive inside! We've only had three balls kicked in so far. Lads at the back, youse are soloing the ball out. We need to be footpassing it up to midfield or the half-forward line. Get the ball in earlier now!'

I don't tend to single anyone out in front of the group; I might just have a quick quiet word with them on the side. I'd be conscious of that because I'm a striker and I've done more commercial work and media through the years than other lads, so there's a slight possibil-

ity for someone to misinterpret my motives; I leave the calling out
to someone like Kevin Mc whose motives will never be questioned.

I'm also mindful of how football and the team has evolved the
last few years and don't want the likes of Ciarán Kilkenny and
Brian Fenton thinking I'm having a go at them in team meetings
just because they're the ones holding the ball up around the middle.
I appreciate they're the core of the team now, the main men. This
year in particular there's a real emphasis on retaining possession
until a high percentage shot opens up, even if it means keeping the
ball for two to three minutes at a time. And it's working. We're now
the best in the country at it and it's probably what we're now best at:
controlling possession, the tempo, the game itself. But I've said it in
a couple of team meetings this summer, I still feel that when there's
an opportunity to play it inside, it needs to go. That's what Dublin
have been brilliant at over the years – lads cutting inside and the
boys outside then feeding us – and this year more than ever we have
the players to get it in to early and often.

It actually helps that I've been out injured while making that point.
I said it after one of the games in Leinster. 'Lads, I know I've been
preaching this forever and at times you might have thought, "Ah,
Berno, you're just being fucking greedy, you just want the ball."
Well now I'm not playing and still I'm saying it! Defenders want you
playing out there beyond the 45. I know we usually break them down
eventually with runners coming through. But when you release the
ball inside, it turns their halfbacks, they're back running towards
their own goal, they don't know where their men are and it causes
havoc. We need more of that.'

Today I'm preaching to the converted. When myself and the rest
of the subs come in from the warm-up room and I join the forwards'
huddle, Flynner and Kevin Mc are making that very point. Keep

getting it inside. The Roscommon lads can't live with EOG's power. Feed the beast.

And that's what the lads go back out and do. Within fifteen minutes O'Gara has bagged two goals to stretch the lead to nineteen points.

Jim begins to run the bench. Paddy Small comes on for Cossie, who kicked nine points, seven from play. Mark Schutte comes in for John Small. That's fine; I said it to Jim that evening in Parnell Park that being fifth or sixth sub was grand with me and that's just four that have gone in now.

Then he takes EOG off and it's Conor McHugh that gets the call.

Again, I'm okay with that. It was always likely to come down to the last sub.

Something Jim said the other night at training though does crop up in my head. Something a bit odd. After telling me I was on the twenty-six, he then added something like how he wouldn't want to put me in a position where I let myself or the team down. But let the team down how? We're nearly twenty points up. It's not like I'm going to cost us the game. Surely he'll put me in now next here.

But then, with ten minutes of normal time left on the clock, Seamus 'Shep' McCormack, our media manager who on match day sits in with the subs, gets word in his earpiece.

Andrew!

My heart sinks.

Andrew is Andrew McGowan. I'd say he must be either twenty-one or twenty-two years old. This will be his championship debut, just like it's Paddy Small's. Paddy is younger again. And I'm thinking: They have forever to make their championship debut! I was twenty-three making mine! Now I might never play for Dublin again!

I know. I know. Jim's always keeping an eye on the future. It's a key reason why he's managed to sustain the success. He's friends with Stuart Lancaster in Leinster rugby who talks about the "performance clock" and how you should avoid letting a team grow old together. You don't wait until midnight to make changes. The best managers make changes before it becomes obvious that change is needed. I know that those of us at the back of the bus can't stay on it forever. I know in the near future we'll be getting off it for good.

But that's all the more reason to play us today. All the more reason to play me today. After all the effort I've put in to get back. After he told me in the Clayton Airport hotel: *There. The first weekend of August. That's when I'll need you.* We war-gamed this. And now we're…

Berno!

I'm jolted out of my inner rant. Shep is calling again, only a couple of minutes after giving Andrew the shout.

Berno! You're on!

Through a quirk of fate, Mark Schutte has got a bang to the head, requiring a temporary blood sub.

I bolt up from my seat, and as I rapidly shuffle across towards the aisle, I can feel O'Gara and a few of the lads behind slap me on the shoulder and shout: Let's go, Berno!

I hot-step down to Jim who instructs me to go in at corner forward and tell Kevin Mc to move out to midfield.

And then I dash on, down towards the Davin End. And while I can hear the huge roar that goes up from the thirty-thousand-plus who've turned up today, I'm oblivious that most of them are on their feet giving that ovation. All that's on my mind is getting to Kevin Mc.

At first he thinks I'm coming on for him. No, I tell him, Schutte's gone off – blood sub. You're out to midfield.

I spit into my hands and rub them together. It feels good being back out here. I'm not going to try anything stupid or spectacular.

BERNARD BROGAN

I just want to show Jim and everyone else that I'm moving well and back in the mix. So I start running across the line, corner to corner, like I've been telling Mannion to do when we're on the attack, so I can maybe get a strike off on the run. I'm not going to be able to stand anyone up and spin him left or right. My planting and turning isn't sharp enough yet, and if I tried, I'd only get blocked down and look an eejit. So I keep moving. I get on a ball, and just pop it off. I make another run, this time to the left off Conor McHugh. He has a chance to slip it off and allow me a clear strike on goal but he gets tied up and the chance passes.

I just move on to what I can next control. I sprint back the field, chasing a Roscommon man, again to show Jim that I'm moving well, only for Paddy Andrews to roar at me. What are you doing?! Get back inside! Flynner's yelling as well. Get the fuck back inside! I don't know it right now, only later, but they're afraid I might break down injured and are only trying to protect me from myself!

And then I'm making another run, only this time back over to our dugout in the stand. After my little five-minute cameo, Schutte is good to go back on again.

The game peters out. Roscommon string a few scores together to make the scoreline a bit more respectable but with the last shot of the game, Conor McHugh points to leave it 4-24 to 2-16.

We make our way back into the dressing room. Lads clasp my hand, pat me on the back, or in Mick's case, throw an arm around my neck and rub me on the head. James Allen and I catch each other's eye and exchange a nod. You made it back. James, you got me back.

Then Jim comes over, as he does to everyone.

Great to see you back out there, he smiles.

'Thanks a million,' I instinctively reply. But within a millisecond in my own head, I'm thinking, Well, no thanks to you! If Schutte hadn't to go off, I wouldn't have got back out there!

I'm not going to upset the mood though. Jim has an All Ireland semi-final in six days' time, a game I've already told him I have nothing to contribute to; instead I'm going to play a game with the club during the week. And right now I just want to bask in having been back out there, and being back here in this dressing room in Croker with my boys.

On the bus to the hotel, the quips are flying, some at my expense. Jaysus, Berno, what was with that run? That's the first time you've tracked back in ten years!

We all disperse pretty quickly from the Gibson once we've ate; there'll be no pints together tonight with such a short turnaround to the semi-final, against Galway. But after calling home and hanging out with Keira and the boys for a while, I meet a couple of friends in the Carpenter bar nearby for a quiet celebration and a few "sleepers" as I like to call a few pints of Guinness before bedtime.

With me are my mate Joe from Donegal, a big GAA man who lives close to the bar here, and Shep, the same man who called my name to come on today in Croke Park. But I make no secret that I feel I should have got the call earlier. Shep is Jim's best mate but he's a great friend of mine too and an honest ear so he puts up with me venting about Jim.

I'm pissed off – and I'm proud. I did it. I got back out there. I might not have kicked a score, I may barely have touched the ball, but running onto that pitch and getting that reception from the crowd may just be my proudest ever moment in blue. Because up to that moment I was never sure I'd play for Dublin again. There were times over the last five-and-a-half months when I seriously doubted I would. And yet I did.

But will I ever again play for Dublin now? In fact, another depressing prospect is now dawning on me: I might not even make the twenty-six for the final.

For all the doubts I've had this year, they've been overpowered by my positivity, my belief. And in my head I've always seen myself on the first Sunday of September on that bus, on the twenty-six, and in the closing minutes, out on that field, helping us win the race.

But after Roscommon, I'd say there's only a ten percent chance I'll feature in any final. If Schutte hadn't to go off, there'd be zero.

The following Saturday the lads deal with Galway comfortably in the second half. Mannion in particular is brilliant, doing all those things we talked about in the Bunker and more.

That evening Mick texts me. Well, any buzz?

I send him a selfie of little Donagh on my chest.

Has to be done, he texts back. Rest up, big dog.

'You on the soup?'

Yezzir.

'Have an expensive whiskey for me.'

Mick actually checked in on me before the game as well. On the bus into Croker, he sent a pic of someone sitting in my old seat. Well, sort of someone: the smiling sunglasses emoji customised with a Dublin blue tee-shirt.

I laughed, then sent another emoji back, one with a teardrop.

But the tears will be real if it's not me in that seat the next day.

11

In Ongar We Went Longer

AT THE START OF 2009 A FEW OF US HAD THE IDEA of getting a house together: myself, Ross McConnell and Éamon Fennell. But we still needed someone else to complete our Fab Four and eventually we identified our man: Clucko.

He had played with Ross and myself in DCU and we got on well so we broached it with him one night at training and he said yeah, he was up for that; in fact his sister actually had a spot in Ongar that she was looking to rent out. And so before we knew it, the four of us were in my parents' back garden with our screwdrivers, dismantling the old gym myself and Da had built. Then we loaded it into Éamo's van and moved it in our new gaff.

What way can I describe that place the year we were there? It was a lads' pad, a high-performance hub and a party house all rolled in one.

Downstairs we had a room that we converted into a gym. All the equipment from Dad's shed was in there. We used it every day. And yet that same room was the one that boasted the infamous graffiti wall. If you visited our house, you had to sign your name on it. The first person to do so was Da when we moved the old gym gear over. By the end of the year it was virtually covered, we had so many people over after games.

It was a similar story with the attic room. We turned it into an exercise studio. Twice a day Clucko religiously did his core work up there. Éamo used to wear this body suit while on the bike and when he'd pull his arm out of the thing, almost a litre of water would spill out. But that same room also had a fridge. And the day before every championship game we stocked it with what we'd be necking down after the match: most of us had this cider called Kiss you could get in all kinds of different flavours, and we'd grab Clucko a couple of bottles of Blue WKD as well. That's where our heads were at! Planning what we'd be drinking the following night!

The way we saw it though, we had been cooped up for three or four weeks since our last game and blowout. Most lads our age were out every weekend. We had trained really hard for this game, so we were bloody well going to party hard after it. Back then it was common for two-day drinking sessions after championship games, and if you were a Dublin footballer in 2009, it was common for each of those nights to roll into the next day out in Ongar. We prided ourselves on it, coming up with our own little motto: In Ongar We Go Longer!

A few times alright Clucko had to sit us down and tell us that his sister had received a complaint about the noise from some of the neighbours, especially after we had the Donegal boys over, but we'll come back to that later. Generally we were all models of restraint and good behaviour that year.

Everyone took their turn with the cooking. It maybe wasn't as diet perfect as we'd have it now but we made plenty of pasta, lumping in some meat or fish to go with it. The Friday before a championship game then, we'd treat ourselves to a big box of popcorn each and some jellies in front of the telly. At the time Stephen was the only one of us going steady, he was already seeing Joanne, now his wife, so she'd join us, and a couple of us would go down to the UCI cinema in Blanchardstown to get our treats to bring back to our crib.

And what would typically be the feature film?

Something by David Attenborough. One of his nature documentaries. Actually, not just one of them – volumes of them.

Clucko had invested in the twenty-four-disc boxset, The Life Collection, as well as the *Planet Earth* series and wasn't going to let them go to waste. So it became part of our routine, watching The Hunters and the Hunted, Jungles and Deserts, munching on our popcorn while Sir David spoke in that awestruck hush as lions closed in on zebras and cheetahs stalked wildebeest.

Maybe all that power imagery worked because for a lot of that year some of us were playing the best football of our careers. Clucko cemented his status as the best goalkeeper in the country, keeping a clean sheet all through the Leinster championship. After two years being stuck at full back as our supposed Donaghy Stopper, Ross was playing in his natural home of midfield, keeping All Stars like Whelo and Shane Ryan off the starting fifteen. And I had finally found my groove in a Dublin shirt.

While in 2007 I felt I was being played out of position and in 2008 my summer had been interrupted by injury, I brought my club form from that autumn straight into the national league. In our opening game we played the reigning All Ireland champions Tyrone under lights in a packed Croker after which the GAA put on a fireworks exhibition to celebrate its 125th anniversary. Stephen O'Neill kicked a couple of late points for Tyrone to edge it but there were encouraging signs from us too. Our new manager Pat Gilroy had blooded some new faces, including my cousin James, while I scored 1-5, 1-3 from play, the most I had scored in a single game for Dublin up to then.

I picked up a knee injury near the end of the league but I was back to kick 2-8 in the Leinster semi-final when we blitzed Westmeath for the first time; only a year earlier we had scraped past them by just two points. And then in the Leinster final against Kildare in front of a full house, we pulled through even though we played with fourteen men for the last three-quarters of the game. I ended up scoring five points in the final ten minutes, including the last three points of the game, which ultimately proved the difference between the teams.

It was one of those wins you get in the championship that suggests there's something different about this lot this year. Kildare themselves were becoming a proper team under Kieran McGeeney and yet we had found a way to deny them. We were no long leaking goals the way we had against Tyrone the year before. The consensus was that we had more steel to us. Everything seemed in place heading into the August bank holiday weekend. The Dubs for Sam and the party going longer in Ongar.

Everything was in place alright – for an ambush. While we were stocking our fridge with Kiss cider and Blue WKD, Kerry were on the train up: proud, wounded animals after all the barbs that had been fired their way after losing well to Cork and just about getting over Sligo and Antrim in the backdoor. Only by then they'd finished licking their wounds. They were licking their lips, hiding in the long grass, eyeing up a big blue unsuspecting wildebeest. Out in Ongar we had no idea we were now the hunted, not the hunters.

They had their jaws clamped in our throats before we knew it. After thirty-five seconds Gooch had put the ball past Clucko. By the time Alan kicked our second point, Kerry had racked up 1-10. In his post-match interviews, Pat famously compared us to startled earwigs and he was right. Once Kerry had lifted the rock and the intensity, we were scrambling, clueless, lost. Only it was bloodier than that. We had been torn to pieces, just like twelve months earlier against Tyrone. Pat's first year had gone exactly the same way as Pillar's last.

There was only one bit of any Process we stuck to that day – win or lose, we booze. We went into the Dandelion bar in town and after only a couple of pints fellas were dancing on the tables with their shirts off.

Then we headed to Coppers where we met some of the Donegal lads: Rory Kavanagh, who had played with me and Lally in Maynooth, their goalkeeper Michael Boyle who we knew from DCU, and Neil McGee. The previous day they had also been demolished in their All Ireland quarter-final, by Cork, and they were still wearing the same tee-shirts as the night before. There was only one place to invite men who could last the pace that long.

A little while after they had signed the graffiti wall, we were all out the back garden, along with some other guests floating around – literally: we had a little paddling pool and there were people sitting in it with their bottles and cans. There was a ball somewhere around too, and Lally and Kavanagh started messing around with it, until next thing Lally hit him a shoulder, sending him crashing through the wooden fence and into the neighbours' garden!

The next day, probably around the time those neighbours were putting in a call to Clucko's sister, we were in another bar with the Donegal boys: there was still a two-day drinking session ritual to maintain in our case, while our guests obviously prided themselves on going longer than the boys in Ongar. Both parties were still reeling from what had just happened in Croke Park; between us we had been beaten by a combined thirty-one points. Neil McGee was trying to describe the power and size of that Cork team: Canty, O'Leary, Miskella and Kissane bombing up from the back; Alan O'Connor and Nicholas Murphy at midfield; Pearse O'Neill tearing through the middle: not men but giants. It was like… it was like… being trampled by a herd of elephants! McGee spluttered. And Donegal had been mere mosquitoes caught in the stampede.

So there in the Grasshopper bar you had the startled earwigs along with the mosquitoes that had been trampled by elephants; there were so many wildlife analogies going around, we could have asked Eamon if he wanted to watch one of Clucko's *Planet Earth* DVDs with us. You'd have got some odds back then that after our respective tormentors that weekend had shared the following two All Irelands, ourselves and Donegal would carve up the next two. And that every subsequent year, one of us has featured in the All Ireland final.

Everything changed for them with the appointment of Jim McGuinness. Things changed for us too, though it didn't take a change of manager for it to happen. At least nominally there wasn't one. But after the startled earwigs debacle Pat Gilroy was a changed man and change was something he was fearless about implementing across the board. The partying culture was one of the biggest casualties.

Looking back now on my first five years on the panel, we had the greatest craic. Heading back as a unit to the Sunnybank after a big game in Croker and meeting our family and partners; heading into town and being treated like celebrities wherever we rocked up in our O'Neill's team tee-shirts, usually Coppers; they were great nights, great times.

And the Mondays were even better – less hectic, less noisy, just the lads. We'd golf in Hollystown, then maybe go to this lovely quiet pub called the Strawberry Hall and play credit card roulette; all cards thrown into the pot and the last one pulled out had to buy a round of shots. Or we might go into town and the Quay's in Temple Bar where Jayo could swing a keg to be dropped off and we'd drink Becks for free for the evening. And then we could well end up in Coppers again – and on to Ongar.

Even on the Tuesday we were still easing ourselves into next-match mode. The management alright would run the shite – and alcohol – out of us that evening and you'd have lads puking up. But then straight after training a gang of us would go to a fast-food spot. Alan and Mossy loved their McDonald's, while Clucko and Mark Vaughan loved their bacon and cheese fries in Eddie Rocket's. So the rest of us would tag along with them for our last little guilty pleasure before the next championship game and the two-day drinking session that followed.

But it was as if we were caught in this perpetual cycle. We were still heading out after a Leinster semi-final as if we had finally won an All Ireland semi-final. Then we'd get beaten in August and booze for days. And that was just in Dublin. A gang of us would head off to Marbella before coming back and sobering up to play for the club. We became almost accustomed to it, this routine, this identity. We're the Dubs: win all round us in Leinster and booze for two days, then lose in the All Ireland series and booze for longer, home or abroad.

When Keira and I got back together in 2013 she couldn't believe how different the Dublin setup was. In Pillar's time she'd meet my mam and da in the Sunnybank after games, then join me and the rest of the team in the VIP area in the back where there were baskets of fried food – wedges, chips, chicken wings.

The scene in the Gibson Hotel under Jim was like a whole other world. A plush, international hotel, not an old-school boozer; no fried food, only what would meet the approval of our nutritionist. Everything was more sedate. If anyone did go out, it was for just the one night. The Monday Club had long been disbanded, and with it Tuesdays in Eddie Rocket's.

The Startled Earwigs moment was the turning point. In the autumn of 2009 we each had to go out to St Clare's and sit across from Pat and Mickey Whelan. And one of the things they asked us was how did we spend our Mondays after championship games? And do you think that is helping with your recovery? What do you think other counties might be doing on the Monday?

They weren't telling us explicitly what to do but the inference was obvious. Not only were the likes of Kerry and Tyrone still well ahead of us but Cork had clearly overtaken us. The likes of Graham Canty weren't still drinking the day after a championship game. Football had gone to another level of preparation, so we would have to as well.

Ahead of the 2010 championship we had a camp in the Cooley Peninsula and in a team meeting in the Ballymascanlon Hotel, Pat once more floated the topic. Again, he let us do most of the talking but after an hour and a half it had come round to where he had wanted it to go all along: the two-day drinking sessions were over.

By then the Fab Four were no longer in Ongar either. We had already painted over the graffiti wall and laughed about the names that had been up on it.

And all these years later the memories from that place still bring a smile to my face.

MID-AUGUST, 2018, and instead of being in Marbella as was once the norm for us at this time of year, we're in Doonbeg, west Clare, where Jim tends to bring us for a retreat a fortnight ahead of an All Ireland final. His parents are from around here, so he has a deep affinity to the area, and it's an ideal place to escape from all the talk of four-in-a-row that's rampant in our own town.

We're staying on the grounds of the local international hotel and in the same house as me is an old flatmate.

As well as Darren 'Butsy' Daly, Philly, Conor Mullally, Mannion, Eoin Murchan, James McCarthy and myself, Clucko is here too.

This evening we're a team within a team. Jim and the management have come up with a Dubs version of *MasterChef*. Each house has to cook up a special dish with Jim as one of the judges deciding which house wins.

It may not strike you as the kind of team-bonding task that the boss would assign but actually, it's classic Jim. He regularly references Maslow's hierarchy of needs and whatever about winning this competition and triggering a sense of belonging or esteem, or even self-actualisation, we've to first of all meet a more basic physiological requirement. We've to eat whatever we make here. If we get this wrong and serve up shite, we'll be going hungry for the night!

Clucko will be up for this as much as anyone. Contrary to the public perception, he's actually quite bubbly with people he's comfortable with, dropping lines from *Family Guy* and *The Simpsons* in to the conversation. He'll slag me as much as anybody. He notoriously shies away from commercial and media gigs while I obviously haven't; as Pat and Jim have told me in the past, so long as you're producing on the field and something is going back into the pot for the group, gig away. And it gives him ammunition to slag me unmercifully. What are you doing that for?! Sellout! Greedy bastard! I'll wind him up then, telling him he's a boring dryshite. The Masterchef Challenge tonight will be another chance to hop a few balls at one another.

A few days ago I was planning on driving down this evening and heading back up again tomorrow night so I could help out Keira with the two lads. As well as that, my mood was cranky enough. I came on for ten minutes for the club against Kilmacud during the week but even warming up my leg didn't feel right. I ended up just popping off a couple of balls and limping around the place. I was scared I was going to hurt myself in a game I shouldn't have been playing anyway. Yet my thinking was, if I couldn't play in it, what chance had I of playing ten minutes in an All Ireland final in a few weeks' time?

Then Dad called. Go down on the bus with the rest of the lads, he said. Don't just come and go; it'll seem like you're just a bit part. Go down and show intent, show them that you're fully invested.

So that's the approach I'm taking. It's probably my last ever camp with Dublin. I might as well make the most of it and enjoy it and give it my best.

We had a couple of team meetings earlier on and I contributed quite a bit in them. I made the point that because a lot of us have been in so many finals we can sometimes overlook that a few lads haven't and we assume they know things they might not. So we covered the basics. Designate a family member – like I have my dad – to distribute your tickets if you somehow haven't already; don't be wasting energy or time on that. The same with people on the street talking about the four in a row, the five in a row even – be polite but quickly change the subject: And how are you keeping yourself anyway?

I also mentioned a hard lesson learned from the Ongar days: don't get caught up in all the talk about possible individual awards. In 2009 I allowed my head to be turned with all the talk coming out of Leinster of how I was favourite for footballer of the year. Then against Kerry I fell flat on my face and didn't even end up with an All Star. It's natural more than selfish to follow speculation like that but you're best tuning out from all the paper talk and social media. Once we arrived down here in Doonbeg, I deleted my twitter app. It has nothing to tell me over the next fortnight.

Now that we're having this cooking competition, I'm going all in with it too. Our performance nutritionist Daniel Davey has left us some ingredients and instructions to go with them. So it's time to get out the pots and pans.

Myself and Philly take the lead. Right, rule number one – delegate.

Clucko reminds us that his family are butchers. Deadly. He'll cut the chicken breasts up and cook them so.

James is put on guacamole duty so starts peeling the avocados.

Mullally cuts up all the vegetables.

Philly is good at baking as well as cooking so with a bit of help from Murch he begins melting chocolate to make brownies for dessert.

Butsy is on washing-up duty. And then I'm cooking the rice, quinoa and beans, with a bit of help from Mannion.

The place is a hive of activity and communication. How's the guacamole coming along, Maccer? 'Make sure you don't burn that now, Clucko!'

We're going for the fine cuisine experience so Murch pulls out the table and arranges the seats as we await the guests-judges to our little soirée. We're even ready to pour some milk into the wine glasses for their pleasure.

Then there's a knock on the door. Mannion, who has volunteered to be the butler, answers the door wearing only an apron. Ah, lads, come in!

It's the management team. Daniel Davey. Shep. 'Colonel' John

Courtney, another army colleague of Jim's who helps with logistics and opposition analysis. And Jim himself.

John is the nominated chief taster but we invite them all to sit down and enjoy what we've prepared. I assume the role of maitre d'.

'So in this rita bowl we have a Mexican chicken curry, with quinoa and beans. And here we have some roasted hazelnuts with honey…'

We watch as they taste what we've served. They're coming on as gourmands with the most delicate palates and sophisticated taste buds. There are nods of approval. Mmm…. this is quite nice! Very good! Maybe could've done with a bit more seasoning?

A little later they dab the corners of their mouths with their napkins like serious foodies and bid us a thanks and a farewell; they've to sample the delights laid on by the next house.

Then we tuck into what's left, making sure we have enough room left to enjoy Philly and Murch's brownies.

Later we learn that chocolate is all that one lad got to eat. Jack McCaffrey's house had to prepare some salmon. Jack doesn't eat salmon. But lucky for him, O'Gara works for Cadbury's and had a pile of Starbars to keep him ticking over 'til breakfast!

Enough to meet his most primitive of physiological needs, but hardly enough to deny our house being Dubs Masterchefs 2018.

THE next morning we have our first field session of the camp. Since the Roscommon game, or at least since the game with the club, I've decided to be more strategic and selective about how and when I train. I can't go full out in every session. I've to choose my times to peak. On Thursday night in St Clare's I only did half the session. I wanted to be right for this session here in Kilmihil. There'll likely be more of a game and a bigger window to show Jim that I might still have something to offer on Sunday fortnight.

I meet up early with James Allen to get in the best possible activation warm-up. I'm still a bit tentative at the start of the session but as I get into it, I begin to feel better. For the first time I'm able again to get the ball and turn.

We go into a full-scale 15v15 and a few minutes in I clip over a point.

Then I sell Darren Daly a dummy, making him dive full-length, pull it back, skip into space and kick over another point.

Then, with my team two points down, I break through and shoot just wide when the whistle goes. That's enough there, lads. Still, I walk off the field feeling upbeat. The game turned out to be just fifteen minutes yet in that time I managed to score two fine points and nearly a goal.

On the bus back to the hotel, Paddy Andrews slaps me on the shoulder. You're back.

THE rest of the weekend is hugely enjoyable. After lunch, we avail of the fine links course attached to the hotel and play a fourball scramble. I'm in a group with Butsy, Mannion and Con O'Callaghan. Mannion says he hardly plays but he can drive the ball a mile. We end up using nine of his tee shots to go for five under, but Flynner's group beat us by two shots.

Paul is in lively form that evening at our table when we all go for a meal in the local bar and restaurant, Tubridy's. We all have a few pints as well. In fairness to Jim, he treats us like adults and knows that enjoying each other's company like this will do the group more good than harm. As old-school and unscientific as it may be, there are few better ways to engender the 'esprits de corps' he talks about.

The following morning we have another pitch session behind closed doors. But Jim also believes that there are times when the drawbridge should be lowered. Before we finish up, there are nearly a hundred local club members and children engulfing the field. So when we're warming down, I invite the kids over.

'Right, who's all togged off? Want to come down and do a few stretches with us?'

They're delighted. They warm up alongside us, then a few of the lads take them for some skills. We stay on for about forty minutes, mingling, standing in for photos, signing jerseys. It's just a nice way of giving back to a community who have been good to us, especially one that means so much to Jim and his parents, Jim Senior and Ann.

On the bus back to Dublin on the Sunday afternoon, my mood's much better than it was heading down on Friday morning. I'm now actually thinking I could play a few minutes in two weeks' time. My confidence is coming back. I was looking around during our field sessions over the weekend and thinking, I'm moving as well as most of these lads.

Now, do I believe the management will play me? No, I don't. But right now that's outside my control. I'm going to just focus on what's within my control. I'll do a strength session with James Allen on Tuesday. I'm going to load up right and rest and look to impress on Thursday; then attack next Saturday when there should be thirty or forty minutes of a game.

Then I'll talk to Jim in the final week and make my case: Jim, I'm tuned in for this. I'm back. You might not think you need me to get over the line but Tyrone are going to throw all kinds of curveballs at us and when it's in the melting pot I know I'll make the big plays for us.

And that genuinely is my thinking. I just feel that when it comes down to it a few of our younger lads could get anxious because the four in a row is on the line and they haven't been in the position before of being three or four points down in the last quarter the way we've been in games against Kerry or against Mayo.

Two things above all else have served me very well in my career. One: my ability to intuitively pop up and get the ball in the right place at the right time to create or finish a score. That knack might be what's needed near the death the next day.

And two: I haven't known when to give up or go away. I didn't make all those underage teams. I was the longest maturing Dublin footballer ever. And I wasn't meant to be back already from this cruciate. Yet there I was yesterday morning, selling dummies and splitting the posts down in west Clare. And I'm ready to do the same if called upon on Sunday week in Croker.

12

No.27

THE BUNKER PREDATES JIM WITH ALL HIS military analogies but this past fortnight especially it has resembled a war room.

Tyrone and Mickey Harte demand that level of attention to detail. They do not have the same talent level as us, or indeed Mayo or Kerry who we've played in our previous finals. But they compensate for that through tactical smarts.

With Kerry and Mayo it's more of a mix of a shootout, a footrace and an arm wrestle. Northern teams, especially Donegal and Tyrone, have no interest in taking us on that way. Instead they invite you to a table and challenge you not to an arm wrestle but a board game. And if you're not sufficiently prepared, it'll be too late by the time you realise that you've been playing draughts while they've been playing chess.

It happened to us in 2008 against Tyrone, prompting Pat to reconfigure how we set up at the back. When Donegal outwitted us in 2014, Jim likewise rebalanced how we were geared between defence and attack. But another significant shift he made was to have us take greater ownership in analysing our opponents.

Again, it stems from his military background; as a flight instructor in the Air Corps he learned that the more active people are in their learning, the more they retain and ultimately better perform. He has an expression: Hand Up rather than Hand Out. He wants us to put the hand up and give our observations rather than passively take the handout.

Before the 2015 All Ireland final we had a camp in Powerscourt in Wicklow, having already been in Doonbeg for our pre-championship retreat. We were all broken into groups and spent ninety minutes poring through video of our direct opponents prepared by the management. And from it we identified lots of little tendencies of Kerry's. I remember Alan's group identifying how Killian Young liked to hang out on the fringes of the play, looking for an out ball on the left wing. Now, management probably recognised the same thing themselves which is why they had prepared those particular clips, but because we discovered it for ourselves we were more invested in the final in making sure to bottle him up so he didn't get the chance to bomb forward.

Our most exhaustive camp on that count was last year's (2017) semi-final against Tyrone. They had been devastating all season with their mass defence and blistering counterattack, a sort of Donegal 3.0. It was the litmus test of how much we had really evolved and learned from 2014 and we were genuinely worried about the challenge they presented. Then we went for a camp in Carton House and forensically watched tape of them before presenting back how we could disrupt them and hurt them. On the field those of us on the B team set up just like Tyrone. I'll always remember us gathered around in a circle in a meeting room before we headed home and Jonny Cooper saying, Lads, this completely blows away everything we've done before. A few weeks later we completely blew away Tyrone.

That's not going to happen this Sunday. They're bound to have learned from last year. Harte always throws a spanner in the works for a final. We have to expect anything and everything. We have prepared for chaos. We have war-gamed the shit out of this.

My group, which Kevin Mc presented for, mentioned how we shouldn't even be surprised if they've discreetly brought Seán Cavanagh out of retirement just like Stephen O'Neill was parachuted in for the 2008 final. They could switch Peter Harte to full forward so in A-versus-B mini-games we've had another red-head, Conor McHugh, play there, just as in previous years we've had Bastick and O'Gara at full forward simulating the role of Kieran Donaghy or Aidan O'Shea. We've gone through what we might do if they form not just a wall inside their 45m line but another around the 65 to try to prevent the outball and trap us along the flanks to stop us recycling and reversing the ball. In another period of the game they might go man-to-man. A big word Jim has used is agile. We've to be agile for whatever they throw at us, tactically, verbally, mentally.

The downside of all this war-gaming is that our sessions on the pitch have been more rehearsals than auditions. By rehearsing scenarios that Tyrone might pose, we haven't quite had the uninterrupted stretches of football I had been hoping for to move up the grid some more since Doonbeg.

This evening, the Friday before the match, I'll learn if I've done enough to make the twenty-six.

There's a vast difference between making it and not. If you don't, you don't even travel with the team. Most county setups bring everyone but Jim believes that anyone who has no chance of playing just isn't going to be on the same wavelength as those who are and their presence can dilute and even contaminate the focus of the group: there are simply too many bodies around the hotel, the dressing room, the pitch itself for the warm-up: people are almost tripping over one another. And of course that chasm between being on the bus and not means there's an even greater scramble to make it.

The strange thing about it is that as ferocious as the competition is to make the twenty-six, as much as it's an achievement in itself, it's not broadcast who actually is on it. This evening just before training starts we'll gather in a huddle and Jim will announce the starting fifteen, but anything else he has to say will be said one-to-one. You can leave St Clare's not knowing who has and who hasn't made the bench.

I still think when it comes down to it that I'll make it onto that bus. I'm even hopeful that I might get on the field and be what Jim calls "a finisher". That's been my role the last two finals against Mayo when we needed to carve out a couple of scores and keep the ball in those crucial final minutes.

Training starts in about half an hour, so I'm expecting Jim any moment now to pop the head round the dressing room door and ask me in to the management's changing room which doubles up as his office. That's where he told me in 2016 that I wasn't starting for the final replay against Mayo. It was my first time in ten seasons being dropped for a championship match but of course Jim didn't phrase or frame it in such blunt terms. I want you to finish the game for us, he said. I want you on at the business end.

It was naturally disappointing but I took it on the chin. Over the years you'd see lads in that position be thick about it but as a senior player I felt I had a responsibility to heat the building, not burn it down. So did Mick Macauley who was in the same boat. I said it to Mick when we were going out onto the training field. 'When the team's being announced, stand tall and strong. Don't be looking at the ground. When lads are watching for our reaction, we look them back in the eye and let them see that we're not throwing any toys out of the pram.' Afterwards several players said it to me that they took strength from that show of unity that we displayed.

Now, two years on, Jim is gesturing for me to come into the office. I head in. It's just me and him, none of his selectors.

Unfortunately, Bernard, he says, you're not on the twenty-six.

I'm gobsmacked.

'Are you joking me, Jim?'

No, he says, I'm not. We've been watching you and you're moving well but we had a meeting and just feel this one has come a little too early for you. There might still be a role for you if there's another game, like there was in 2016, but for this one, we don't think you're ready yet.

All kinds of thoughts race through my mind. All that bloody rehab. I put my life on hold to get back here. And now I'm not going to be there with the team on All Ireland final day. I'm going to be making my own way into Croker with the rest of the crowd.

I can't just take this lying down.

'Jim, I can't believe you're saying this to me. I'm after breaking my arse to get back. We war-gamed this at the start of the year. And now I'm back out there, moving well, causing our backs problems…'

I want you to come with us, he interjects. I want you to travel.

'What do you mean? Like tog out? Be on the pitch?'

Yeah, he says. I want you to warm up with the lads. I want you to be number twenty-seven.

It catches me off guard. It's a strange one, totally out of leftfield. I have to think about it for a few seconds. Has he just made it up now on the spot? That's unlike Jim but maybe he's been taken aback by my reaction. Whatever, he's offering it now. It's some gesture of respect, I suppose.

"Alright, Jim. Fair enough. Look, you've probably other people to talk to, so....'

After training there's a message from Dad, wondering if I'm on the twenty-six.

But I don't want to get into it all with him. I simply text back: I'm travelling.

SO I'm here: the Gibson Hotel a few hours before the All Ireland final. On Friday evening in those surreal few seconds between Jim telling me I wasn't on the twenty-six and me wondering what to say to him, another thought crossed my mind: what do I do with my overnight bag for the function? Do you head around early to the Gibson, drop it off there and then make yourself scarce so you don't distract the group? Do you haul it around with you while you're at the match and then head to the hotel afterwards? I've never known what the logistics are for the lads who don't travel with the team. And I still don't.

Today I'm the Limbo Man. Unfortunate not to be on the twenty-six, but fortunate enough to be here to drop that bag off and more importantly be with my boys on the biggest day of the year and hopefully see them finish what we started back in Innisfails last January. So I'm going to try and embrace this and make the best of it.

It's still a bit strange though. At times I feel like a bit of an impostor. Usually in this big open floor room we have to ourselves here in the hotel, I float around the physio tables and put my name down for either Dicey or James to strap my ankles or a masseur to give me a rub. But today when James asks if I want anything, I tell him no, I'm fine. He probably doesn't even know I'm only number twenty-seven and I'm not going to go into it now.

I've told only a few of the lads: Flynner, EOG, Paddy, Mick. Other

lads probably think I'm on the twenty-six. Later tonight I'll meet
Denis Bastick at the function and shortly after telling him I was actually No.27 today, I'll cop: 'Was that you last year?' And it was; last
year he wore twenty-seven too. At the time I didn't even notice. I
thought he was on the twenty-six like the rest of us. So it's probably
the same with me now for other lads. They might even think it's a
good thing I'm there to come on if the team needs me, so again it's
important I radiate good, positive vibes in keeping with the match-
day climate we like to have.

Elsewhere around this big open floor room, some lads are chill-
ing out on the bean bags with their headphones on. Mannion and
Scully are playing FIFA. Mick and Paddy Andrews are foam rolling.
And then there's the crowd converged around the table tennis table.

Clucko and Jack McCaffrey are going at it. They'd be two of our
best ping-pong players, along with Mannion, but the biggest shark
over the years has been Bernard Dunne. If you don't keep track
of the score, you'll find yourself on the verge of losing a game you
thought you were winning. He'll distract you, disguise quick serves
to catch you out, trash talk – anything to win! And he laps it up when
we're all rooting for whoever it is he's playing.

Some of his games against Clucko have been just war: probably
the two most competitive and head-strong men in Dublin, around
the same table. I usually get a ring seat for that one.

It's strictly a spectator sport for me now. Early on when we moved
here for match days I used to play but found I was expending too
much energy. I don't know. Maybe it helps some lads get in the zone.

A bit later on, we're called into the meeting room. It's all very task-
specific. Clucko and Declan Darcy reaffirm what we're doing on our
kickouts and the importance of maintaining possession. Lads stand
up and walk through where they're to be on our kickouts and theirs.

Then after a few final words, it's on the bus, beside Michael Darragh. We make our way to Croker, through the streets and the heaving crowd, then slowly drive through the stadium gates right up to the dressing room entrance.

When we're in there, there's another awkward impostor moment. All the jerseys are hanging up in sequence but I can't see any number twenty-seven. Jesus, this is embarrassing. I'm meant to be running out on All Ireland final day and I've no bleedin' jersey! I'm walking around, trying not to be idle, trying not to inconvenience anyone, but I spot Davy Boylan. Davy and his father, Tony, look after the transport of our kit and equipment, and poor Davy, he's mortified when I mention my predicament to him. He runs off to try and get something sorted but while he's away, I finally spot it – there was no need to alarm Davy. Between himself and his da, Tony, they already have it up, sandwiched between numbers twenty and twenty-one, possibly so it didn't stick out at the end like a sore thumb.

Thankfully for the warm-up I can immediately spot my name and number up on the board and that I'm in a group with a few of the other forward subs. That makes me feel more comfortable and I feel even better again when we eventually head out the door. I let the lads out before me but once I turn the corner, I bolt out of that tunnel and onto that field and this wave of energy and noise just hits me.

I'm going to surf it, enjoy it. When we break into our groups for a small-sided possession and tackling game, I give it plenty of welly, trying to help lads get to the intensity that'll be needed later on. I even strike a few frees into the Hill, because who knows if or when I'll ever get the chance again.

Then it's down to business.

Tyrone start well and race into a five-one lead. They're pushing up on Clucko's kickout, putting massive pressure around the middle third. But then he picks out Jack, bombing up the left wing, with a sublime ball, taking out ten Tyrone men in the process, and setting in motion a score finished by Kilkenny. A minute later Mannion is brought down for a penalty he puts away. That's like a trigger: Okay, we're settled now; let's go. And that's what the lads do.

They smell blood. Tyrone's curveball has been to throw no curveball. Amazingly, outside of Colm Cavanagh sweeping as usual, they're pretty much playing us man-to-man. They're going with the Mayo template when their only chance was to turn this in to that board game. It's only a matter of time before our runners are overpowering them and acres of space open up. Scully and Con combine for a team goal. Mannion is devastating. Dean curls over a couple of beauties from play and frees. The lads have copped on to their movement on Niall Morgan's kickout and shut it down. At halftime we're seven up, in total control.

We maintain it in the second half; at one stage the lads keep the ball for almost two minutes before Fento spots the gap and coolly strikes the ball over.

There is the odd blip on the horizon. Eoin Murchan joins Cian O'Sullivan injured on the sideline. With three minutes of normal time left, Tyrone win a penalty and Peter Harte puts it away. Then John Small is shown a red card and they point the resultant free. With six minutes of time to be added on, our lead is down to four.

But then come the Finishers. Kevin Mc kicks a fantastic score and then with virtually the last attack of the game Michael Darragh surges through to fist over the bar.

By then I'm down on the touchline. All day I haven't gone for a stretch; we have a rota of three lads warming up at a time and there's been no point clogging up their space. But now we've used all of our subs. And Flynner hasn't been one of them: with Cian and Murch and later Jonny having to go off, we've had to bring on more backs than usual. Flynner's greatest strength is how heartfelt he is about things, so I can see that he's pissed. I'm shocked as well. In every other All Ireland final we've been in, he's played at least fifty minutes. He's played at some stage in every game this summer. He contributed with scores in every game in the Super 8s and the semi-final against Galway. He must be wondering what more he had to do to be brought on.

I nudge him. 'Here, it's not over. There could be a blood sub. Stay with it. You might have a job yet. I'm going down for a run. Want to come?'

Initially he declines, but I head down anyway: this could be my last time here so I might as well bask in the buzz. I'm stretching, sometimes glancing up on the big screen, sometimes looking out on the pitch, just enjoying being on the turf and knowing that any minute now we're going to win the All Ireland. Next thing, Flynner's down along with me. I don't know if he got a call to warm up, or he just decided to join me, but he's there towards the end which is nice.

The whistle goes. We've done it. It's a different sensation to having played and that outpouring of ecstasy and relief you get after scraping over the line as we have in previous years, but it's still satisfying. I go round congratulating the lads: Brilliant, well done. Then after the lads bring the cup onto the pitch and up to the Hill, I go looking for Keira and Donagh and Keadán.

That's been another vision that has sustained me all summer and which in those awful few seconds in Jim's office I thought had been taken away. I remember when Alan brought Jamie on and put him in the cup and thinking to myself, I'd love one day if I could do that with my kids. Well, today is that day.

Eventually, after some difficulty, I manage to get to them. I bring them over towards the Hill where Flynner's scowl is now a huge smile, and he holds and dotes on Keadán as if he's auditioning to be his godfather.

Then Mick and EOG join us, with the cup. The photographers take snaps of us with my two snappers, pics for the family album, mementoes we'll have forever.

And to me that's the moment that makes this year of desperation and frustration all worthwhile. There with the boys and my sons – and Sam.

TONIGHT Jack McCaffrey is the man.

The man of the match.

The man who for the second year in a row steals *The Sunday Game*, this time for receiving the bit of crystal just as the temporary tent overhead buckles under a torrent of water (which drenches poor Butsy's back).

And the man that I'm now entrusting as my successor as chairman of our social committee.

I don't know if it was because of our track record of going longer in Ongar but a year or so after our stint there, Éamon Fennell and myself were tasked with finding some venue where we could all go after the hotel and before heading on to Coppers. But then when Éamo went, it all fell on me.

The last couple of years we've been going to Xico on Baggot Street, an underground cavern that used to be the old Baggot Inn. My business partner Alan Clancy is behind it and places like House and 37 Dawson Street, so he's swung it that we have the place to ourselves. And this year it's where the lads want to go again. I've barely been out this year with Keira being pregnant and then the two babies coming along, but still lads have been coming up to me the last few weeks: Are we good for Xico?

So, the answer is yes, we're good for Xico. I have the wristbands organised for everyone to show at the door, and the drink tokens as well, only I'm not going round distributing them. I'm thirty-four now, married with kids! I feel like Danny Glover in *Lethal Weapon*: I'm getting too old for this shit! So in the Gibson after dinner, I plonk the box of wristbands and drink tokens on Jack's table. 'Jack, congratulations! I'm passing the social committee over to you!'

The outgoing officer still have certain obligations though. Dad and Mam drop Keira and myself off to Xico where we're the first of our gang there; the band are just setting up. But after a while, the whole team arrives down with friends and family and the place is hopping.

At about 3.30am, me and Keira bail. The rest are going on to Coppers but sure time evaporates in there. We've to get back to the two boys who are being minded by Keira's mom in our place. Besides, we'll be all week on it.

The Tuesday night is a particular highlight for me. In a possible nod to the Vengabus tradition, Butsy organises a party bus. So we go round town in it before stopping off in the Dropping Well over in Milltown for a sing-song.

Kevin Mc's band, The Solids, are there, with Kev on the mandolin and vocals. I must be their biggest fan! I had them play at my wedding and also the day after my friend Cush's wedding. Over the winter I sometimes pop in to the Temple Bar on Mondays to see them play, covering anything from The Pogues to Kings of Leon. Now, here in Milltown, they're joined by a couple of special guests, Kevin's housemate, Danny O'Reilly from The Coronas, and Danny's mom, the legendary Mary Black. And soon we're all joining in with them, singing along.

It's just the best of times, together celebrating the journey, the win, life.

THIS part of the journey has been different to the others. I'd be lying to you to say 2018 has been the high of previous years, having played so little. But at the same time I have a new sense of self-accomplishment.

I would have had myself down as naturally lazy: while I've always kept trudging along the rocky road because I had a set of goals and values that I'd be passionate about, I wouldn't be a process ninja like a Jonny Cooper who lives to be in the gym and eats up video analysis. And yet I toiled every day to try to get back. Was I sure I would, at thirty-four, only five-and-a-half months after doing my cruciate? No, I wasn't. And there's no way I would have if I was just a club player and hadn't the support and expertise of a James Allen. But I did make it back and I'm proud of that. I'm a grittier bastard than I had myself down for.

Last winter the goal was to get back on the starting fifteen, be a key contributor and that pivot man inside, like I was in the opening league game against Kildare. But after the injury I kept trying to help my teammates in other ways. In Doonbeg, Mannion spoke to the group about a point he got against Galway, running across the line, and how it was something he had been working on with me. Seeing him go to another level the last couple of games has been pleasing to see.

So, overall, I still ticked a lot of the boxes I'd have drawn at the start of the year. I played a part, just a different and smaller one than I had hoped for.

The morning after the final, Declan Darcy was surrounded in the Gibson by reporters that produced headlines concerning me being left off the twenty-six: 'We don't do sentiment.' And that has irked me. Eventually, I'll cool down and appreciate that the rest of his quotes were very respectful and measured, but at the moment I'm thinking: Sentiment doesn't matter, Dec?! At one level it's what it's all about. It's what we've been toiling and training for the past fifteen years. Our whole culture is based on legacy: representing our families and communities; playing for the same jersey our fathers played for and hopefully our children might someday too. We bust our guts for one another, our boys and brothers in that dressing room. So in a way it is about sentiment!

I'm well aware this is high-performance sport. I've been around it for a long time and know you don't compromise a team's performance to play someone who shouldn't. But I don't like the idea of management possibly getting off on this image that they're so "ruthless" and 'don't do sentiment'.

Deep down my anger is probably more a residue from the Roscommon game. At least they made some gesture by making me No.27 against Tyrone. But Roscommon was the chance to give me a freebie. They knew how much I put in to even get back on the field. And yet if Schutte hadn't by freak chance to go off with his blood injury, I would not have got on that day. I would not have been able to say I got back.

In the dressing room after the final when Jim went round to shake each of our hands as he always does, he said to me, We'll go for one more. But that's easy to say in a moment like that.

Right now I don't think I'll have the energy for it. I don't think I understood just how much goes with having kids, especially two of them together. Keira has been a warrior but it's been tough on her, while I've been away or trying to get my sleep.

The easy thing would be to go back for a crack at the five in a row

BERNARD BROGAN

but that in itself is not a real motivation for me. I've already won six.

The main thing I want in 2019 is just to get a run of playing football again. In Plunkett's we've probably lost our chance to win that elusive championship but another league wouldn't be beyond us. I'd love to have a crack at that and get back to just playing and enjoying it. I don't want to go through another year of training just to be No.27 and the only football I really play is in AvB games.

It's just that while we were in the Dropping Well that Tuesday night after the All Ireland, James McCarthy said to me, Stay with me on the journey. Give us one more year. We started this run together, let's finish this run together. And God, that's wobbled me a bit. I didn't need that! To basically be told, Look, six All Irelands is fine, but it doesn't really mean anything. Five in a row is history. Let's go for it.

Coming from a fella like James, it's powerful. He's so passionate about Dublin football, about what his father and his peers created in the 1970s and our part now in honouring that tradition.

And that is what this is all about. The management are excellent at what they do, which is to facilitate us. But it's about the guys you go to war with: your Cian O'Sullivans, your Paul Flynns, your James McCarthys. And when one of our greatest soldiers says, Come with me on the journey, what do you do?

Sentiment has everything to do with it.

13

Tough Love

WHAT THE HELL'S KEEPING HIM?!
It's just gone six o'clock on a freezing December morning, and I'm bleedin' standing here in my shorts on the side of the road, around the corner from my house, holding a hanger with my shirt for work later on.

I'm waiting on a friend, Declan Lally. For the past month we've been doing these early-morning gym sessions three times a week together in the gym in Westmanstown. We're finding out if we really have the stomach for one more year: in his case, with the club, in my case, with Dublin.

He's collecting me this morning because I had a couple of pints last night with the rest of the Legacy management team in the nearby Strawberry Hall. Only for him, I wouldn't be bothering with a session this morning. But as I was heading out the door last night, I got the usual text: You still going tomorrow morning?

Now I'm the one texting: You know I'm here freezing my balls off?!

A few minutes later he arrives, all apologies: he had to go back to get his guitar for the Christmas carol choir he's helping with at school.

There was never a question whether he was going to show. Declan Lally wouldn't be as well-known as other Dublin players through the years; he was that kind of player who would start regularly in the league but in the summer would be mostly coming off the bench. But there was a reason why his senior county career spanned ten years. Within the group he relentlessly drove standards. And he wasn't afraid to have hard conversations. In DCU that time when Declan Brennan said in front of everyone that if it had been up to him he wouldn't have picked me to start our first-round Sigerson game in 2006, Lally stood up in the middle of the dressing room and told him he was out of order, that it was unfair to the player and the other selectors to talk like that on the eve of a championship match.

His honest, fearless nature means he's been willing to stand up to me as well as for me. A few hours after the 2016 drawn final against Mayo when I went scoreless, I got a text from him: Give us a ring and we'll get in a few kicking sessions between now and the replay. But first, get rid of those bleedin' plastic boots!

Only someone who knew both me and his football could have spotted it. A couple of months earlier I had got this pair of light, stylish soccer boots. Lally wouldn't have been able to see them from where he was sitting in the stand, but he could just tell from my kicking why it was off. The same day it was pissing rain and I was missing shots I'd normally put over in my sleep because the ball was skewing off the wet plastic. A leather boot would have moulded more around my foot and given me greater control.

I ditched the plastic boots for some blacked-out leather New Balance ones and we hit the field out in the Garda club in Westmanstown. The rain that week wasn't much better than it had been in the drawn match but my kicking was. I was dropped for the replay but came on and kicked a point. We won by a point.

Now, two years on, he's out there again with me, only this morning we're in the comfort of the gym.

I'm working mostly on my leg, rehabbing and strengthening it again. I had a bit of a lull once we finished with the club. If I was a robot I might have pushed on and be gunning to play in the O'Byrne Cup but between the kids and work and just not knowing what way I feel about 2019, I eased off for about six weeks.

The last month I've cranked it up again, linking up with James Allen, rehabbing the knee every day, and teaming up with Lally here. Because as he says to me, I know you have the two lads now but you're going to have to squeeze in all the extras. Otherwise, don't bother your bollix trying to come back! You're just going to be a journeyman when you're better than that!

THE start of 2010 was a lot like this as well: plenty of early mornings and plenty of hard truths and uncomfortable questions.

After the startled earwigs affair, Pat Gilroy had no more time for any bullshit. It applied to anything and everything: how we played, how we prepared, how we behaved. He started to stress a value that's all the rage now but was rarely heard in dressing rooms back then: humility. Before we ever swept a shed, we first had to sleep on the streets, outside Arnott's, on a twenty-four hour fast to raise money for the Simon community; instead of swanning around Coppers, a few of us had to go round there, shaking a bucket.

If you won any man of the match or player of the month award or any other kind of individual honour, you had to bring it back into the dressing room at the next session and leave it there until the end of the season when you could then take it home.

We needed to become more grounded, more trustworthy, more accountable. Pat had a very good S&C team in place for his first season, with Sammy Dowling from Leinster rugby in charge and Dr Niall Moyna helping out in the background. We were each given a set of ladders, a medicine ball and an individual gym programme and expected to pretty much do it in our own time but Pat realised after the Kerry game that obviously not everyone had been adhering to it. By November we were all in DCU under the supervision of Sammy and Niall – often at 6am.

But those gym sessions were positively cosy compared to what else we did that winter as well as the preseason of 2011.

A typical day would start with a 5am alarm call. It got to the point where I'd sleep in my compression gear, armour for the cold that awaited, just to buy myself an extra couple of minutes in bed. The gear bag would have been packed the night before. Then you'd steal out the front door, get into the car and drive through a city still in slumber after the Christmas.

You'd turn off the Clontarf Road into the car park at the Alfie Byrne Road complex. In the dressing room there'd barely be a word, just the odd grunt. You'd walk out onto the floodlit all-weather county council pitch which would be completely white from the frost. You'd pick up a ball and start kicking it to a teammate but you couldn't be sure who they were because they were wearing a snood and a hat. There were mornings when your hands would be numb from how wet and cold it was and your feel would only return from the sting of trying to catch the ball; lads would even have a pair of woolly mittens on under their football gloves to provide another layer of warmth.

Then Mickey Whelan would blow the whistle. We'd go into a warm-up, clouds of steam floating from every breath, not knowing what would be coming next. Sometimes we could go into some drill or small-sided game. Mickey might introduce tennis balls, throw-

ing one between each pair and get us to try to strip it off each other
to improve our tackling. Or it could be a gruelling series of ladder
runs, sprinting from the endline to the 21 and back, then to the 45
and back. And repeat. And repeat. Sometimes we were even fired
straight into a beep test, which is never fun but particularly torturous
that early in the day.

Other mornings we ran the North Bull Wall through the snow and
the dark.

The weekends could be just as gruelling, even if they were in day-
light. I'll always remember with the pitches all frozen Pat took us out
to the beach in Donabate where the sand was covered in ice until it
began cracking under our footfall; then we had to repeatedly run up
this hill, ploughing through the frozen sand, an arctic wind blowing
in from the sea and Mickey Whelan roaring in our ears: Get the fuck
up there!

They were knocking the shite out of us to bring us out of our
comfort zone, to weed out those who weren't fully invested, and
bond those of us who were. A few lads came up to Pat after those
sessions and told him: This isn't for me. But for those who stayed
on, there was a real satisfaction in leaving a frosty pitch or a freezing
beach with our footprints everywhere and the steam rising off everyone. We'd go over for our breakfast to the Yacht in Clontarf or have
the DCU canteen kitchen to ourselves, and there'd be a fierce buzz
about the place. The harder the session, the sweeter our porridge or
eggs and beans seemed to taste. And there was no one rushing off or
any phones going off. For that half-an-hour before we all went our
separate ways to work or college, we had each other's full attention.
That's where I got to hang out with some lads for the first time:
James McCarthy, Kevin Nolan, Mick Macauley, Mick Fitzsimons,
Rory O'Carroll, Philly, EOG, Kevin Mc.

BERNARD BROGAN

They were a new breed. Some of them may have been a bit raw and unpolished but that was what was needed. They were hungry, unentitled, out to make their mark.

The beep test was a measure of that. To Pat it was as much a gauge of your mentality as your fitness.

In case you're not familiar with how a beep test works, basically you've to run back and forth between two points twenty metres apart at an increasing pace; the longer the test goes on, the less time there are between beeps and the quicker you've to go. When you twice consecutively fail to reach the opposite line before the beep, your test is over. Each level takes about a minute and there are twenty-one levels in all.

Once during Pat's first season we were all struggling a bit at about level fifteen but we pressed on, not wanting to be the first to drop out. Eventually, at about level sixteen, one of the sub goalies fell out, understandably, as they wouldn't have had the same stamina as the rest of us. At that point we would have all ran about 3.4 km. And yet not even forty metres later, eight more of us had dropped out.

It was a long ingrained mindset. Lally recalls when in the winter of 2001 it was a dream for him when one night out in the barracks in Rathmines he was pulled over from the U21s to train with the seniors. Lally was seriously athletic and soon was setting the pace. But then he heard a voice in his ear: No one likes a hero. The inference was clear. Fall back. Stay in the pack. This is how we do it here.

Pat Gilroy was having no more of it. That day of the beep test he stormed onto the court in DCU and went ballistic. What the fuck's going on here? Is this what youse are about, just doing enough to get by? Youse should be pushing yourselves to the limit! Do it again! All of ye!

And so we all had to start again from scratch.

In a way he was educating us about The Process even before Jim came along. Around that time the Alabama college football coach Nick Saban had started using the term and when asked to explain what it was, he gave the analogy of a forty-metre sprint. The Process was trying to run as fast as you could, regardless of the man next to you, as opposed to doing just enough to beat him. Yet here we were, not even sprinting those forty metres after the goalie had dropped out. We weren't being the best we could be. We were putting these limitations on ourselves, more concerned about not looking bad rather than being committed to excellence. There was still a residue of that old mindset: Don't Be a Hero, Fall Back, Stay in the Pack.

From there on under Pat, if anyone couldn't reach level eighteen on the beep test, they couldn't train with the rest of the panel for the rest of that week. There was a retest the following Saturday and if they hit the required level, then they could re-join.

In Pat's effort to get us to smash those ceilings and transform that mindset, there were casualties. A couple of the eight lads who dropped out that day didn't come back for the next session. But there was another wave of players only willing to step in and replace them.

On one of those early-morning beep tests in Clontarf, three men were still going while the test was nearing level twenty: Flynner, mad to establish a starting spot on the team; Lally, ten years on from that jog around the barracks in Rathmines, and this human wrecking ball called Michael Darragh Macauley. Lally could feel his hamstring at him but kept going. Afterwards he asked James Allen to look at it and James said to him: Sure what were you doing, taking on Mick Macauley in a beep test? He's a basketballer! Up and down is his game. You'd made the last three. Your hamstring was at you. You should have just pulled out.

Of course James was right. But it showed Lally was still up for pushing the pace. And now there were new lads willing to join him at the front rather than hope that he fell back.

PAT was not afraid to have hard conversations and make hard calls. Mark Vaughan, a fantastic character that we were all very fond of, has spoken about how in 2009 he was caught by Pat having a drink in Café en Seine with some work clients in the lead-up to the Kerry game. Pat rang him the next day and we never saw Mark with Dublin again.

Even after I scored two goals against Westmeath the previous month, Pat had a problem with me – or at least how I had celebrated them. I had given the big hands-out gesture to the Hill after one of them, and hopped on Darren Magee after he had found the net as well, as if we'd scored to win the All Ireland, when all we'd done was rack up the score on a demoralised opponent. I did a media gig ahead of the Leinster final and admitted that we had over-done it; it was just that it was Darren's first-ever goal in championship while it had always been my dream to score into the Hill. 'Whether you're forty points up or five points down, when you score a goal into the Hill, it's a big moment,' I said. 'You do get lost in the moment.'

The next night in the Bunker before training, Pat produced a copy of the interview and told everyone to have a look at it. Then he turned to me. So you honestly think it's okay to be celebrating like that after you score?

I said, 'Well, it fires our crowd up, maybe takes some oxygen out of them. Why not?'

Pat wasn't having it. You literally admitted you get lost in the moment! You're supposed to stay in the now! Okay, you scored, you did your job for the team. But then get back out for the next kickout,

backline to be totally exposed. Heads rolled: all of them except Alan were dropped for our first game in the qualifiers. Pat brought in a lot of new lads: Kevin Nolan, Mick Macauley, Eoghan O'Gara, Kevin McManamon.

The qualifiers suited me down to the ground. There were no three-week gaps between games, nor constant training and meetings and talking. All we were doing was what I love doing most: playing football, week in, week out.

While I'd like to think I backed up 2010 in subsequent years, I always found myself chasing that 2010 feeling without ever quite finding it again. That was the only year where I felt I just could not miss. Any time I got the ball inside the 45, left or right, from frees or from play, I felt it was going over the bar. I knew it was going over the bar.

It showed in the scoring stats: 2-4 against Wexford, 2-3 from play; 0-3 against Meath, two from play; 0-7 against Tipp, four from play; 0-9 against Armagh, five from play; 0-3 against Louth, one from play; 0-9 against Tyrone, no wides, four from play; then 1-7 against Cork, 1-6 from play.

But what pleased Pat even more was how my tackle count had soared. I had become probably our best tackler upfront, along with O'Gara once he broke into the team. There was still the odd time that summer where he called me out in front of the team but what the rest of the lads wouldn't have known was that I was in on it and that earlier in the day Pat would have rang me: Just to give you the heads up, I'm going to have a lash at you tonight in training, alright?

By then I understood what he had been trying to do all along. He'd wanted to make it clear that no one was sacred, nobody's place on the team was secure. And I'd been sort of his sacrificial lamb. By dropping me, he'd sent out the message that he could drop anyone;

by insisting I had to tackle, it meant everyone had to tackle. By taking away what I loved most – playing football, as much of it as I could – he gave me back so much more. You could argue that he risked alienating me, that I could have stormed off and walked out, but Pat knew my nature. He'd heard in those sessions with Caroline Currid just what Dublin meant for me. But what he knew that I probably didn't know myself was that good can be the enemy of great. By making me not settle for being merely good, he brought out of me football that I didn't even know I had.

As that year went on, he allowed me more and more into his inner sanctum. One evening he invited myself, Éamo, Ross and my cousin James over to his house for a bite to eat and let us in on some of his plans for Dublin: tactically, commercially, mentally. The team was taking a different shape now. Whelo's body was creaking so he had stepped away. Jayo hadn't been asked back while Shane Ryan had gone over to the hurlers. It was up to us now to drive it like they had for so long. One of the nights coming back from training in the car, I remember saying to Ross, 'God, it's kind of our team now, isn't it?' We were no longer just the young fellas. We felt empowered, that it was our team, our time, even maybe our year.

We thought it all the more after the All Ireland quarter-final win over Tyrone. They had been our bogey team for years, especially at that stage in the championship. In 2008 they'd ransacked us down the middle, scoring 3-10 from play within the central scoring channel. In 2010 that was down to 0-7. Our defensive system forced them to take shots from where they didn't want to shoot.

But the most telling stat was the tackle count. In 2008 they had pulverised us in that category. In 2010 we either blocked the ball or stripped it off them twenty-four times. The spirit of Inniskeen had translated to Croke Park. Whatever luck we got with the ball coming off the upright for O'Gara to fire in that late goal, we had earned.

In the Cork game I felt simply unmarkable and for a long period I thought we wouldn't be stopped either. But we were. We still had more to learn, lessons that Cork had picked up the hard way from reaching All Irelands the previous few years. That pure experience told. They nabbed us at the end by a point.

That autumn I was awarded the Footballer of the Year, the only time such an honour has gone to a player whose team hadn't reached the All Ireland final.

But at those All Stars I was struck by just how much the night really belonged to whoever had won the All Ireland. Cork hadn't walked away with as many All Stars as they'd have liked but almost all of them had been nominated, nearly all of them were there, basking in their status as All Ireland champions. Only myself, Philly, Rory O'Carroll and Mick Macauley were there from Dublin. And then I was the only one of us to get up on the podium. And at one point while I was standing there, sandwiched between Gooch Cooper and Benny Coulter, I had the thought: I'd give anything for there to be more Dubs up here.

Next year. Next year.

14

Monday Night Football

WE'RE ONLY BACK FROM THE TEAM HOLIDAY in the Caribbean when the text drops from Jim.

'I'm delighted to invite you to DSF 2019. Attached is our POA for the first 90 days. Preparation for NFL campaign starts tomorrow evening with a gym session in the Shed. Complete your online Survey Monkey reviewing last year.'

So tomorrow evening I'll be in the Shed, the gym in Parnell Park. I'm accepting the invite to be part of the Dublin Senior Football team of 2019.

I met Jim a few weeks before Christmas, again at my request, and again at the Westin, as has become our little annual custom. It took a while to pin him down. Sometimes when you ring him, he's in the air, flying a plane, especially during the offseason when he tries to get in most of the flight miles he has to clock up in a given year, so I asked him about that and the rest of his work with the aviation authority.

He also enquired how everything was with me. At his very first presentation to the DSF team back in 2013 in the clubhouse in Parnell

Park, he showed us this slide with a triangle. At the apex was your family and personal relationships, which he likened to a glass ball; you didn't want to let it drop. Then in the bottom left corner was your professional or academic career; he wanted you to win at that as well. And then there was you as a footballer. That was important too, the reason we were all in the same room, but he understood at different times in our year that there'd be "pinch points" where you might have to miss training, because of exams or something at work or at home. And to be fair to him, he's kept reiterating it and valuing it all these years later even though he demands so much from us. In the Westin he was asking, How's Keira? And little Donagh and Keadán? He likes to keep an eye out on what we're doing in Legacy and PepTalk and has always been willing to help us, giving a few talks on leadership for both companies.

The purpose of our meeting though was to talk about that third point in the triangle: me as a footballer. At first it was more of a sales pitch. I told him how I now felt I had the hunger to go again, that I still have a point to prove after how last year went. 'I think I can add something. We didn't have to go to the well last season but there's going to be a war in 2019 where you'll need experience and depth.'

That's a strong hunch I have. Last year for the first time we didn't have to go through Kerry or Mayo. At least one of them will be back, standing in our way, if not both. There will be a war and whenever we've had any before, I've been there in the fray, either to the front or as part of the cavalry. I'm ready to enlist again.

After a while, I'd to check myself. 'Look, Jim, I probably waffled a bit there. Just tell me straight: Do you want me back?'

He said, Yeah, definitely. I think there's a place for you. But I know you have a lot on with your family and with work, so you need to be sure that you're fully up for the challenge.

BERNARD BROGAN

I made it clear that I'm coming back to play, not just to be some passenger on the drive for five. And I repeated what I said to him last year: judge me on my form, not my birth cert. I know he thinks that he already does but we all have some unconscious biases so I want him to be particularly vigilant about that one.

He gave me a bit to think about too. He didn't say it in so many words but he seemed to infer that I could up my input when it comes to our post-match reviews and our opposition analysis. I suppose it's a fair point. Last year was tough, between sometimes not feeling fully part of it with the injury, and then Donagh and Keadán coming along. Jim did acknowledge the work I did with lads individually, especially the younger fellas, but in terms of being more detailed about specific matches and opponents, that homework piece is something I'm going to have to go after more.

After a while then we got up to leave, and as we were walking out, he again told me to pass on his regards to Keira.

He saw her a good bit with myself and the twins on the holiday. We spent the first couple of days in Orlando before getting a bus down to Port Canaveral and embarking on the Oasis of the Seas, one of the three largest cruise ships in the world. People think cruises are for pensioners but this was like a boulevard in Vegas with all its bars, clubs, restaurants, shows and a couple of casinos. It was only when I felt a sway two days in that I remembered we were at sea.

We stopped off at three islands: Barbados, Saint Martin and Saint Thomas. Saint Martin was fascinating. It's basically divided in half, one part a former Dutch colony and the other still under the auspices of the French – and the EU – four thousand miles away. We took a water taxi across and a few of the lads then hired out quad bikes to discover the rest of the island, although myself and Keira and the boys mostly stayed by the port and the beach.

People were great though to help out and allow us some time to ourselves. Paul Flynn's wife, Fiona, kindly volunteered to be our babysitter while we headed down to the adult-only part of the boat for a few drinks. Others like Philly McMahon's wife Sarah also took them for walks so we could get a bit of lunch on our own.

Every morning Keira would bring the lads for a few laps of the ship's walking track as I headed into the gym trying to steal a march on the others. There was only one morning on the cruise where I wasn't in it. And I'll be in the one in the Shed tomorrow night as well.

A MONTH later and the sun and the sea of the Caribbean have long faded into the cold and the rain of Innisfails.

It's actually a year ago this week since I did my cruciate. We joked about it our first week back. We were walking from one station over to do the same diagonal drill where I lost sight of Mannion's pass in the lights. I had a flashback, so I shouted over to him, 'Hey, remember this drill last year?!' For a moment he didn't know what I was on about but then an Oh shit! look came over his face. Jesus, I do, yeah! And then when it came to my turn, who was kicking the ball into me? Paul Mannion.

He pinged it almost exactly as he did last year. But this time I saw it all the way, caught it, landed smoothly, turned and banged it over the bar. It felt great, another little box ticked, especially for the head.

I've kept moving through the gears. For all the gym work I did with Lally and on the holiday, I hadn't done any running since September.

When we got back from Orlando, I decided after talking to James Allen and Bryan Cullen that instead of running on the side of the pitch with James, it was better if I just joined in with the group. Even if I was towards the back, I was going to just push through and finish everything.

The first couple of sessions I was still wary about turning sharply and taking on my man; I was just getting the ball and popping it off on the run. But then our second week back Flynner played a little one-bouncer down the line. I came running out from full forward to collect it ahead of Mick Fitzsimons. Mick assumed I was going to just lay it off to the runner but instead I spun, cut along the endline and popped it off to O'Gara for the palmed goal.

We knocked a bit of craic out of that. Mick Fitz is ferociously competitive and almost anal about the art of defending, so in the dressing room afterwards, I was slagging him. 'Where were you going for that one, Fitzy?!' He just laughed: I thought you were going to go on the outside! I was almost expecting him to ask me to stand up and walk him through it because he's that kind of lad; he's as humble as he is proud and will often ask you questions if you get a score off him: What could I have done there? Should I have stepped up to you? Should I have stood off? But this time he just let me enjoy my moment and O'Gara and James McCarthy beside us chuckle away.

The last session before the opening league game against Monaghan, Jim called me aside. Just letting you know out of respect, you won't be travelling to Clones but you're moving well. Keep driving on. There'll be game time for you coming up.

I got energy from that. I hadn't been expecting to get a look in until the third or fourth round of the league. He gave me a real carrot with that promise of game time.

The Monday after the lads lost in Clones by a goal, anyone who played less than twenty minutes or didn't play at all up there participated in a full fifteen-versus-fifteen in-house game in Innisfails. Jim called up about a dozen club players to ensure we had enough numbers and afterwards thanked them in the huddle for coming along. You guys are among the top fifty players now in the county. This is a chance for you to break into the main panel. I'm watching you here and I'll be following you with your clubs.

It's another little process Jim has added this year to shake things up and keep everyone on their toes. Normally after a league game at the weekend, the panel would have had a bit of a game among ourselves on the Wednesday. But now again, the Monday after the lads beat Galway well in Croker on Saturday night, he's called in those club lads for another full fifteen-on-fifteen game. We won't see the lads who started at the weekend until tomorrow night for some gym work and then we'll have a collective field session two nights out from the next league game.

The standard of these internal Monday night games is high. In the one after the Monaghan game James McCarthy, Jack McCaffrey, Cian O'Sullivan and Eoin Murchan were all playing to help with their transition back into the playing rotation against Galway. I left that night feeling ten feet tall. I kicked five points and set up four goals, two of them for O'Gara. He was buzzing as well in the dressing room afterwards. The twin towers from 2010 are back, he was saying. Jim has to bring us in the next day! We come as a package!

I thought Jim might call me up for the Galway game after how well I moved that night, along with the fact the lads lost up in Monaghan. But he didn't, so here I am tonight back again for some more Monday night football.

Something I'm really going after is the forward mark which has been brought in on trial for this year's league. Some people don't like that you get rewarded with a free kick for cleanly catching a ball inside the twenty-metre line from a kick delivered beyond the 45, but I'm rubbing my hands at all its possibilities. Every year I like to look for ways to optimise opportunities and evolve and bring something new to my game, and the mark is another way to expand on being that pivot man inside that I was trying to be last year.

I'm well familiar with it from my time playing for Ireland in the International Rules. To be honest, I'm a bit deflated the rule's not in place for the championship, but it's still a means of getting into the team and building some form through the league. As a group we've yet to do any work on it but in these Monday night games I'm making a point of having a word about it with some of the half-forwards playing on my side. Last week Seán Bugler from the club hit me beautifully with one but he's not here tonight as he came in and started against Galway. Shane Carthy is though. He has a lovely left foot, just perfect to play that ball in, so I've said to him and young Aaron Byrne from Na Fianna that if they think it's on, hit me with it.

The night ends up being a mixed bag for me. I score a goal and a couple of points, one from a mark after a lovely ball in from Carthy. I pull off a lovely basketball-style crossover dribble to go through a gap and win a penalty. And yet I drive home feeling quite frustrated. If anything I've probably moved down the grid. We squandered some of those goal chances I helped carve out. I kicked a few wides, especially off my left, because I haven't got in enough shooting on my own, while down at the other end O'Gara and Paddy Andrews were on fire, scoring about six points each. I don't know if I've done enough to travel to Tralee next Saturday. I have a feeling I haven't.

I'm not going to get too down on myself though. I'm back competing, back enjoying my football, back moving again with a bit of freedom and a zip in my step.

Jim has promised me game time in the coming weeks. I'd be looking to feature in our fourth game, at home to Mayo in Croker, a fortnight after the Kerry game. I love playing them. They usually set up man-to-man, especially under James Horan who is back over them, ideal conditions for me.

I've also ordered a bag of balls from O'Neill's that should be with me next week so I can sharpen up my kicking. It's one of the best investments a footballer can make: if I could recommend anything to a young footballer, it would be to fork out on your own bag of balls. That way you don't have to depend on anyone or anything else to get in your practice; you can just grab them and go.

About ten years ago Dad bought me a set of ten balls as a present and over the following few years I'd say there was hardly anyone in the game who could have made better use of them. I practised and practised to the point I felt I could not miss in a game. But gradually the balls started to become yellow and worn and unused. And to be honest, I haven't replaced them. And it's probably shown. Even in 2015 when I averaged nearly six points a game from play in the championship, I didn't feel as confident in my shooting as I had in previous years. I've had some good shooting days since, like kicking five from six in the 2017 Leinster final, but they've been less frequent, so my accuracy needs to sharpen.

It's just that it's bloody hard to get in the extra practice these days. When I arrive at training, I have to spend more and more time inside having to prehab and warm up before I can get in some shooting at all. And pretty soon there are fifteen other lads out with you and instead of having five balls to yourself, you're having to scamper and retrieve your own ball. By the time the whistle goes, you've only got in about fifteen shots, so then you're pissed off and you say to yourself, I'm going to go out and do some kicking on my own. And you might; you'll make arrangements with the kitman, like I do with Davy Boylan, to collect and drop off a bag of balls or sometimes you'll get someone to go along with you. But then you don't get out the next week, especially in the winter when there isn't much light and the weather is shit. Plus, the older you get, the harder it is to keep juggling all those glass balls as well as your football. Life can get in the way.

Now I'm just going to have to find a way. As Lally said to me on one of those early mornings before Christmas, if I'm not going to do the extras, I shouldn't have bothered my arse this year. He suggested I should get the name 'Brogan' labelled on those balls, similar to how you can now get a county or club crest stamped on them: he just feels it'll help make them a bit different and special and motivate me that bit more to take them out. And so I'm going along with it. Next week I'll be out in Westmanstown again on my own, kicking those Brogan's O'Neill's.

And hopefully the name Brogan will be back on that Dublin team sheet pretty soon as well.

15

The Times They Are A-Changin'

W HEN WE THOUGHT IN 2010 WE'D NEVER again have a tougher preseason we were badly mistaken. For 2011 the workload and the hardship doubled. Literally.

As well as sleeping in our Under Armour and setting the 5am alarm for more winter morning punishment, we had to train again that night. Two-day drinking sessions were long gone, two-a-day training sessions were in. Some of the teachers on the panel would head straight home from school and jump into bed for a few hours, knowing we were going to be put through the mixer again that evening, possibly pulling ploughs and pushing sleds and puking our guts over in Clan na Gael or somewhere. There was one week that January where we had a gym session on the Monday morning, a two-a-day on the Tuesday, a rescheduled O'Byrne Cup game on the Wednesday, another two-a-day on the Thursday, another session on the Saturday and then an O'Byrne Cup Shield game on the Sunday. It was all consuming. Savage. But for Pat and Mickey, absolutely necessary.

We'd nearly won the 2010 All Ireland but nearly was no bloody good to anybody. To go the extra mile Pat and Mickey drove us to the ends of the earth.

Mickey was remarkable. Still is, now in his eighties and still coaching teams in Vincent's. He's both old school and new school, Old Testament and New Testament. He can hold court with scientists and scholars, citing academic references to beat the band, and can curse like a sailor: Ah, for fuck's sake, Berno! There's an endearing gruffness about him but back then there was also a hurt in his soul. He had been a hidden figure in the glory years of the 1970s, the consigliere to the Don that was Heffo, his great friend and old Vincent's and Dublin teammate. Then when he came to the fore taking over the team that had won the All Ireland in '95, it went horribly wrong. Players felt he changed too much too soon when the old formula had worked and after a section of the crowd turned against him, he sadly walked away a few games into his third national league. Coaching Vincent's to a club All Ireland in 2008 helped heal a lot of those wounds but going back in with Dublin, with Pat as a more natural frontman, offered him a shot at total redemption.

A big theory Mickey had about Dublin teams was that in the big games we didn't keep going right to the end. We always seem to falter or ease up before the finishing line, never power past it, and for all the progress we had made in 2010, the semi-final against Cork was another in a long litany of fadeouts.

Philly explained it well in his book, *The Choice*. With four minutes left we were still two ahead. He remembers looking up at the clock and thinking, We could be in the final in a few minutes. He'd started to think of the outcome, not on the process, what still had to be done. He was counting down the time. Wishing it was over. Like a lot of us were.

One of the ways Mickey drilled into us to keep going and to keep going in matches was to have us keep going and keep going in training. In almost every other setup, training consists of a warm-up, some skills and drills; then you play a game, warm down, shower, have a bite to eat. You can nearly set your clock by it. With Mickey we could play a game and then have to do ten runs. And then maybe go back into a small-sided game. You never knew what was coming next and you never knew when it would end. A session could go on for an hour and twenty, or for two hours, or an hour and forty. All we knew was to keep going, and keep going and keep going. It led to an important realisation: we had a lot more in us than we ever thought. And in 2011 it started to transfer into games. Instead of wanting games to end, we wanted them to last. We were becoming steeled and conditioned to play to the last.

His coaching was simple but brilliant. We played lots of small-sided games where you had to make loads of decisions like you would in a game. He kept linear drills to a minimum because to him they were pedestrian and predictable and didn't resemble what you'd be encountering in Croke Park in August and September. I remember us throwing a tennis ball around in the snow in Ballymun, playing a possession game. Mickey was a fierce man for the tennis balls. We'd use them for walkthroughs as well. He'd line us out in our positions, then fire it to Clucko. Right, where are you looking to kick it out to? Okay, Maccer has it. What options are ye giving him? He wasn't telling us what to do, he was getting us to come up with the solutions ourselves. All the time he was developing smarter, steelier footballers.

It seemed to be all coming together that league of 2011. We went unbeaten in our seven round-robin games, winning the first six and drawing a dead-rubber in Salthill. And we had to go to the wire in most of those wins. A huge one was beating Kerry at the death on a Saturday night in Croke Park – that was our first year taking league games outside of Parnell Park and bringing them into Croker. Kerry had come back to level the game while Marc Ó Sé had held me scoreless from play going into injury time. But then I managed to get a shot off my left foot with his fingers on my toes to give us the win.

We were playing for each other and we were playing for Pat. Although he was ferociously demanding, he had a very open relationship with us. He wasn't afraid to develop a rapport with players because at the end of the day, we still knew that wouldn't stop him from giving us a bollicking. In fact it allowed him to challenge us all the more because we knew it wasn't personal and we knew that he wasn't a bollox. He had no hesitation telling Alan for example he needed to work harder and be more of a leader for the team but that didn't stop him sitting down with Alan when we were eating after a game. Jim doesn't work like that. And as genial as Pillar was, he didn't either; when we'd go back to the Goblet after games, you'd have the management at one table and all the players at other tables. Pat and his management team could sit anywhere.

Our opening league game of 2011 had been a Saturday night up in Armagh, the kind of game and place in the noughties we'd have lost. This time we won by four. Afterwards we went back to a nearby hotel for a bite to eat and Pat came down to sit beside myself, Alan and Lally. You know what, he said, I should have organised for this to be an overnight trip and have us go for a few pints; we're not playing for another two weeks. Wouldn't have been a bad idea, said Alan. But then Pat did the next best thing. He got up and organised a couple of bottles of beer for everyone. And they were a couple of the sweetest beers we've ever had. We'd earned them: he and Mickey had driven us like dogs in preseason and here was a little reward.

We had something the same twelve months earlier when we beat Derry the week after we'd won down in Killarney. We went back to the Sunnybank and ended up having a sing-song. Flynner led out the *Rattlin' Bog*. Brendan McManamon sang *The Music Man*. But Éamon Fennell stole the show by morphing into Will Smith and rapping The Fresh Prince of Bel-Air! ***Now this is a story...*** We still laugh about that night and Mark Davoren having to go on his Valentine's date the next day still in the same clothes. The two-day drinking sessions were maybe history but Pat understood the value of the occasional night out together.

Well, actually, there was one two-day drinking session during that league – and it tested Pat's tolerance to the limit.

That St Patrick's Day I found myself in the White House along with Eoin Kelly, the captain of All Ireland hurling champions Tipperary, as part of the Irish party meeting President Obama because of our 'excellent individual contributions' to the previous summer's championship. Naturally when I first got the call, I thought it was a wind up, not the actual US Embassy. I didn't even tell anyone until the following week when a written invitation from Barack and Michelle came through the letterbox at home. Obviously, it was an amazing honour and experience. We got to shake Obama's hand and chat for a while with vice-president Joe Biden and various other dignitaries.

The next day I went down to New York where I was flying out from to be back in time for a league game against Mayo in Croker on the Sunday. But seeing as we were in the Big Apple, I decided to take a bit out of it. So me and my pal David Whelan, who created and runs the Dub matchtracker twitter account, hit Pacha, one of the biggest nightclubs in the city. Another friend, Eddie Dean, owned it so we had a heavy night of it.

The following morning Dave and myself were in McDonald's on Times Square when I checked my phone. There was a text from Gilroy: Hey, hope you enjoyed Washington. Still good for the match, yeah?

I texted back: Yeah, can't wait, Pat.

Then I replied to a message from my pal Vinny Tyrrell: In bits after Pasha last night! What a spot! Getting breakfast in Mickey D's now. Where r u?

Only it wasn't Vinny that ended up getting it.

A minute later the phone beeped. Pat Gilroy: WTF?! You're not starting tomorrow anyway!

It got better, or should I say worse. Whelo and myself went to the airport the next morning and discovered our flight wasn't for another twenty-four hours. The day of the game. We'd got our days wrong. So we had to book in to an airport hotel. And I had to ring Pat Gilroy. 'Eh, Pat…'

Not surprisingly, I didn't start our next game either, a Saturday night match under the lights in Croker against Down. It proved to be a particularly poignant occasion for our family.

The day beforehand, our granddad passed away peacefully, the same Jim Brogan who served as a Garda superintendent for all those years and who had a word and a smile for everyone. In a classy gesture the county board during the warm-up posted a picture of him up on the big screen – Jim Brogan, 1926-2011 – prompting a smile from his grandsons down on the field, and then just before the throw-in, a moment's silence in his memory was observed.

Even though I began on the bench, two Brogans still started: as well as Alan, our younger brother Paul lined out at full back, having finally got a run free from injury.

I later joined them on the field and just as the game went into

THE TIMES THEY ARE A-CHANGIN'

added time I kicked a point to draw us level. When Down went back up the field pressing for the winner, Paul intercepted, burst out with the ball and played it down the line to me. I soloed down towards the Nally corner of the Hill before crossing over to Alan on the edge of the square. It got a touch off a Down back but broke to Alan who poked it to the net. Running out he looked and pointed to the heavens. That was for you, Grandda.

We sometimes smile that there weren't just three Brogans involved in that goal but four: Paul with the interception, me with the cross, and then it was Grandad who tipped the ball out of the Down defender's hands for Alan to finish.

It's a special memory for us. We only wish he had still been around for that September.

WE may have gone to the end in that Down game but the league final was a painful lesson in how far we still had to go.

With half an hour left we were eight points up on Cork. I'd scored a goal which Dermo followed with another point. We were ripping them apart. But just like in the All Ireland semi-final the previous year, Cork began to chip at our lead. Eight, seven, six. With twenty minutes remaining, I pulled my hamstring and had to hobble off. Cork ended up winning by a point, without having to score a goal.

We took serious flak afterwards. Some pundits said a 'monumental collapse' like that could break us and that we hadn't the mental toughness to win national honours. But straight after the match Pat went out to bat for us.

'This team has character and guts to put up with the kind of stuff that surrounds them every day, and they get back out there and they train and they work,' he told the media when asked if we had a mental block. 'And I tell you, they're the most honest guys. They'll

199

get stick for this but we'll deal with it. And when we have the All Ireland – someday – that's when we'll stop hearing that.'

He went several ways about 'dealing with it'. A few players who came on that day didn't make the cut for the championship panel, including Paddy Andrews. But the biggest change was probably in our mindset.

A few weeks later Pat brought us over to London for an intense pre-championship camp where we basically had London Irish's rugby grounds to ourselves. And that's where he introduced us to this idea of "emotional hijacking".

Pat had done some serious self-reflection in the wake of the 2009 Kerry game, and upon hearing of this model, identified that he as much as the team had been emotionally hijacked. He started working with this performance and business consultant called Bart McEnroe, meeting him for a series of brutal four-hour sessions every week for ten weeks. At their first meeting out in the Citywest, this Bart fella apparently tore into Pat, saying he'd brought shame on his county for overseeing that disaster in Croker. You're only a novice! Bluffer! Choker! Your team can't tackle! You can't coach! You can't manage! He kept on abusing Pat and his team right until they were nose to nose and Pat eventually snapped and pinned him against the wall. Bart just smiled. Pat, look at yourself! You've allowed yourself to be emotionally hijacked again!

Pat went away to read a lot on psychology and this human needs approach which Bart advocated – Pat would be as big into his Maslow as Jim is – so he gave us his own crash course over in London Irish. But first for effect he needed a prop and a sacrificial lamb. I was sitting in a chair at the front when before I knew it, he'd given some cue for Philly McMahon to grab me by the neck from behind. WTF?! I didn't know what was happening and just went into survival mode, and began grappling with Philly so I could breathe. I ended up pushing him back against the wall.

After we'd resumed our seats and Philly had stopped laughing, Pat explained that what had just happened to me was a bit like what had happened to us in the league final. And the 2010 All Ireland semi-final. And when we were hit for five goals by Meath. And the Kerry game in 2009. We'd been startled earwigs because we'd been emotionally hijacked. Or, to use the neuropsychological term, we'd fallen victim to an amygdala hijack.

The amygdala, as we'd learn from Pat, is the emotional part of the brain and designed to alert us to potential harm. It can be your best friend and your worst enemy. It was very useful back when wild animals and rival tribes were roaming around and it'd trigger the stress hormones to activate you to either fight or flee from such danger. But the downside is that it can exaggerate threats. Instead of merely alerting the rational part of your brain, the neocortex, it can override or even bypass it and you're unable to think logically and clearly.

What Pat was teaching us was similar to the chimp management model that Dr Steve Peters was using around then with leading British athletes, though few people, including us, would have known of it back then. The amygdala was essentially like a chimp: excitable and impulsive. And we were letting it hijack us. Whenever we were hit with a sucker-punch – like a Tyrone or Kerry or Meath banging in a goal, or Cork coming back at us in a big game – our thinking could become foggy. Lads were overlooking the pass. Not enough of us could properly follow the game plan.

That workshop was the first time that we discovered the critical difference between reacting to a situation and responding to it. Too often in big games we had been reacting. Just because the smoke alarm had gone off didn't mean the whole house was on fire. Just because a team had scored a goal against us didn't mean a lion was about to eat us up. We could respond, not react.

Pat then threw it back over to us. One of the other realisations Pat had from his serious introspection following the 2009 Kerry game was that he and Mickey had assumed that the players were as clear about the game plan as they both were. But it's like that line of George Bernard Shaw's that I came across at a conference with work: The single biggest problem in communication is the illusion that it has taken place. The Kerry game had shattered that illusion for Pat and so from then he decided to give less team talks and more team "asks". He'd just given the team a talk about emotional hijacking but to cement it he gave us a team ask. He broke us into groups and got us to discuss and present how the brain worked under stress and strategies as to how we could respond rather than react. So we got out the flipcharts and Clucko, who is a science and biology teacher, drew up the different parts of the brain with arrows going here and there showing how they worked together.

We came up with various scenarios we could encounter. An opponent mouthing or nipping at you was basically trying to hijack your amygdala. But by even having that awareness you had a greater sense of control and capacity to respond, not retaliate and lash out.

We talked some more. If we concede a couple of scores, especially a goal, stay calm. It's okay if for a moment you think Oh Shit. That's just your amygdala giving you a signal you might want to lift things or improve things a little here. But Oh Shit doesn't mean OH SHIT! Make one or two simple plays. Stick to the Process, although we didn't call it that back then.

The workshop dovetailed nicely with some of the work we were doing individually with Caroline Currid. She helped some of us come up with our own personal triggers to keep us present and in the right emotional state and prevent any emotional hijacking. Flynner drew a smiley face on his wristbands. Éamon Fennell would pick up a blade of grass and let it blow away; that's gone now, next play.

My thing was to click my fingers. Keep cool. Deflect the energy. Any man-marker trying to get at me, just look past them, as if they're not there. I'm the one in control. Not him or my chimp.

THE league final also taught us that our game management as much as our mind management had to improve. Once again we'd failed to control and kill a game. It's something the current team excels at but back then it was something we had to learn and that began in 2010 and 2011. In previous years we'd keep playing the same way regardless of the score. Alan had been on the Dublin team for ten years by that stage and only knew how to play at a hundred miles an hour; every time he got the ball he wanted to take on his man or give it inside as fast as he could. Eventually we copped that you couldn't keep doing that against the better teams because it would only invite them back into the game. While your competitive intensity wasn't to drop, it was okay if the pace of the game did. Pat and Mickey started to talk about and rehearse situations where we were five or six points ahead in certain games. Take the sting out of it. Keep handpassing sideways and backwards around the middle. Draw them out, wait for the gap, then take your shot. It might have been two minutes before you did but you'd been in control of the game all of that time.

That summer of 2011 was also the start of our A versus B games being ferociously competitive over the course of a championship. A problem in Pillar's time was that the longer a summer went on, the more demotivated lads outside the top twenty became. If you hadn't featured by the second game in Leinster you pretty much felt you were out of the equation for the rest of the year. There was never a bolter from the pack.

With Pat everyone genuinely felt they could get minutes the next day out if they performed in those training games. A few weeks before our first-round game against Laois, Éamon Fennell emailed all the lads on the B team saying he for one didn't want to be stuck there for the rest of the year: let's push these guys to either take their jerseys or at least get the most out of them. They beat us well and from that Barry Cahill came back into the starting lineup. Éamo didn't feature against Laois but was the first man off the bench the next day and then started the Leinster final. Cian O'Sullivan's first bit of championship action that year was the All Ireland quarter-final when he came straight in at corner back. Lally started the year on fire but then tore his hamstring. He came on a few times in Leinster, then didn't feature in the All Ireland quarter-final or semi-final, but before the final Pat called him in to his office and said if Paul Flynn didn't pass a fitness test, he was in. There was just one rub: he was the one who had to run along with Flynner in that fitness test. And Flynner passed it. But it was Lally who pushed him. It was the bench who pushed us all year.

Paul Conlon didn't see the field after starting in the Leinster final but he was in my face and in my jocks for every A versus B game for the rest of the summer. Down at the other end of the field Mossy Quinn was regularly schooling Mick Fitzsimons. Mick wouldn't have been the player he was for us that summer if it wasn't for Mossy and no one knew it more than Mick. When Mossy stepped away from the panel at the end of the 2012 season, Mick pleaded with him to stay on for one more year because he felt he was learning so much from him. Within the group and on the training ground in St Clare's, the players who commanded the most respect were the likes of Mossy, David Henry, Paul Casey, Ross McConnell. All of them had been regular starters during Pillar's time. Now they were fighting for scraps of game time but their influence had never been greater because of how they were setting the tone before and during those A versus B games. They were like championship games to them. And so they began to resemble championship games to us.

IF any team ever set themselves up to emotionally hijack Dublin, it was what Donegal threw at us in the 2011 All Ireland semi-final.

In our previous game we gave what Alan often says was the best Dublin performance he was ever involved in. Although Tyrone weren't what they had been even twelve months earlier, that night was more about us than them and how much we had progressed under Pat: in our tackling, foot-passing, movement, scoretaking. Dermo was on fire, finishing with seven points from play. I kicked four, Alan, three. Nine of those fourteen points were with our left foot. Flynner scored one off his left as well. For years people had said Dublin hadn't enough technically-sound, two-sided players to win an All Ireland but that night suggested that we now had.

But that night we'd encountered basically no sweeper. Against Donegal we were coming up against fourteen men behind the ball. *Fourteen.* Mickey Whelan had us steeled to meet a massed defence by having our starting fifteen play against eighteen men in train- ing but this was beyond what he or anyone except Jim McGuinness could have envisaged. According to Kevin Cassidy's account in that *This Is Our Year* book which eventually got him on the wrong side of his manager, McGuinness told his players that they were geared to win by something like four points to three. 'They'll start kicking crazy wides,' he said of us. 'The Brogans are going to shoot from anywhere. They're going to get frustrated and they won't be able to understand why they can't break you down. Diarmuid Connolly is not going to get a kick on goal. And every time they hit a wide, they'll be reminded that they're not playing Tyrone now.'

By halftime it was as if we were all just actors in his script. The scoreline was a ridiculous 0-4 to 0-2 in their favour. Personally I couldn't see where we were going to get another two scores. Alan had already kicked four wides from all angles. Dermo had been able to get one kick on goal but it trickled wide and he'd had another blocked down. I'd blown a goal chance when they were going to be as rare as hen's teeth and I'd dropped a shot short and ballooned another. I had Neil McGee in my face, and Mark McHugh playing right in front of me, and time and time again when the lads had tried to kick it into me in the D, McGee would break it down and there'd be three Donegal men to hoover it up.

So I was frustrated alright. But maybe not to the point McGuinness had been hoping for. I hadn't been emotionally hijacked. I'd kept clicking my fingers, kept seeing past McGee and deflecting the energy when he'd try to stare me out, and I'd still worked hard, making good, aggressive runs. Our two scores had come from frees which I'd won and tapped over. I was still getting in tackles, making them turn and slowing them up as they came out. Halftime allowed us to reset. The message was to stay patient. We don't need to be shooting from forty yards, Alan. Let's try to get the ball inside. Let's try to turn their backs. We'll keep at it. We'll go right to the end.

I got a boost too from seeing Kevin McManamon coming on. Early in his career Kevin tended to doubt himself too much but from the first time I ever saw him play for DIT with my brother Paul, I thought, God, this man's a dancer, he's got a bit of magic about him, he's going to be a difference maker with Dublin. Like me, he had to put up with people thinking he didn't pass it enough but I loved how he'd just put the head down and burn lads on the outside. And that's what we needed to prise Donegal open.

With twenty minutes to go, Donegal's lead was out to three when I got my hands to a ball boomed into the D by Bastick and was fouled. Then Clucko converted a 45. Even when Dermo was harshly sent off, we felt the momentum was now with us. They were just trying to hang on but were losing shape and space was opening up. Kevin Nolan booted a ball that hopped in front of me and I managed to flick it overhead into the path of Kevin Mc who went on and kicked our first score from play all day. A minute later when O'Gara got blocked down, I pounced on the break over by the Nally corner, picked out Bryan Cullen across goal with my left foot and Bryan put us ahead. Then when I ran out to a ball Flynner had played into the corner, McGee pulled my shirt and I swung over the free with my left. Eight-six. Which is how it ended. We'd found a way. We'd kept going right to the end, reeling off the last five points. We were through to our first All Ireland in sixteen years.

It was the kind of game we'd have lost a year earlier. We wouldn't have had the tactical awareness or psychological clarity to cope. I used to almost define my performance by how much I'd scored from play. That day I didn't score anything from play. But I'd found other ways to contribute, winning the four frees I'd put over and laying on the pass for our two scores from play. I've learned that Jim McGuinness's right-hand man that season, Rory Gallagher, told a paper shortly afterwards, 'There were days in the past that you might have felt that if Bernard wasn't going to be brilliant, he wasn't going to be good at all. But while he wasn't brilliant against us in the way people normally associate with brilliance, he was still the most influential player on the pitch. Given the pressure he was under, I thought he was unreal. He became Gooch-like in his influence. He kept his composure and I thought he showed more leadership than I've seen anyone show for Dublin over the last fifteen years.'

Some of that was going too far. But I'd chipped in for the team in a way that I couldn't have before.

IN the lead-up to the final against Kerry, we were all gathered in a circle in the Bunker when Dr David Hickey felt he wanted to say something. Dave is one of life's exceptional people, an incredible man who just radiates wit, warmth, humility, compassion. He's been one of the leading transplant surgeons in the world. He's campaigned for the end of the blockade of Cuba, a country he took to his heart. He's survived several health scares of his own, including brushes with cancer. And back when he was a young man, he played and won All Irelands with the likes of my da. The respect and fondness the group had for him was massive, which was why Pat had brought him in as a selector after his first year, and why Jim kept him on as team doctor for a number of years, and why we hung on his every word when he spoke to us this particular time in September of 2011.

Earlier that year we'd all picked a song for a team CD, as a lot of teams used to do around then. Dave's choice had been the old Bob Dylan song, The Times They Are A-Changin', which came out way back when Mickey Whelan and his old mucker Heffo were All Ireland champions as players. But to Dave its words and message were as relevant now as ever, at least to us. Lads, the times are a changin'! Believe me, ye're better than the team I was on. I'm looking around this room and the talent there is and the bond that ye have and it's incredible. Ye're special players. Ye're special men, good men. Ye're going to do special things.

Lads were welling up, biting their lips as he was talking. About how the last decade may have belonged to these Kerry boys we were about to play, along with Tyrone, but this decade was going to be ours. This game was ours. Didn't matter that people outside this circle couldn't see that yet. They would.

Come writers and critics/who prophesise with your pen
And keep your eyes wide/The chance won't come again
And don't speak too soon/For the wheel's still in spin
And there's no tellin' who that it's namin'
For the loser now will be later to win
For the times they are a-changin'

Before we boarded the bus to head to Croker on All Ireland final day, Pat presented us with a couple of stats. The first was our tackle count from the night we first played Monaghan in the shit and the rain in Inniskeen. It was double what it had been in the startled earwigs game. Then he mentioned our tackle count against Donegal: 120. More than double what we'd put in up in Inniskeen.

He didn't have to say anymore. We were a different animal to the one Kerry had last seen in the championship. And we were ready to hunt and to chase to the death.

Gooch would again side-foot a first-half goal into the Hill and then with sixty-three minutes gone on the clock, threw over a point to give them a four-point lead. But this time there was no emotional hijack. We responded, not reacted, with big play after big play which almost every Dublin supporter can still rattle off by heart, along with multiple unheralded plays and little wins that they didn't spot, driven by voices – Pat's, Mickey's – they couldn't hear.

Alan getting a hand to a Declan O'Sullivan pass to deflect it to Cian O'Sullivan: *Alan, you've got to start tackling like everyone else!* Cian's quick free back to him, Alan popping it off to Kevin Mc, and Kevin, you little dancer, you, with a shuffle of his feet, firing it low into the Kerry net; then pointing to his head running out, the trigger to remind us that while the Hill is going gaga, we can't. *Okay, you scored, you did your job for the team. But then get back out for the next kickout, not still be stuck in something that happened twenty seconds earlier!*

From that Kerry kickout, Kevin Mc along with O'Gara burst themselves and made the receiver, Marc Ó Sé, have to run right across the twenty-one metre line instead of just come straight upfield. Another little invisible victory; Pat with Ray Boyne had redefined a tackle as whenever you made an opponent turn around or change direction and do something they hadn't wanted to do, so that was a massive tackle on Ó Sé.

Kerry managed to work the ball past the 21 to Tom O'Sullivan, who I'd allowed go all the way upfield to kick a point in 2009. But this time he'd have caught something in the corner of his eye closing in on him. *Okay, so, if your man breaks forward, you think someone else should cover your runs and you can save your energy, is it? That's complete bullshit! 'Oh, I'm Bernard Brogan, I'm special!' You do have to track back and tackle!*

I clattered into O'Sullivan as he tried to offload to Anthony Maher, enough possibly to put it slightly off-track and for Michael Darragh to intercept and win a free. Alan took it, found Dermo, who found Kevin Nolan. You know the rest, at least if you're a Dub. Kevin thumped over the equaliser. Then I squeezed over a point off my left, identical to the one that had given us the win over them in the league nine months earlier. Donaghy equalised for them with an outrageous score under the Cusack. But then Éamo beat him to a jump ball. Kevin Mc drew a free. And then I ran over, crouched down to pat him on the shoulder, took the ball, and then motioned for Clucko to come up and kick the free to win us the All Ireland.

WHEN we were all living in Ongar, we came to learn from Clucko just how important it was to have routines and rituals, and just how important they were to him. We'd even come to abide by some of his for fear of upsetting him. For the first time in years outside of Christmas, myself, Éamo and Ross found ourselves in a church, shuffling in to the back row, because Clucko was literally religious about getting in Sunday mass the morning of a championship game. But the thing he was especially a stickler about was being first to training.

Back then I was working as a trainee chartered accountant in town. Any night we weren't training, I could be in there until nine at night. But any night we had training, I'd to leave at five on the dot and hop onto my red Honda CB125F motorbike and speed back to the house in Ongar because at 5.45 on the dot the rest of the lads would be leaving in Clucko's car for training. Any later and I knew he wasn't going to wait. Even if you were just in time you risked a dirty glare. I'd pack my gear bag the night before, and place it in the hallway, so while he was tapping his steering wheel, I could just pop in and pick it up and hop into the car.

Sure enough, we'd be the first at training. And the two of us would go down to the far end and practise our frees until others would arrive. Even though he wasn't on the frees for Dublin then, he'd religiously go through his warm-up: twenty frees from across the fourteen-metre line, then move out ten yards and hit another twenty; then strike another twenty across the forty-five. Honing his craft. Mastering his technique. Preparing for the moment.

Now this was it.

A county held its breath. But really there was never a doubt.

The next thing, there was this explosion of noise. Pandemonium. Elation. Liberation. Redemption. Self-actualisation. History.

The times they had a-changed.

16

Line In The Sand

C ROKE PARK ON A SATURDAY NIGHT IN MARCH,
but if you were to go by the team Jim has put out here against
Tyrone, you'd almost think it was last September again.

Twelve of the side that started against them in the 2018 All Ireland
final are starting again tonight. In our first couple of games of this
league, Jim started a few young lads and some veterans like Flynner
and Michael Darragh who spent most of last year on the bench,
but since losing in Tralee in round three, Jim has kept the experi-
mentation and rotation to a minimum. There is no more margin
for error. Drop another point against either Tyrone or next week in
Cavan and we miss out on the league final. We've yet to miss out on
a league final under Jim, and in the six we've contested, we've won
all bar one.

There was a time not long ago when the league for Dublin was
"only the league", but like a lot of things, that all changed with Pat,
even though we didn't win one under him.

It used to be that we'd all have our pre-match meal at home. If it
was championship, we'd meet up in Parnell Park to do some mobil-
ity work and kick a few balls around before getting on the bus for
Croker. If it was the league, we'd just go straight to the dressing

room in Parnell about an hour and forty minutes before the throw in.

After the startled earwigs fiasco, Pat was leaving nothing more to chance. We had to arrive to every match, league and championship, as a unit, not as individuals coming in dribs and drabs. We began meeting up three hours beforehand in DCU and having our pre-match meal together. Instead of some lads having a fry-up at home and listening to their family and friends talk about the game, we were now in our own bubble where Pat didn't have to worry if lads were getting in the right nutrition and we could just chill in each other's company. That routine remains in place today, even if it's now the Gibson where we meet up.

The 2009 Kerry game brought home to Pat that if we were going to beat the top teams in the championship, we'd have to start beating them in the league. When the heat came on in August, we didn't have a reservoir of confidence to draw from because we had little to no experience of beating those teams. Even after we won the Battle of Omagh in 2006, we got hammered the next week in Parnell by Monaghan. We were too up and down and too easily brushing off defeats in the league, persuading ourselves that it was "all about the championship".

In 2010 and 2011 the likes of James McCarthy and Mick Macauley had no baggage going into big championship games against Tyrone or Kerry. They only knew what it was like to beat them – in Killarney, in Omagh, in Croker – from the league. That was the only history that mattered to them. And that fearlessness rubbed off on the rest of us.

Winning is a practice. The more you win, the more you will win because when it comes down to it in the last five minutes and it's all in the balance, you believe you'll edge it. You'll be more composed and make the right plays and keep going to the end, out of pure habit. And that habit is ground out in the league, giving yourself no excuse to lose.

You also don't want to give any opponent oxygen so come the championship they can say, We beat this crowd already this year, so we can beat them now. In 2012 we lost heavily to Mayo in Castlebar and it emboldened them that summer to build up another big lead on us which we couldn't overcome. When you have teams down, you keep them down. And that's where we must keep Tyrone.

I'm in the twenty-six for the first time this year. The confidence has taken a dent after I was overlooked for our round four game against Mayo. It's a vicious circle: when you don't play, you have less confidence, and if you have less confidence, then you're less likely to play. I've tried to hide my disappointment from the group but I'm battling with myself, trying to stay motivated when there's been no encouragement from the management.

It's been a frustrating time for a lot of the 2011 boys but especially the full-forward line that finished that final. O'Gara hasn't played a minute this year either. Kevin Mc got on for the last ten minutes in Tralee but that's been it. Last week we had a training game, just eight minutes each way, and two minutes after halftime Kevin and myself were both taken off so some young lads could get a run. Kevin was seriously pissed off, saying it was the first time he had been taken off in training since he was twenty-two. The previous week I didn't start in a fifteen-v-fifteen game for the first time since I was twenty-one. There are whispers of a big cull coming and a lot of us older boys are thinking we mightn't be around much longer, including Flynner and Mick who have been feeding off scraps since starting the first day in Clones. We're all talking to each other, trying to support one another because there's little love coming from Jim, but sometimes you wonder are we helping each other or are we only bringing each other down? I don't know. Maybe tonight will change things. I actually haven't been moving that badly in training or in the couple of games I've played with the club. And Jim did promise me in Innisfails before the league started that there'd be game time coming up.

So here in Croke Park I stay ready all night. Watching what angles I might run if I get a chance. There's little ball getting through with it being so crowded in the Tyrone backline, in contrast to the other end of the field where we're way too open to cope with Cathal McShane and Mattie Donnelly. We're not composed, we're taking too many bad options. We need a few scores to catch up. I'm still ready. I can see possibilities, like running diagonally across the pitch through the traffic, prompting my man to ease off the further I get from goal, then turning on the loop, taking a pass off our runners attacking the massed defence and shooting.

But the call doesn't come. Instead, with sixty minutes gone, it's O'Gara who comes on for Dean. So that's where things stand. When Jim can see his league final disappearing and he has the choice between two fellas who haven't been good enough to feature this year but one of them might dig him out of this hole, he goes: Eoghan. He might get us out of this, he might get us a goal, he's maybe the answer.

And I'm not.

We don't get out of the hole. Tyrone win and deservedly so. We were naïve and complacent in our preparation. We thought we just had to show up. We thought they were going to do what they've always done and we just needed to do what we did last year and everything would be fine.

Back in the dressing room, you can tell Jim is annoyed. There's going to be a league final here in two weeks' time with another team in this dressing room, he says. I want that to sink in with you. I want you to remember what this feels like. Someone else is going to be going up those steps and taking our cup.

The mood isn't any lighter back in the Gibson. It feels heavy. Like the end is nigh. I don't hang around. I just eat and go: I'm out of here. I could be out of here for good.

I HAVE to talk to Jim.

It's something I'm saying all the time now, far too often anyway. Keira is sick of me saying it. When I learned I wasn't travelling to Tralee, I said to her, 'If they don't play me in the Mayo game, I'm gone.' Then when I wasn't on the twenty-six for that game either, I came home, fired the gear bag on the floor, threw myself back on the couch and turned to her. 'Am I wasting my time here, do you think?' I can't answer that question for you, she said. Sure I thought you were gone weeks ago! 'Well, if I'm not picked for the Roscommon game, I need to have a conversation with Jim.'

So I did. I owed it to Keira at least. Mickey Whelan used to say to us that players don't make sacrifices: we're pursuing our dreams, playing the game we love. It's our loved ones that make the sacrifices: all the time we're away from them, the things they selflessly put in place and work around to facilitate our goals and, I suppose, our selfishness. That's why when we had training camps in Portugal and La Manga, Pat and Mickey used to allow partners and kids to go too. So when I spoke to Jim after I wasn't picked to travel to Roscommon, I told him that I – or at least my family – was sacrificing as much as anyone here. I've two young kids and two young businesses but I'm here because I want to be here but only if I can add value. I don't want to be a passenger; if it means at the end of the league we shake hands and say goodbye, that's fine with me.

Jim told me not to worry about that, that there'd be no passengers. He wanted me to talk up a bit more in the group, that I had gone quiet recently. And he said the reason why he didn't bring me to Roscommon was because it was better that I got sixty minutes under my belt with the club that morning than maybe just getting ten minutes in Hyde Park.

His logic might have been sound on that one but at this stage I definitely need some game time with Dublin. I was all over the place at training on the Wednesday between the Tyrone game and our upcoming dead rubber in Cavan; an old shoulder injury is at me again but my biggest problem is my head, scrambled from wondering am I just wasting my time. So the day of our last session ahead of the Cavan game, I ring him.

'Look, Jim, I don't know whether I'm in the mix right now for the weekend but I think I need half an hour on Sunday to change your perception of me. I know I haven't been training great but I was flying it a month ago and thought I'd be in for the Mayo game and that would lead to a few more half-games but you haven't given me a dickie. My head is all over the place at the moment although I'm trying to stay positive around the group.'

I go on, making my case. And not just for me. For a lot of us.

'I'm a footballer. I need to play football. I need game time to get momentum, to get my kicking in and get my scores. The same with the other guys on the bench. You haven't been playing them enough. You played all your main players in the league and they didn't come up with the goods, yet for every game you went back to them because you wanted the result. And that's fine; I understand there's a hierarchy there. But this [the All Ireland] isn't going to be won by twelve lads. You've been devaluing the bench.

'We turned Dublin football around by the power of the bench. By empowering it. By bringing on four or five lads with twenty minutes to go who were fresh and had enough game time under their belt to make an impact. Now we're leaving it to the last minute or for someone to be injured to bring them on. How can Kevin Mc and Paul Flynn come on and play well when they haven't been playing much in the league? The likes of Kevin have won All Ireland after All Ireland for us because in the league they got their starts, they got their reps in, they felt empowered. They weren't coming in feeling they had to impress or wow you; they just had to do a job. There were no obvious tiers which is the way it's looking now: there's these lads and then there's the rest of us.'

Jim, measured as always, says he appreciates my honesty and insight. You only talk when there's something to be said, he tells me, we've a good working relationship and that's something I value. We talk for another while. Then, if I've heard him right, he seems to imply that I'm not even in their plans for Cavan after how I trained the last night. But I'm not letting that go either.

'You're judging me on Wednesday night in training? That's a joke! I've played with you for six years. We've won five All Irelands together. Don't be judging me on one night of training. You've played lads in this league who haven't exactly lit it up but you've kept giving them chance after chance. Give us our chance at the weekend.'

I GET a chance in Cavan. Well, only five minutes, but with it, one chance.

I'm not in a great headspace coming on. For most of the game I've stayed positive and tuned in, looking at who I might be coming on for and where I might make an impact. But the more the second half wears on, the more I've looked at the clock and the more I've been thinking, I'm not going to have enough of a window here to make an impression, the only impression I might make now is a bad one. And when it goes past the sixty-minute mark and Collie Basquel gets the call to come on for Mannion, myself and O'Gara beside me start grumbling: Ah Jaysus. And that's where I tune out, just like in the Roscommon game last August when Andrew McGowan got the late call. So when I do get the call a few minutes later to come on for Michael Darragh, I'm as caught unawares as I was when Schutte had to go off with the blood injury that day.

I run around Breffni Park like an eejit, a bag of nervous energy. Just trying to get on the ball, trying to do anything to impress.

And then the chance presents itself.

Dean runs down the left and pops it back to me around fourteen yards out from the posts. I've my back to goal so I turn and wind up to drop the ball onto my right foot. And…

I'm blocked down.

John Courtney, the Colonel, who'd be one of the most popular and respected figures in the backroom, has said to me numerous times over the years that in all his time watching football he's never seen anyone to get ball to boot and get a shot off quicker than me.

And now I'm getting blocked with the one chance I've got in this entire league campaign. Because I telegraphed it. Because I'm not playing instinctively, naturally. If I was in flow, if I was sharp, if I felt backed, I'd have thrown a dummy-solo, cut back in on the left and fisted it over the bar. Instead I'm tentative, second-guessing and overthinking everything.

All that visualising how I could use the mark, all that waiting and worrying and work since the start of the season and it's all reduced to that moment.

So this might be it. That blocked shot may well be my last act in a Dublin jersey. I've been around long enough to see things for what they are. When Jim gave me those five minutes, it wasn't to build me back into the team. It felt like a tick-the-box exercise: Here, told you I'd play you in the league.

Jim is very reluctant to tell a senior player straight out that he's finished. A few years back a veteran who had got virtually no game-time the previous season arranged to meet Jim over the winter to tell him face to face that he was retiring. But before he got the chance, Jim began by saying, I'm delighted to invite you to be part of the Dublin Senior Football Team of.... The player couldn't believe it! But sure you didn't give me a dickie-bird last year! Actually, Jim, thanks but no thanks; I'm hanging them up.

And maybe that's what Jim wanted: for the player to make the decision for him. Is that what he wants a few of us to do here? To take the hint and simply walk away?

That's very much the way I'm leaning now. I'm going to think about it some more over the coming days but I'm pretty sure I'm going to tell him I'm done. We all come to the end sometime. I don't want to hang on just for the sake of it and to see if we win the All Ireland; I don't believe in that. I only want to be around if he wants me to be around and he wants to play me. If he doesn't, well then, I don't want to be around either. He should be the one selling me on a role to go after, not me being the one constantly selling him on this role I have in my head: the pivot man inside, winning ball, using my guile and vision.

I'm tired of selling it. I'm tired of selling myself.

I'm just tired...

THE next morning, before I know it, the alarm goes off. It's 5.45. Hours after the bus getting back from Cavan and dropping us off in Abbotstown, we're back out there for a dawn swim in the National

Aquatic Centre. Our league may be over but our championship preparations start now – right away.

Jim has always had us right up to the league final before we go back to the clubs and he's decided that there's no reason that should change just because we're not in it this year. And so, just before we got off the bus last night, he dropped it on us that he'd see us all back here at first light.

Back when we used to be gasping for air during those savage early-morning and two-a-day sessions, Mickey Whelan used to say to us, Money in the bank, fellas. Money in the bank. This year, between the holiday, and the league being that bit earlier and the games coming so thick and fast, we haven't yet had the window to make those kind of deposits. Now we can. It's a chance to catch up with our competitors and a chance to get a jump on them – and a chance for Jim to test us and find out: Do they really still want this?

After the swim on the Monday morning, we're in the Shed on the Tuesday evening for a weights session that doubles as a fitness test. We have the Wednesday off but the Thursday in Innsfails is an absolute ball-breaker.

We begin with the Bronco fitness test: a twelve-hundred-metre run where you've to go to a twenty-metre mark and back, then a forty-metre mark and back, and then a sixty-metre mark and back, five times in all, continuous running, no break. Towards the end I'm chasing down Mannion and while I don't quite catch him at the end I've obliterated my time from January. Back then I did it in five minutes twenty seconds. Now I've done it in 4.47.

So I'm energised from that and bring it into our next station even though it's torture too. It's the tackle box: ten yards by ten yards, a man in each corner, two lads in the middle, two balls on the outside and sixty seconds of murder. And the way it's worked out tonight, the last two men to step into a box are myself and Ciarán Kilkenny. Everyone else has already had their turn, so everyone is gathered round watching us, including the management.

I'm tackling Ciarán first. He tries to shake me off to receive a ball from one of the lads. He gets it but I'm all over him, making contact, and at one stage push him out of the grid.

We swap around: he's tackling me. And Ciarán is just like Ciarán Whelan all those years ago: a bull of a man, ready to give you the car wash treatment whenever you step into a tackling drill with him. But I'm able to get the ball, then pop it off and go and receive the second ball. I even give Ciarán that little basketball crossover bounce and twirl past him before popping it off and going again. I'm wrecked towards the end, but feeding off the energy from the lads around us. And when we're finally done and we're moving onto the next station, a few of them come over, slapping the shoulder. Fucking great stuff, Berno. And while it shouldn't make that much of a difference to someone who has been around for fifteen years, it does. I get a huge lift from it. And a bit of juice too that Jim and the management would have seen it.

We go into another Bronco test. And then another tackling drill before a cross-field match. It's animal. But that's exactly what we need. That's exactly what we want. At one stage we're in a circle and James McCarthy, that great big silverback gorilla of ours that rarely says a word, is stomping around, grinning, gritting his teeth: Fuckin' love it! This is what it's all about, lads! This is what it's all about! And it is.

The weather has been brutal all month but this evening the sun is shining and the promise of summer feels just around the corner. Walking off the pitch in Innisfails for the last time this year, the whole group is feeling electric, me included.

The next morning it's another early alarm call, for a 7am gym session in St Clare's. I'm bollixed from the night before but we get through it okay and then head to work.

And the next morning, a Saturday, it goes off an hour earlier again. We're on our old stomping ground of Bull Island, back where I'd have first come across James McCarthy as he was starting out on his journey.

We do a series of team-building challenges on the beach. I'm in a group with Clucko, Mick Macauley and Brian Howard. We roll tyres. Run along the ground on all fours. Carry a log about a kilometre down the beach and back. Then we split into pairs. I blindfold Howie and we run waist height into the freezing water where I guide him around a buoy and then guide him back to shore where he empties a watering can into a bucket; then we'll start again, roles reversed. It's all a bit of craic to go with a bit of hardship, all part of a week creating a memory and a spirit to sustain us over the summer.

We then retreat to Clontarf Castle for a small brunch, followed by a session with Gary Keegan, the high performance advisor. The right man at just the right time.

Only last week I was bemoaning to Mick and Flynner that there's no conduit between us and the management. In Pat's time lads could go to Caroline Currid and she'd filter accordingly our observations as well as hear out our fears and concerns. Bernard Dunne isn't around this year because of his commitments as performance director of Irish boxing. But now here's Gary. And while it's not like he hears us out – he's the one that does all the talking – it's as if he has. It's as if he's talking to me. By the time he finishes up, so many of my doubts and worries have evaporated.

We were introduced to him in 2015 down in Powerscourt after the drawn semi-final with Mayo. That's where we first heard of The

Process, a concept which helped keep us on track when things got shaky in that replay. And he's been into us five or six times every season since while consulting quietly away with Jim in the background. I can hardly think of a session when he didn't hit the mark but today is probably his best yet. He knocks it out of the park.

In the hands of someone else, some of it could come across as abstract and pure corporate speak, but with him, you know he lives it, that he's so passionate about it. He asks us to reflect on what are our distinguishing characteristics and values – humility, commitment to a higher purpose, continuous improvement. How are we nourishing them? They're not just something you write on a flipchart and put up on a wall. Farm Your Culture, he says. Don't neglect it. You've to care for it, water it; sometimes when there's been challenges and change, you might need to re-sow it. But always nurture it.

Other little lines resonate with me. Worry Only About Character, he says. That's all that matters. That's what your legacy will be – your character. Your service to the team and the purpose.

He reminds us of the journey. Cherish it. Will I Look Back and Smile? Create Key Moments Every Day.

And then wrapping up, he has on a slide: WIN. What's Important Now. The league, the past, whatever was off, it's gone, done. Draw A Line in the Sand, he says. Then step forward. Go forward and leave your legacy. Go farm your culture.

When he finishes, there isn't just a round of applause. He gets a standing ovation. I go up and shake his hand. 'Brilliant. Thanks for that. I got a lot out of that.'

And then to nicely round off our week before we go back to our clubs for the month, we head over to Scoil Uí Chonaill, a small club on the Clontarf Road, for what Gary would call 'the humility piece' and train their kids for an hour.

Helping Hand: Myself, Flynner and Mick, along with Donal Óg Cusack on a 2012 GPA All Stars tour assisting with the clean-up in Breezy Point

Unrivalled Blokes: Jonny Cooper and Paddy Andrews had their experience of the rocky road, but it only made them more resilient

Twin Towers: Eoghan O'Gara's loyalty and service to the cause has personified what our group is about

Neverland: In Mick Macauley's back garden, where time just disappears, in 2017. From left: Darren Daly, me, Mick, Clucko, Ciarán Kilkenny, James McCarthy and Flynner

Forbidden Fruit: At 29 I was able to attend my first music festival along with my friend Jude Clonan, Flynner, Éamon Fennell, Ross, and that mad fella on the right – Clucko

Viva Las Vegas!: On my stag with my buddies

The Miss: In Maynooth College, David Clarke and myself repeatedly practised one-on-ones with each other – but he wasn't meant to save it when we eventually came face to face in 2012. The Miss haunted me that winter

Striking Back: Twelve months later I'd thankfully atone for The Miss by pouncing for two goals against Mayo in the All Ireland final

Big Brother: Alan inspired me to want to be a Dub while we'd also share some great – and some tough – days with the club as well

Back In The Clubhouse: With all the boys from Plunkett's

MasterChefs – And The Naked Chef: In Doonbeg for our 2018 All Ireland final camp

Five For Five: Butsy, Mick, me, Dermo and Cossie after the historic 2019 final replay

Up In Lights: I've always felt that GAA players, as much as rugby and soccer players, should have the chance to promote their sport as well as brands

What A Way To Go: With Alan after the 2015 final

Leading It Out: Captaining Ireland in the 2015 International Rules series

Comeback: Just 23 weeks after doing my cruciate, I got back on in the Super 8s

Jim And Me: At times over my last two seasons in blue I was frustrated but Jim Gavin and myself have had a hugely-successful and mutually-respectful partnership

Blocked: Against Cavan in the 2019 league

All Worthwhile: With Flynner, O'Gara, his daughter Fiadh and my two boys

The Last Dance: Against Tyrone in 2019

My World In My Hands: With Donagh and Keadán only months after their birth and only moments after Dublin have won Sam in 2018

Love Of My Life: Keira and me on our wedding day in December 2016 (above); at the All Stars (top right); and when she was pregnant with the lads and I was having cruciate surgery in February 2018

Best Men: All my teammates and friends at my wedding

Hands Full: Feeding Donagh and Keadán

Twins And Trebles: With Mam, Keira, Dad, the two lads, and a trio of trophies

Blue Steel: The lads striking a pose. I wonder where they learned that from?!

Welcome To The Family: Me with Keira's brother Colin, mother Liz and father Martin

The Clan: With all the Brogans after our traditional GOAL Mile run

Club Is Family: Playing with Alan and Paul again was an unexpected joy in 2019

All On Board: Back playing my first game of football post-Covid lockdown, with a couple of biased fans

Generation Game: Dad, me and the twins – and in the back, the great team he played on. No pressure, Donagh and Keadán!

My World: Keira, me and the two lads

Soldier Field: Witnessing Ireland beat the All Blacks in Chicago in the company of Richie McCaw and Brian O'Driscoll was a special experience

All Business: At the Pendulum Summit, representing Legacy and PepTalk

Before we left Clontarf Castle, Jim said to us, Remember, we shouldn't be here, we should be getting ready for a league final tomorrow. And that definitely would have been his preference; that we'd have been there going up the steps to get what he calls 'a piece of tin' instead of the Mayo lads who beat Kerry.

But this past week might have been just what we needed. It has literally been a wake-up call for us; it has shaken off any semblance of complacency there might have been.

It's definitely jolted me out of whatever state I was in. I was feeling hard done by, feeling sorry for myself, too preoccupied about the management's perception of me, not controlling all of the controllables.

Now I'm drawing a line in the sand and leaving all that negativity behind. When we come back from the clubs in a month's time, Jim might sit down with me and tell me it's the end of the road. If so, we'll shake hands and part ways. But this week has given me a fresh perspective and appreciation of just what a special place we're in, of what a special group I'm part of, of just how lucky I've been to be part of its journey.

There was a line Gary had in his presentation: Hard habits are hard earned. And they are. This culture, this winning habit, we planted it and cultivated it and dug it out on early mornings like this past week; and in places like the beach on Bull Island; and on the training ground where the Mossy Quinns showed me how to side-foot the ball past the goalie and tutored Mick Fitzsimons even though we were playing major minutes and he wasn't.

In 2012 we went down to Dingle on a camp before the All Ireland semi-final against Mayo. We were doing these runs up a hill on the side of the pitch and you could tell Paul Casey was gassed: his face was all red, his legs looked like they were pulling a sleigh and he was

225

panting hard. Yet he not only finished every run, he was pushing on everyone else, telling them to keep going and not to be crouching down, putting their hands on their knees. Come on! Just the last few now! Stand up straight, don't be showing any weakness! Keep going, lads! Keep going!

After Paul had thrown himself over the finishing line and we were all gathered around, Pat Gilroy pointed to him. Look at that poor bastard! He's after giving it everything he has! He kept going, kept going, right to the very end. That's what we're about!

Paul had played only five minutes that whole year. And he didn't see the field against Mayo either, a game we ended up losing. But we kept going right to the end, and though Paul retired that winter, that spirit of Dingle carried into the following season and beyond. That 2012 season was Ciarán Kilkenny's first on the panel. He ran up that hill that day. And he'd have seen Paul Casey, a veteran of twelve years, most of them as a starter but now a fringe player, yet never more central – still setting the standard, still wanting it, still going to the bitter end, still planting seeds and helping farm the culture.

So here in 2019 that's what I'm going to do. I'm going to give to the group all that I can while I can. Whether that's through game-time or scores or just motivation and leadership, I will help farm this culture. I will help leave a legacy for this group. And show and remind some of the new lads: This is what we're all about.

17

Legacy

TO WIN ALL IRELANDS THIS MILLENNIUM YOU need to have everything in place.

The technical. The physical. The mental. The tactical.

And the commercial.

Pat Gilroy identified the latter in a way no one really had before.

Tyrone and especially Kerry weren't just beating and outwitting us on the pitch. They were outperforming and outsmarting us off it. And there was a correlation between the two.

One night Pat pulled myself and Éamon Fennell aside and showed us a chart of what counties had spent the previous year on their county teams. Kerry were on top, having splashed out over €1 million, leaving us in their wake. Though their summer had lasted six weeks longer than ours which explained some of their extra expenditure, they weren't having to fund a competitive hurling team like Dublin were. In a typical week the Kerry senior footballers were spending roughly twice as much as we were. We needed to close that gap, Pat said, because we needed the extra resources and support.

For 2010 we were able to have a second physio so more players could be available to play. Chris Farrell came in to not only video and analyse all our matches but our training sessions as well. We could bring Caroline Currid in as an embedded performance coach, just as Tyrone with their Club Tyrone supporters' fund had in 2008 when they went on to win the All Ireland. Dr Crionna Tobin came in as our first-ever nutritionist, something the Kilkenny hurlers already had for over a decade. And by then the Bunker had been built, a base we could finally call home.

It was a challenging time trying to raise those funds. The Celtic Tiger had not only stopped roaring, it was dead. Virtually at the same moment Pat was appointed, in October 2008, the economy crashed. If you were going to attract businesses to come on board with you, you were going to have to be creative.

Luckily Dublin GAA had the right leadership for those times: John Costello as CEO and Pat as senior football manager. Both understood the power and potential of the Dublin GAA brand. And Pat also identified that if we were to bring in money, he needed the players to help get it.

That meant another form of tough love for me. By 2009 I was being asked to do quite a few commercial gigs, probably more than anyone else on the panel except maybe Alan. I was now established in the team, getting scores, had the famous family name, and if you look half-presentable, that's half the battle. And I felt, well, if I'm being asked to do them, why not? I didn't mind.

But a few lads did mind: Why is he getting all the gigs, just because he's a forward and a Brogan and had a decent season? And Pat felt it needed to come to the surface. So he had this thing in the Bunker, not unlike a truth session, where three players had to offer up something about a teammate that was annoying them. Sometimes it could be something silly, like saying they hated a hat a lad was wearing. But one day it raised its head: Berno can't be talking about some sponsorship gig he got when other lads aren't getting any.

I was a bit shocked but I had to take it on the chin. Then Pat came in. He said it was important that I appreciated I was getting a lot of these gigs and attention because there were fourteen other men working their asses off and helping get me the ball. In future, a percentage share of whatever anyone got for doing a commercial deal would go into the team pot so that everyone would get a slice of the action. But equally, more lads needed to step forward and commit to appearing at some of our fundraisers and events put on by our sponsors. Instead of a golf club calling Alan or myself because they knew we'd oblige and show up, other lads needed to get their names and faces out there and meet and greet and play a few rounds and say a few words after dinner.

And that's what happened. More of the workload and the lime-light was shared and more finance was brought in for the group. By 2011 our income and expenditure was more than any other county in the country, a position we haven't relinquished since.

Pat was brilliant in how he wove it all together. He got in people like Mark Doyle and Podge Byrne, a Vincent's clubmate and business partner of his who is now a mentor to Philly McMahon, to help manage some of the commercial matters of the team as well as offer career advice. Very few GAA managers thought like that. One exception was Tommy Lyons, who innovatively raised funds to help with the team's preparations and also emphasised the career development of his players – and still looks out for them as I know from personal experience.

And then there was how Pat dealt with the Brogans. Because while he'd appeased those lads by being seen to have brought us down a peg, he viewed our marketability and knowledge of the corporate space as a strength, not a liability, and duly tapped into it.

One day we had a brainstorming session out in Swords in the

boardroom of Dalkia, the successful water, waste and energy management firm that Pat would later sell to Veolia.

Around the table were Pat, his executive assistant Aileen Burke, Podge, me, Alan and our cousin James. Alan had been dealing with sponsors for almost a decade and was a commercial manager in his day job. I already had quite a lot of experience of interacting with sponsors too, as well as having a masters in business management and specialising in sports taxation in my work as a chartered accountant.

James, a solicitor, specialised in sports law. Although he was out injured after doing his cruciate, Pat had kept him around because of his positivity and passion for Dublin GAA, so himself and Paul Griffin, who was in a similar boat, were helping Ray Boyne with the stats. Pat had already got him to look over a couple of proposed sponsorship agreements he'd lined up. He knew from previous conversations that James had big ideas on how Dublin GAA could optimise its commercial potential. As far as they were concerned, Dublin GAA had been underselling itself. While it had secured €800,000 a year from its main sponsor, Vodafone, which had succeeded Arnotts, there was still so much more we could be doing.

So Pat got up with his marker and approached the whiteboard: a blank canvas to create a template to optimise the Dublin GAA brand and give its teams the best chance of success. Right, what does this team need? What are the key performance inputs that could be put in place to let the players be the best they can be? What industries and companies can we look to form partnerships with to provide these?

We started firing out ideas.

Nutrition. How about we get onto one of the suppliers and offer them the chance to partner with Dublin GAA instead of lads having to go out and spend €30 a month of their own on a big tub of protein?

Gear. Okay, we get our tracksuits, tops, shorts and socks like every other county, but what about compression gear? The science shows it helps you warm up quicker and move better and aids recovery. And we're wearing it in games, warming up, warming down. The supplier's brand name will be visible in photos.

What about warm-weather training camps? Kerry go on one every year. Cork most years. It's a real chance to get in a block of training and bond the group even more. It might cost up to €80,000 taking forty-five people away for the week but let's talk to an airline about doing some deal with us to help with some of that cost. Berno, you're a brand ambassador with Aer Lingus, aren't you?

Yeah, I know Seán Murphy, their head man in HR. I could talk to him.

Great. What about a hotel to partner with? You keep on hearing about the Kilkenny hurlers and Langton's. Before a big championship game in Killarney, the Kerry boys are cocooned away for hours in the Europa, that plush hotel by the lakes. That's what we should be looking at. We're in Dublin! The place is coming down with hotels!

Jesus, we've been only scratching the surface, haven't we?

Yeah. We've been asleep. A sleeping giant.

Well, we're awake now.

From that meeting and a few more like it, a new commercial model was hatched, basically the first of its kind in the GAA. Instead of just having your main commercial sponsor as had been the traditional template, we could have multiple associate partners, like Manchester United for example had long been doing. James became a de facto commercial manager as an aside to his day job. We established a Dublin players' foundation which operated with the support of the county board; I initially helped manage the bank account and funds along with Aileen and was a signatory on the account.

When it came to personal deals, the percentage split was carved in stone; if I or anyone else entered into a commercial arrangement with some company on the back of being a Dublin footballer, a share of that would go back into the players' foundation which would be split evenly among the panel at the end of the season to cover expenses. If the players' foundation had a fundraising event, a share of whatever was brought in went to the county board.

We knocked on doors and found potential associate partners that were glad to open them. Renault became our commercial car partners. Aer Lingus came on board; while we didn't go on any warm-weather training camps after 2010, we've thankfully since gone on multiple team holidays with them after winning All Irelands.

Even when Pat stepped away after the 2012 All Ireland semi-final, he sat down with James and myself numerous times in the following months to solidify the players' foundation. And Jim Gavin was happy to keep it in place, especially certain protocols like the percentage share split. Although he didn't want to ever distract from on-field performance, he understood that Dublin was a commercial monster that needed a structure put on it. James was trusted by the players because he'd soldiered with them and so they were comfortable talking about money with him and offering their ideas as to how they could engage as brand ambassadors with potential partners. In Jim's first year, James was able to negotiate multiple partnerships: the Gibson Hotel, Skins compression gear, ROS Nutrition.

It grew to the point that it needed to become a full-time in-house position, run directly by the county board. James by the end of 2013 was too busy growing his own company to continue in the role and so it was advertised, and Mossy Quinn, our old teammate, landed it, becoming the first commercial manager appointed by a GAA county board. He's taken it to another level again. Mitsubishi Motors are now our commercial car sponsors. Intersport Elverys are our retail partners. But again, so much of it is a continuation of Pat's vision of finding partners that can directly aid our on-field performance. As of now Kinetica are our nutrition providers, O'Neill's lay on the kit, Ballygowan and Energise Sport are our official hydration partners, the Gibson Hotel is where we begin our match-day prep, and then you have one of the most fundamental and costly aspects of inter-county preparation – food, provided by the Gourmet Food Parlour.

A concept we'd adopted from the All Blacks is that as a player you leave the jersey in a better place. The same goes for the Dublin managers I've played under: they've each left – or will leave – the bainisteóir bib in a better place for the next man. Pat's contribution to Dublin goes beyond just being the man who was at the helm when we made the breakthrough in 2011. At the start of that year he championed John Costello's concept of the Spring Series, taking our national league games out of Parnell Park where we never played in championship, and bringing them into Croke Park where we shared several double bills with the hurlers, bringing on them as well: all these years later, that's where we still play our league games. We still use the Bunker as our base, once the league is over. And he initiated a transformative commercial model the likes of which the GAA had never seen.

Now that is legacy.

A FEW days after the 2011 All Ireland semi-final win over Donegal, I handed in my notice at Farrell Grant Sparks where I'd trained as a chartered accountant and worked as a tax accountant. They had been very good to me, especially one of the partners, Éamon

Griffin, father of Paul, but I had an itch to do something where I could express myself more and maybe start a business of my own.

James was in a similar headspace around then. He found working in law very linear with little room for the kind of creativity and dynamism that his spirit craved, so he reached out to me, saying he was thinking of starting a sports agency. I knew he'd be good at it. When companies would want me to endorse their product, James often advised me and negotiated on my behalf: Well, there's his time, his profile and travel expenses: he'll need a bit more than that. So when he asked if he could dip into my contacts book and get on to some of the soccer and rugby as well as GAA lads that I knew, I said I could go one better: I'll go in with you, let's do something together.

David Clancy, a tax consultant and a friend of my dad's who mentored me through my accounting exams, also came on board as a director and gave us an office space out in Lucan. We called the company Legacy, or to give it its full title at the time, Legacy Sport and Entertainment Consultants. We were basically a PR agency. James understood the agency space, while from interacting with various sponsors as a player, I had seen the good, the bad and the ugly and felt there was a gap in the market to do it better. At Legacy we could promote brands in a more effective, energetic and impactful way.

So we went for it. We'd advise players, work with brands seeking to invest in sport, host corporate hospitality events and pretty much everything in between. We were hungry, determined, ready and happy to get our hands dirty to make it a success. All we needed was a chance.

But that was a problem. We struggled to get that chance. It was fine when we were representing the Dublin players' foundation and helping to land deals with the likes of Skins and ROS Nutrition. But when we were going in as simply Legacy, we weren't being taken seriously. We were just seen as football players, not real players in this very different ball game.

A CEO or marketing manager would happily meet with us for a coffee but while we'd explain what it was we were offering, they were less interested in doing business with us there and then as they wanted to talk about football: So, tell us, will ye win the All Ireland again? Some of the time you were meeting decision-makers with only a passing knowledge of the GAA and assumed I was a full-time athlete. They didn't understand that I was trying to make a living here, that this was actually the day job.

It was eighteen months before we could take anyone else onto the staff; we didn't pay ourselves a salary for the first two years. James had been living in Smithfield with Niamh, his now wife, but they each had to move back in with their parents because they couldn't afford to stay where they were. It was a testing time, especially when his friends and colleagues from the old job were moving up in the world and into nice pads around town.

We had to have a couple of hard conversations with ourselves: Are we doing the right things? Do we need to pivot here? And I had serious doubts about myself: have I the credibility to work in this space? Have we any chance in this market? But those wobbles were only temporary. Whatever about having faith in myself, I had huge faith in James. He was a bit like his dad, Jim, who was on the Dublin panel for ten years under Heffo and was a selector with the 1995 All Ireland team and a few of the U21 All Ireland teams that Jim Gavin managed: loyal, sensible, bright, patient. With him on board, we'd figure it out. We'd get a break and we'd take it.

And we did figure it out. And we did get our break.

It came in the autumn of 2013. A few weeks earlier I'd scored two goals in the All Ireland final. This was a similar moment: I'd stayed patient, spotted the opportunity, then pounced.

AIG had just been announced as the new main sponsors of Dublin GAA after Vodafone had stepped away. I was at the airport when the news broke, about to fly out to Marbella with my brother Paul and Éamo, Ross and Mick Macauley. I made a few calls, got the number of AIG Ireland's general manager Declan O'Rourke, and rang him while I was at the door of the plane. The cabin crew were frantically gesturing, saying they were closing the doors, but I told them I'd just be one more minute. So I got talking to Declan, and as the flight attendant ushered me to my seat, I congratulated him on securing the deal, that we were delighted to have a big global brand like his on board, and that I'd love to meet him when I got back. My company Legacy was just the agency to get AIG's brand and message into the communities of Dublin.

I firmly believed it. A concept I was big on from my studies as well as my experience of sponsorship was brand "activation". The traditional sponsorship model was that you paid a certain amount of money to get your name on the front of the jersey of the team in the sport that you followed, you'd have a press launch to announce it, you'd get to sit in the box at the match and that would be it, more or less. But there's limited value in that. You'll get a far greater return by spending that much again on activating the sponsorship: where you create experiences and interactions and ultimately a relationship with your targeted customers and build brand affinity that way.

I was a main ambassador for Vodafone when they were sponsoring Dublin and initially they were quite inventive and proactive. But once their marketing director left, all the energy and creativity seemed to go with her. They stopped activating the sponsorship and just went through the motions. Vodafone are now a benchmark for sponsorship activation but back then they didn't seem to appreciate what a great asset they had and what more they could get in return for the money they were investing.

I'd worked with other brands like Supervalu which would use bill-boards and TV ads in a way that connected with their customers and portrayed the values of the GAA. You'd meet the store owners, customers, supporters. You'd have a kids' day where you'd maybe coach them or just kick around and there'd be great fun in it and you'd create lots of social media content.

I knew how players thought and what would connect with custom-ers. Players wanted to do things they'd enjoy and which would be relevant to fans, not just give some corporate spin that felt heavy-handed and stilted. That just wouldn't land. But if you engaged with the players, asked them what they liked, and allowed them to be just themselves and authentic, it would resonate much better with customers. AIG in particular were going to have to activate their sponsorship because other than being known as the sponsors of Manchester United, it wasn't a brand or service that most people in Dublin were familiar with.

The week after I got back from Marbella, we met in the Cel-bridge Manor Hotel: myself and James from Legacy; then from AIG, Declan O'Rourke and their marketing manager, John Gillick. They were both very personable and both big GAA men. Declan was from Tipperary and heavily involved in their supporters club. John, like his brother David, the Olympic athlete, was a Ballinteer St John's man and actually had played wing back for them when they'd knocked Plunkett's out of that year's county championship. But while it was all smiles and pleasantries on the outside, inside the butterflies were churning. This was Legacy's All Ireland final and if we didn't get it right here there wouldn't be another.

We went for it. 'Look, no one else in this space knows Dublin GAA like us. It's in our blood. Our fathers played for Dublin. We've both played for Dublin. We're both club footballers. We know the clubs, we know the grassroots, we have relationships with them. We can get you in there with them quicker and better than anyone else. If you're going to get your product and message to thousands of GAA supporters and members, you need us. We're your guys.'

And it worked. Declan and John were won over by our vision as well as our passion and enthusiasm and so they took a chance on us. But now we had to make it work. We had to get down to work, roll up the sleeves, pick up the phone and start hustling like hell.

We got onto someone we knew in every club. Say Raheny. I'd call Ciarán Whelan. 'Whelo, how's it going? Listen, who in the club there should I talk to about…?'

So then Whelo would give me the number of Jimmy, the club secretary or chairman. And I'd call Jimmy. 'Howiya, Jimmy. This is Bernard Brogan, I got your number from Ciarán Whelan. Look, I'm working on the sponsorship for AIG and we'd like to give youse some gear and equipment if we could just put the logo on it and have some signage around the club.'

James and myself would then go to O'Neill's, get bags of balls, order cones, put the AIG stamp on them, meet Jimmy and his equivalent in the car park of virtually every club in the county and hand over the goodies. So the clubs would maybe get fifty footballs and sliotars, cones and bibs and jerseys, all in return for just having the AIG logo on them and an advertising hoarding placed in some prominent spot around the club, saying: AIG: Supporting Your Club. Because it was.

The signage started going up all around the county. In the clubs, as well as on the roads. AIG: Drive Safely. And the message percolated.

They were in the insurance game. And they were in the community. They were adding value to the club and the community.

That connection has only strengthened in the years since. All our county teams have also been heavily engaged. We've organised photo shoots and content days where we've had a player not just from our senior footballers but our hurlers, camogie team and the ladies footballers; AIG have won awards for being one of the earliest sponsors to promote and elevate female athletes. We've had days where the players have met and interacted with clients and supporters. We've produced creative, fun content on social media platforms where you get a sense of what lads are like, such as Paul Mannion doing a Q&A with his mammy, or being frightened out of his wits by having to blindly pick up a (fake) snake!

We actually offered to do something similar for Cork GAA. I felt they were the one brand in the GAA with the potential of a Dublin so I contacted their then county board secretary, Frank Murphy, on behalf of a client when the Cork sponsorship was up. But while Frank was very polite, I got the impression from him that they already had their next sponsor lined up and that by talking about this "activation" thing, maybe I was speaking a different language.

The way it worked out, we didn't need it. But we needed the AIG account. That was the game-changer for us. It allowed myself and James to finally pay ourselves a proper wage. More clients started to come on board. But we were also sufficiently self-aware to know we still needed greater credibility around town and in the meeting room. We wanted to completely shred that perception of being the footballers, the nice lads. So we head-hunted Kevin Moore, the head of sport at the long-established PR firm FleishmanHillard and after about six months finally persuaded him to come over and be our deputy managing director. I'd seen him operate with various brands that I had been an ambassador for and knew he was the perfect fit for us: approachable, genuine, creative, hard-working. And that was the other game-changer. Before, we'd been able to get in the door because they wanted to meet the footballers. Now with Kevin we had the credibility to close the deal.

Along the way we changed our name to simply Legacy Communications. We now employ seventeen people there, to go with the fourteen others we employ at PepTalk. To me, that's the buzz: job creation, more than wealth creation. I live in a nice estate in my native Castleknock and all I want is to be able to pay off the mortgage, provide for my family and my children's education, maybe have a couple of holidays a year. But it's a special feeling when you can employ someone. And bring them on board to join us on the journey and to share our values and vision. We think they'll enjoy it. We pay them well. We give them autonomy, space; we place our trust in them. We've unlimited leave holidays; if you're on top of your account – whether it's Volkswagen, Energia, Glenisk, Amgen, Lenovo, whoever – and want to go away for a day or go home early, that's fine. We find that if you treat people like adults, they won't take advantage of you, they'll repay you – in buckets.

On the journey we've taken several detours, adapting to the environment and marketplace. We realised after a couple of years that we were getting caught between two stools, trying to be both a players' agency and a PR agency, and it was hurting us winning business. So we decided to double down as a PR agency; the sports agency market was too small over here and too shark-infested over in the UK. We focused on working with brands. Our work with Laya Insurance in activating their sponsorship as health and wellbeing partners of Leinster Rugby would epitomise what we're about. At some of Leinster's home matches we've had drummers, entertainment and giveaways to create a fun experience for fans, many of whom are potential customers. Subliminally there's a process going on: That was a bit of craic. What's the name of that crowd who put that on? Laya. Oh, okay…

They're a health insurer obviously, so we've produced content where you're introduced to Leinster's own health and wellbeing team – the physios, the doctors, the nutritionists. Again, it provides insight for the fan, while subtly reminding you of the game that Laya are in. We've ran their super troopers campaign where the brand ambassador Johnny Sexton and some of his teammates have visited the schoolyards, classrooms and playing fields of our country's primary schools to promote physical activity, good nutrition and even a bit of mindfulness. Again, that's activating your sponsorship, not being passive about it.

Some accounts then lead us back to the GAA. Littlewoods Ireland are basically an online department store, where you can go onto their website and either have your order delivered directly to your home or you can pick it up at one of their thousand collect spots around the country – could be the local Centra store or post office, wherever. When they came to us about a grassroots initiative, I looked at a map of where their collection spots were and it was almost the mirror of a map of every GAA club in the country. We knew from conversations with Croke Park that a couple of the anchor sponsors of the hurling championship were finishing up. We also thought the camogie national league was another opportunity to appeal to female customers. So after James negotiated with Croke Park, the parties partnered up and we activated the sponsorship.

We identified Jackie Tyrrell, Anna Geary and Austin Gleeson as perfect ambassadors for that brand: confident, into their fashion and clothes which Littlewoods retail, but also grounded, part of their community, again, like the brand. For the launch Anna and Jackie participated in a fashion shoot by Lough Dan in Wicklow which provided some great imagery and digital content. And at it they made the point: this sponsorship is good for the GAA. It brings a bit of style and a contemporary feel to it. It shows that our players can be looked at as more than just footballers and hurlers. They can be models, role models, ambassadors.

And that's the way I've always looked at it. Ultimately sponsorship is good for the GAA. It helps promote our games and our players, makes them more attractive and more likely that kids will want to play and go to our games. You might still have the odd puritan who has an issue with it, but would they prefer if it was only soccer and rugby players in all the ads and on all the billboards? That attitude is less prevalent now but even starting out I wasn't going to bow to it. I wanted to stand up and help other players by showing it could be done in the right way: that we could be role models as much as any other group of sportspeople. I get recognised more on the street for being that nice lad doing his shopping in Supervalu than for what I've done with the Dubs – but they still know from the ad that it's GAA I play.

Brands want to partner with the GAA because of the values it has. And that sponsorship ultimately goes back into the community and the clubs. Most of the revenue a Supervalu or a Littlewoods pays in sponsoring the GAA championships is ploughed back into the grassroots. You go to a typical soccer club and they have a container box for people to tog out in. You go to a GAA club and they'll have at least one fine pitch with dressing rooms and maybe a stand and a grand clubhouse. Without sponsorship, you wouldn't have that across the board like you do.

The way Legacy has evolved, a lot of our work now is actually unrelated to sport. In this game you have to diversify. The reality is whenever the economy experiences a downturn, sport and sponsorship are among the first places where budgets are slashed. These days we have clients varying from Dublin county council and Pieta House to the self-tanning brand Bondi Sands; restaurants like Fire and Sole to hotels like the Portmarnock Hotel and Westport House; a hardware retail brand like Screwfix to a telecommunications provider like KN Circet.

But sport will always be part of what we do. It was through sport that I learned nearly everything about personal growth and the importance of good values. It's helped me become who and what I am. As a person. And as a businessperson.

18

Summertime Blues

I'M ON MY WAY TO COLLECT THE KIDS FROM THE crèche in the middle of club month when Jim drops a text: Are you able to come out to St Clare's in the next hour or so?

Sounds ominous. Am I about to get The News?

I grab the kids, drop them home and shoot out the door. When I get over to the Bunker, I see that they're setting everything back up for the summer ahead, now that it'll be the team's base for the rest of the year: some new slogans and images are on the wall, leadership books are back on the shelves. This could be the last time I'm in the place. We'll soon know.

Jim motions me into his office. After some pleasantries he explains that he's meeting lads over the next couple of weeks before the group starts back and he'll be telling some of them that he has to let them go for the year.

I'm thinking: Right, and?

I'm not here to put you out of your misery, he says. I'd like you to stay on for the summer. Almost everything is telling me that your time is up but just something in my gut tells me that I might need to call upon you at some point in the championship. So I'd prefer to have you around.

'Okay,' I say, but little more than that. I did enough talking during the league. I can tell anyway Jim has more to say.

Just so you know where you stand, he continues. If we were playing championship in the morning, you probably wouldn't be on the twenty-six travelling. To be totally honest, if we were having an A versus B game and everyone was fit and available, you'd probably be on the bench for the start of it. You mightn't even get to play in that match.

'You're not serious, Jim?' I played well for the club in championship last week: scored a goal, kicked five frees, including one in injury-time from the wing to give us an unlikely draw against a fancied St Jude's team.

I am, he says. That's my assessment of how things stand at the moment.

He takes out a document and breaks it down for me in tiers.

Tier One has twelve players. All fit and well, they're automatic starters. You know who they are.

Then there's the second tier, roughly numbers thirteen to twenty-one. They'd all likely be getting game-time at some point if there was a championship game tomorrow, it'd just be a matter of which of them would start and who'd be the Finishers.

Then there's Tier Three: numbers twenty-two to thirty.

Then there's Tier Four: numbers thirty-one to thirty-six.

And then there's the last tier: the five or six lads outside that thirty-six.

I'm somewhere in Tier Four, he says.

'Alright. Well, Jim, what I need to know is: is there an opportunity for me to change that? If I'm going well in training, is there a chance for me to move up the grid and play?'

He says there is. He was at the Jude's game. Thought I took the goal well, was striking my frees well, came up with some big plays in the clutch when they were needed. I moved up a tier in his head with that performance. So, yeah, if I play well, there is the possibility I will play.

I tell him I'm going to need a bit of time to think about what he said and talk to my family. There's quite a bit to process there.

When I talk to Keira, she says, Look, you just need to be happy with whatever you do. They're not going to fight for you, everything you get will be tough fought. You can't let it get you down. I don't want you coming home in bad humour after a training session or a game like we had through the league. Anything that happens now is bonus territory. Football has been good to you. As long as you understand that and don't let it drag your mood down here at home, I'll back you. And if you decide to go on, then be happy with the decision and go after it.

The following week I ring Jim to tell him I'd like to accept his invitation. All I'm asking for is a guarantee that he's open to me moving up the tiers. And I know I'm not going to crack the top tier. 'I don't want you to even think that I'm aspiring to be a starter,' I tell him. 'I want to be a twenty-minute option for you. Everything I do will be geared around being fit to carry out that role. I'm out kicking every second night so that if I get two chances in a game, I'm nailing both of them.'

He says that's fine, just that if I do play, he wants me to be able to run up and down the pitch, something Paul Mannion does for us.

I check him a bit there. James at work told me Jim might throw my fitness at me and that I'd need to have my ducks in a row if he did. I'm in as good a shape as I can be. He will see that if he checks my GPS unit. We were all given these units before going back to the clubs. We have to hand them over once a week to our S&C team for monitoring, another indication that preparations this year have gone up a notch. I've been rigorous about my nutrition too. I've shed four kg from last year. I'm at eleven percent body fat. I scored well in most categories in the fitness test. And in those few where I was among the bottom five, I was no worse in them than I was back when I was winning All Stars. I'm as lean and as sharp as I've ever been. I don't want them to have it as an excuse for not playing me.

And that's why I check him there. 'Jim, I'll work hard, but I'm never going to have the legs of a Mannion to be running back into our own square. We're different players. The team isn't just a bunch of robots where one fella just slots in the same as the next. We all bring different attributes. There'll be space for different skillsets at different times. And I'm going to offer something different: I'm looking to be that pivot man inside, turn defenders, create goal chances.'

As we finish up, I say that from now on in, I want to do the rest of my talking on the field. Just so he knows that I'm going for this, that I wouldn't be here otherwise. Work is busier than ever. I can't afford to be wasting my time here.

Jim says these are all valid points. Keep going after the frees. Get that accuracy up to ninety percent. Remain vocal in the group. See you next week.

So he does, and he sees Rory O'Carroll as well, back after three years, having travelled and worked abroad. That's a great option for us to have at the back.

But no sooner is one old teammate back then another is gone. The day after our first collective weights session back in the Shed, Flynner calls. He's just told Jim that he's pulling out. He's retiring from county football. He went to the gym session hoping that the energy of the group might spark the fire to go for one more summer but it didn't. Jim had a similar chat with him to the one he had with me. And after the league he'd had, he felt he couldn't spend another three or four months on the bench – if he even made it onto it. His whole game is about manic energy and desire and he just feels the body and mind can't provide that anymore.

He seems at ease with the decision, though. Jim likes to quote the legendary American college basketball coach, John Wooden, who defined success as peace of mind from knowing that you've done your best to become the best that you're capable of becoming. Paul can have that peace of mind. No one pushed harder to be the best that he could be: physically, technically, mentally, personally and professionally. He was initially a plumber by trade, the youngest of a family of eight in which no one had been to third-level. Yet he had the courage to go back to college, get a first-class honours degree, a masters, then become the leading commercial director of a top recruitment firm before his role now as CEO of the GPA.

He's probably been my best buddy on the team, on and off the field. Back when himself and Alan were in the half-forward line, it was a dream for me. It's funny how it works: in the current team, Fento, Ciarán Kilkenny and John Small would be all very tight and it transfers onto the field in how they'll often pass it to each other around the middle. Me, Alan and Flynner had had that kind of understanding as well. Flynner might drop deep to receive a kickout from Clucko. Alan would have told him to just kick it up the line, he'd be there; then Alan would get out in front to take it and invariably look for me. One Touch Football, we called it: Kick, kick, kick – score. And often Flynner would just get the ball and look right away to get it into me. My first goal in the 2013 All Ireland: that wasn't a shot that dropped short: he intentionally picked me out.

Now he's not there to pass it to me.

One by one, the band is breaking up.

IN 2012 we were just that bit off. Flynner powered on, winning another All Star, but as a group there was slippage. And I probably personified it as much as anyone.

I don't regret for a minute heading off at the end of 2011 to Australia and Thailand for a few months with Éamon Fennell, my Plunkett's teammate David Matthews and my flatmate at the time, Jude Clonan. The only regret I have is that I didn't do something like it earlier. Alan went and did his J1 in America during Tommy Carr's time because even though he had already made his league debut, he figured he wasn't going to feature in the championship. Looking back, I should have done the same thing in either 2005 or 2006 when I wasn't getting a look in under Pillar. The trip away with the lads more than made up for it. Revelling with ten thousand others at the Full Moon party on the island of Ko Pha-ngan; then on to the craic in Koh Samui; then over to Australia where we must have gone out forty nights straight. I was meant to stay on another couple of weeks and maybe catch some of the Australian Open tennis but I decided to bail early for home, a broken man. It had been harder going than any preseason at home!

I was back only a few weeks and playing a club game when I felt something wrong with my knee. I went to my friends in Santry for a scan to find there was a floating bone that needed to be removed so I missed the rest of the league.

I've tended to struggle whenever I haven't played much in the league, although I'm trying to tell myself now that 2019 will be the exception to that rule. In the championship of 2012 I was wildly inconsistent. In the first round against Louth I went for 2-5, 2-4 from play. When we beat Meath by a goal in the Leinster final, I finished with 1-7, 1-3 from play. But in our three other games that summer I managed only a total of one point from play.

BERNARD BROGAN

Pat was still as driven as ever in 2012. But by his own admission, in his obsession to try to put back-to-back All Irelands together, he became overly-obsessed with Donegal and how to break down their System.

That summer we were often working more on how to play against Donegal than we were on our next opponent. And that sapped a bit of my juice that year. I wasn't enjoying training and my football as much as normal. I don't play football just to win, I play football because I love it: just the thrill of handling ball, kicking it, going out there, me against my man, and may the best team win. But when you're repeatedly inside in the full-forward line and there's no ball coming in for fifteen minutes because there are three men in front of you, it diminishes your basic enjoyment of the game, as much as you try to convince yourself you relish the challenge of finding ways to break systems down. We ended up spending tens of hours readying ourselves for a game that never came. And as a consequence, we ended up not being quite ready for Mayo.

We still could have beaten them. We still should have beaten them. After being ten down at one stage, we rattled off the next seven points. It all came down to one moment.

Only four of us know this but long before it played itself out to the world and over and over again in my head, that scenario used to repeat itself over and over on the field.

A ball pumped in from the wing. I bring it in to my chest. And then as I close in on goal, David Clarke is closing in on me.

Only it isn't in the hot heat of an All Ireland semi-final with 82,000 in Croker and another million watching on TV.

It's on a quiet field out in Maynooth College where there's only myself, Lally and Clarkie, with our buddy Billy Dumbrell there to retrieve the ball.

Back in 2005 we were all in the same economics class but naturally it was football that we most had in common. At the time we all had our own dreams and goals and also frustrations. Lally was trying to cement a place on the Dublin starting fifteen. I was trying to break onto the panel. Billy would have died happy just to get on the field for our Sigerson team. And Clarkie, he couldn't even make his club team at the time; when Ballina Stephenites won the All Ireland that St Paddy's Day, he was on the bench. Lally and myself couldn't believe it. We thought next to Clucko, there couldn't be a better goalie in the country, let alone one in the same club. We were in awe of how good his kickout was; back in those days, before Clucko started pinging balls to the wings, you wanted the ball to float and hang in the air for your midfielders to rip down and Clarkie was brilliant at landing it precisely into the right pocket of airspace. And his shot-stopping was phenomenal. He would spread-eagle himself like Peter Schmeichel to block out the goal. We had a drill that we'd do over and over again: Clarkie would boom it right into Lally's hands, I'd make a run, catch Lally's pass, and then shoot on Clarkie; then Billy would retrieve it if it wasn't a goal and we'd do it again. There were days I walked off that field having hardly put a ball past him. He was that good.

Fast forward seven years from those college days and another ball is kicked in from the wing, only this time it's pumped in by Ciarán Kilkenny, not Lally, and all of Hill 16, not just Billy Dumbrell, is behind Clarkie's goal as I bear down on it.

I knew he'd come out and try to Schmeichel it, so I said to myself, Keep it low, keep it low. But I ended up taking the shot a tad too early and leaned back too much and it rose enough for him to block it with his hand.

I should have scored – but it was still a brilliant save; it was a brilliant save – but still I should have scored. I should have just taken it around him and tapped it in.

At the end of 2016 the two of us were on an All Stars trip in Dubai and ended up having a couple of beers. I said to him, 'Clarkie, you have no idea how much that save haunted me that winter.'

And it did. I questioned my whole mindset and ability to make clutch decisions and clutch plays for the team; I'd thought after 2010 and 2011 I was a big-game player but my confidence was badly shaken after that miss.

Clarkie said back to me, Well, you've helped spoil a few winters for us in Mayo, Bernard.

And I suppose, I had, especially the one in 2013. After The Miss, I'd bounce back, my confidence restored, in no small part because of our new manager who massively empowered me.

Yeah, Jim Gavin.

EVEN Shane Lowry is cracking jokes about my plight.

The last day of May and twenty-four hours before the team goes into a weekend camp in DCU's All Hallows Campus ahead of our 2019 Leinster semi-final, I'm playing some golf in Milltown at a client day put on by CPL, a recruitment agency that Legacy do some work with. The sun is out and so are some of the stars of Irish sport, like Shane and Peter O'Mahony and Johnny Sexton who are all represented by Conor Ridge's Horizon Sports – we do some work with them as well. I'm about to head out with three business colleagues – Cormac Loughlin, Mark Buckley and Ruairí Kelleher – when Shane comes over with a big welcome and to hop a few balls. Good to see you getting picked for some team, Bernard!

Shane, you don't even know the half of it, bud.

Last night we had thirty-one players fit to train. And when we were going into a fifteen-versus-fifteen game and Jim called out the two teams, I was the one left standing on the sideline.

What did I do? I did what I've been doing all month: I'm well used to the drill now. I said nothing, grabbed five footballs, jogged up with them to the top pitch and started kicking on my own: thirty, forty shots. Then I came back down, did a few runs along the sideline to remind the management I was still around, and finally got on with ten minutes to go.

Our team was four points down but we managed to make it a draw. I got onto a ball breaking off Kevin Mc to kick a point and then won a couple of balls inside to pop off to Paddy Andrews as he ran past on the loop and swung them both over. I made a mess of trying to chip a ball straight off the ground into Niall Scully's hands so it wasn't like I was perfect but I made a contribution and a few of the lads afterwards commented that I was moving well.

It's bleedin' tough, though. Shortly after we came back from the clubs, Jim had arranged a couple of challenge games on consecutive nights. About twenty lads were picked to play against Cork and then there were another eighteen of us for a game against Cavan in Parnell Park. I started on the bench alongside two lads who weren't even on the panel. Actually, one of the lads who started wasn't on the panel either. I came on for the last twenty minutes but we were playing against a stiff breeze and only three balls came in. I got my hands on a couple of them and threw a few shapes, didn't do anything bad, didn't do anything good.

The worst though was the internal game we had a week out from the first round against Louth. We were out in St Clare's, the sun shining, the grass just cut, championship around the corner. Everyone warmed up together, then we went back into the dressing room to hear the teams only for me to find out I was one of the two lads not starting. The other was Paddy Andrews who was just back from breaking his jaw. That was the lowest moment I've ever had in my Dublin career. Like a knife to the heart. I'd been going well in training after the Cavan challenge game, getting scores, moving up the grid – or so I thought. But sure it was easy for Jim to leave me out because in his head he was probably thinking, Well, I did warn him that if we had an internal game he probably wouldn't be starting.

That was the first day I went up to the top pitch to do some kicking to make the best use of the time; Paddy came along with me too. I suppose it's now become a common sight at training: in the last four internal games, I've been left off for three of them.

I don't know what the other lads make of it when they see me up there. Are they getting energy from it? Does it impress them that I'm still grafting away after fifteen years? Or do they pity me more than anything? That I'm allowing myself to be subjected to this after fifteen years?

I hope it's more of the former. I hope they don't think I'm just sticking around in case we do the five in a row. That's my worry now. I don't think the team thinks that but the public and supporters might. The truth is I couldn't give a flying fiddler's for the five in a row right now; it means nothing to me. This is all about process for me now, not outcome. Doing things the right way. And that's why I have to park what people might think. As Gary Keegan said to us in Clontarf, Worry Only About Character. And that's what I'm doing. I'm not sulking. I'm not giving out. I'm controlling everything that I can.

I rang Lally on the way home from training last night and he offered a great perspective on it all. You've probably only about ninety days left as a Dublin footballer now, he pointed out. Maybe thirty field sessions, that's it. Then you're gone. So enjoy every session while you can. Make the most of it. Keep going, keep reacting positively for the sake of the group.

I've also recently reached out to someone else I've soldiered with for club and county. Over the years Jason Sherlock has been a teammate, mentor, coach, friend. I remember when I was starting out with Dublin, he advised me to just focus on three things I wanted to do in a game – like, say, showing for the ball, taking on my man, striking the ball well. Other players may have been setting targets like kicking three points from play but as Jayo pointed out, that was only something you could achieve near the end of the game. Get into it right away. Control only what you can. Just little nuggets like that, he was great with.

Even after he finished playing with Dublin and before he came in as a coach with Jim, I'd sound him out for his observations. And he'd always come back with some gem: You need to make harder runs. Your striking could sharpen up a bit. Are you getting in the practice you need? The same when he came in as our forwards coach: we'd go out shooting before training started, we'd collaborate about my runs and the movement of the forwards as a unit. When I did my cruciate last year, Jayo was one of the first people over to the house, with some lovely healthy chocolate brownies his son Joshua kindly made for me.

Since then our communication has been more sporadic. But it lately dawned on me that's probably been more on me than Jayo. So the other week I decided: You know what, I'm tired of talking to Jim. Jayo might give me a better steer.

So I went over to him. 'Look, Jayo, I'd value your opinion on something. I know I'm not going to start this year, no matter what happens, but I'm going after being as effective as a twenty-minute man as possible. What do you think I can work on so that with twenty minutes to go, you can say in your head, "Yeah, we can go to Berno now"?

Well, he replied, the last three times you've come on for Dublin, what's happened?

It took me about three seconds to answer him. Even though I suspected his maths might have been a bit off and I'd never thought of it before, I could just tell by the tone of the question the answer he was looking for.

'I was blocked.'

Yeah, he said. That's what's in my head when I see you. That's something you have to work on.

I thanked him for the feedback and went on and trained away, but in the car going home that night, it struck me: Christ, we've been living in parallel universes, me and the management, for nearly two years.

In my head is the player from our last two games against Kildare: the 2017 Leinster final when I came on and kicked five points from play, and the opening game of the 2018 league, days before I did the cruciate, when again I would have been in the running for man of the match. Being an impact sub, being that pivot man inside: creating goals, kicking points. That's the role I've been envisaging for myself, that's where I think I can get back to again, that's the footballer I see.

But Jayo – and obviously Jim too – have been looking at me in a totally different light.

I did get blocked down alright by Keith Higgins when I came on in the 2017 All Ireland final; I made some other big plays but yeah, Higgins smothered my shot that day.

Then I got blocked down when they gave me those token five minutes up in Cavan.

I'm not even sure what the third game he'd been referring to would be. The 2016 final replay, when Brendan Harrison got a block in on me as well after I got a point on him? Maybe, though I've played other games for Dublin since then in which I haven't been blocked. Anyway, I'm being pedantic. What matters is what Jayo thinks. While I've been trying to keep my confidence up, reminding myself of those two games against Kildare, the men who really matter – the men who make the decisions – seem to have me down as this has-been who keeps getting blocked down.

There's a chasm between how I see myself and how they see me. And when that dawns on me, it's demoralising. For some time now the management have made up their minds on me. And when they gave me those five minutes up in Cavan and I came on lacking in confidence, it confirmed their bias: There he goes again – blocked. Finished.

At least now I know what they're really thinking: they don't trust me to make the right decisions in a big game. It's going to be a real uphill struggle to try to change their minds.

I can take hardship. I took plenty of it from Pat back in 2009 and 2010 when he was constantly dogging me and calling me out. But that was tough love. This is different. It feels like there's no love at all.

There's a motto I've had for most of my career: Play Like A Kid. I remember when I was about twenty, the club had a game against Naomh Barróg on a beautiful evening. I ended up kicking something like 1-13. Their club chairman, the late Jim Fitzmaurice, as well as his wife Marian, was a friend of my mam and da; when he passed away too soon in early 2012, I brought the Sam Maguire to the altar on his day of rest, knowing it would bring a smile to a proud Kerry-man who lived so much of his life in Dublin. And whenever I'd meet Jim, he'd say, God, I remember that day you played us: everything you touched turned to gold! To me, that was the ultimate Play Like A Kid game. It's one I've often gone back to, even in big games in Croke Park, trying to reconnect with that sense of freedom I played with that evening.

But now it's very hard to tell myself to just go out and Play Like A Kid. Because everything's pressurised. Right away I'm on the back foot. The management don't seem to trust me. It's as if they're expecting and waiting for me to mess up. I know when I go out playing with the club and have a ball in my hands I'll match any other forward on the Dublin bench. I've enough cop on and humility to know there are better forwards around now than me.

Con O'Callaghan is the main man; he's obviously ahead of me in the pecking order and rightly so. Mannion and Dean too. But after that? Give me sixty minutes in a blue jersey against Louth who the lads smashed and I'd do just as much damage.

But I won't get that chance, so I have to do it in five- or ten-minute windows – and that's just in training. And it's tough. Because you're trying to both make an impact that they'll notice and yet trying to do the right thing.

Look, it's an embarrassment of riches Jim has to pick from. If they were in any other county fellas like Conor McHugh and Collie Basquel would be automatic starters, known all over the country. I did a media gig yesterday for Supervalu with Andy Moran and the thought struck me: Andy's the same age as me yet he's either still starting for Mayo or he's the first man off the bench for them. I can't even make our starting thirty for an in-house game.

That better change at the weekend now during camp. If I'm on the bleedin' bench again there, Jim's going to hear about it from me. I've helped win All Irelands for him. And if he were to open his mind, I think I can play a part in helping him win another.

ONE of the first slides Jim showed us upstairs in Parnell Park when he got the job in the autumn of 2012 was Dublin: All Ireland champions 2013, 2014, 2015, ?, ?

It was a ballsy statement to put up there. As a county we had only won one All Ireland over the previous seventeen years. Outside of the 1970s, we tended to win only one a decade. And the football landscape at the time he got the job was highly competitive. The public perception at the time was that Donegal were this invincible force with this unbreakable System. Cork had won the previous three leagues and an All Ireland. Mayo, you could already tell, were built to be around for a long time while Kerry never go away. Yet he was basically saying, we're not just out to win the next All Ireland but multiple All Irelands, at least the next three; we're not just here to compete or to win, but to dominate.

It was exciting, as was the way he talked about how we were going to go about it: after floating the idea of all those All Irelands he wanted to win, he barely mentioned the word 'win' again. He wanted us playing a fast, attacking style of football. While Pat had decided we weren't going to be suckered into a shootout with Kerry in light of what had happened to us through the noughties, Jim was more than happy for us to take them, or anyone else, on toe to toe. We were the ones now with the superior firepower. He totally believed in our skillset as players and totally believed it was the right way to play football.

I thrived under that approach. On our way to winning that 2013 league, the first Dublin had won in twenty years, I was averaging eight points a game, more than half of that from play. When we played Mayo under lights in Croker, I finished with 1-10, 1-5 from play and pointed a sideline ball. I felt electric, in a way I hadn't since 2010.

The coaching was excellent. A lot of it was back to basics: stations, with every coach and selector taking one apiece, including Jim himself: he was very hands on back then. Mick Bohan used to have us handling two footballs simultaneously so we'd all be comfortable passing off either hand and foot and soloing and shooting with both feet.

He'd set up the Shooting Challenge where before training, all the forwards would each shoot from nine spots, four times, starting in front of the posts on the thirteen metre line, then working our way out to two spots on the twenty, then back out another seven metres and then back out another seven to thirty-four metres out. It wasn't a case of just sauntering up and casually trying to kick them over the bar. This was designed, focused, competitive, match-like – and fun. He'd chart our scores, pinning up how much we each got out of thirty-six shots, so we'd all be trying to beat one another and better what we'd clocked up the previous night. It really sharpened the mind – and our shooting.

I had a mini-slump midway through that summer, scoring only a point in both the Leinster final against Meath and the All Ireland quarter-final against Cork. But Jim never doubted me. And his faith was rewarded: in the semi-final, I kicked four from play and another two from frees as we took Kerry on in a shootout – and won.

The final with Mayo was more of a slugfest, a war of attrition. But we shaded it by one. And I managed to carve out 2-2 from play.

The Miss had been exorcised from my mind. And Jim had the first of those multiple All Irelands on the board.

BIT by bit I'm moving up the grid.

A week out from the Leinster final against Meath and I'm starting in the A versus B game. No prizes, obviously, for guessing which one I'm on, but that's okay for now.

It has that crackle of intensity that reminds me of those A versus Bs we used to have when we started out on this journey: the likes of Paul Casey, Ross, Éamo, Mossy bristling at where they were in the pecking order and vowing to harden these boys for what they'll get the following week in Croker. Kevin Mc is chomping; he didn't get on the last day against Kildare. So is Dean, having been out injured the past couple of games.

We tear into them, rip them apart. Deano goes for 1-6. I go for 2-2. At one stage we're up seven, and when they begin to chip at our lead, Kevin Mc halts both their momentum and Brian Howard in his tracks, clattering into him as he comes tearing out with the ball. Howie is raging and they go to ground, wrestling one another, but Kevin Mc is unapologetic. That's what you're going to get next Sunday, Howie! Learn to deal with it!

It's a timely reminder for the whole group. So far this summer the lads have been cruising. But we hold them off, win, and shake them up. The following week they play a tight, claustrophobic game against Meath where the score is just five-one at halftime but they remain composed. The third quarter and Meath are still within distance but then Dean comes on to kick four points and set up a goal for Con. Kevin is unleashed as well as part of the surge that sees the lads finally win by sixteen points.

And me, I stay sitting where I am, at home on the couch.

A few of the lads couldn't believe that I didn't make the twenty-six. Bryan Cullen came up to me and said, Look, I won't spoof you: after the league I had you completely written off. But you're right back in the mix now. You're unlucky to miss out for this one. Keep at it. You're going the right way.

I got some love from Jayo after that A versus B game. A big thing he preaches is the palmed goal, or a team goal as he calls it, like the one Scully scored against Tyrone in the 2018 final, or like my second goal from Bastick's pass in the 2013 final. In the As against Bs, both my goals were palmed efforts at the back post so he came straight over to me afterwards and patted me on the back: Great to see you getting on to the end of those moves. Fair play.

I don't know if I hurt my chances when the Wednesday before the Meath match I asked Jim if I could be released to play with the club instead of training that night. I just felt to keep the momentum going I needed another sixty minutes of ball under my belt. So he gave me a free pass, said it was going to be just a light session anyway, working mostly on kickouts. I went away and kicked 1-4 against St Jude's, then was back at Dublin training on the Friday. Jim didn't say anything to me so I was the one who approached him. 'I presume I'm not travelling on Sunday.' He said, no, you're not, but keep up the good work, you're flying.

I'm still a bit pissed though that he didn't take me. I say it again: if I was twenty-three or twenty-four, playing the way I am, there's no doubt I'd have got a game against Meath.

I wish in Jim's head he could just erase every detail on my application form. Blank out the profile pic. Forget about the All Irelands and All Stars won – if it means you'll also forget about my date of birth.

That night after the lads beat Meath, we all go out, not so much to celebrate becoming the first team to ever win nine consecutive provincial titles but to give Paul Flynn a proper send off. We're in Huck's, a bar and restaurant on Camden Street that three of the men of 2011 – Éamo, Ross and Mick Macauley own. The craic is good and Flynner is in great form, all the more comfortable with his decision.

Should I have gone with him? I can't think like that. There's no turning back now. I've to keep going, keep trying to move up that grid.

IN 2014 we played probably as good football as we ever have. Dermo and Flynner were at the peak of their powers. Alan was back, orchestrating everything again after missing most of 2012 and 2013 through injury. And once I returned from a groin surgery that ruled me out of the group stages of the league, I hit a groove, going for 1-6 against Derry in the league final, the same against Meath in the Leinster final and the same against Monaghan in the All Ireland quarter-final.

But waiting for us once more were Donegal, with another game-plan which we'd never encountered before. And this time we weren't ready for it, even though we thought we were.

It's well documented by this stage: how we started out on fire with Flynner and Dermo kicking bombs from outside their mass defence to put us five up; how we should have scored a couple of goals to kill the game off but didn't; and how they then broke our high press by hitting Neil Gallagher on their kickout to tap down to their runners, putting them through for three goals on the break.

Heading into that match I thought I'd almost mastered the mental game. But during that second half I found myself over a couple of frees, thinking, Jesus, I actually don't know if I'm going to be able to kick this over the bar. It was the first time I'd ever doubted myself over a free. In 2011 I had a kick at the top of the D to win a big match against Kildare: I didn't even flinch; I just got up, took my steps, bang, done. But that day against Donegal, I started thinking, Am I going to miss this? They were both tricky enough but on any other day I'd have nailed at least one of them. I was just in shock at how the game had unravelled. My amygdala had been hijacked.

Donegal hadn't been able to emotionally hijack me in 2011 but now they had in 2014.

With everything else that went on that day, those couple of wides weren't as glaring as The Miss against Mayo in 2012. But privately, it was just as tough and had probably an even more negative effect on my confidence. When the game had been going against us, when the team had needed leaders to stand up, I'd wilted. I felt a guilt for letting the team down. Jim's vision of back-to-back titles was gone: 2014 now had a big red cross over it.

How he responded to that defeat is probably the greatest measure of him as a manager. In that book, *Extreme Ownership*, that I took from our leadership library in the Bunker, one of the co-authors, Jocko Willink, talks about a mission that went wrong when he was over a SEALS unit in Iraq. A litany of small errors added up to his unit losing a man and several others being injured. There was plenty of blame to go round yet when Willink reported to his superiors, he baldly stated, 'There's only one person to blame for the entire operation: me. I am the commander. I am responsible for every action that takes place on the battlefield. There is no one to blame but me. And I will tell you this right now: I will make sure that nothing like this ever happens to us again.'

That was Jim. A few weeks after the Donegal defeat, he publicly stated, 'I accept full responsibility for that performance. And I accept full responsibility for the philosophy and for the way Dublin play their football, for the attacking style we play, and sometimes for the vulnerability that it brings.' He shielded the players and then went about making sure nothing like that ever happened to us again.

His aviation background kicked in as well. In that industry, the culture is that mistakes are inevitable but can be minimised once everyone learns from them.

Jim forensically went through the wreckage of the Donegal game and found lots of little faulty processes that needed to be addressed.

We needed more protection at the back, so that was the start of us playing with a sweeper, or a Plus One as we called it, allowing Cian O'Sullivan to drop back deeper and sit in front of our full-back line.

Jayo was brought in to help us break down mass defences.

And Dean was drafted into the starting lineup to take over the frees from me. I couldn't argue. Dean's a more accurate freetaker than me. He's also able to kick it off the ground. After my first cruciate, I couldn't do that anymore: my knee would get too sore from the repetition of practice required.

For most of 2015 I didn't feel anywhere near as confident as I had in 2014. But I was still racking up big scores: 1-6 against Longford, 2-3 against Kildare, 1-1 in the Leinster final against Westmeath, 1-6 in the All Ireland quarter-final against Fermanagh, all from play. A bit of me was thinking I was winging it a little as for some of those goals I just had to palm the ball into the net. But Jim and Jayo were more than happy with me: those team goals were just what they were looking for.

In the All Ireland semi-final replay against Mayo, I had been quiet enough for the first three-quarters of the match. Another manager might have looked to take me off. But Jim trusted me, looked at me as a big-game player. Within two minutes I'd scored the equalising goal and set up a team goal for Philly. In the first half of the final against Kerry, I could hardly get a ball to stick in the torrential rain, but management kept me on for the full game. I even took over the frees from Dean when he went off and then played that one-two with Alan for the insurance point he kicked.

They nearly trusted me more than I trusted myself.

Back then.

BERNARD BROGAN

DERMO'S back.

The morning after the lads pull away from Cork near the end of our opening game of the Super 8s, those of us who didn't play are on our way over to Scoil Uí Chonaill for a workout when Jim rings and includes me and Kevin Mc in a group chat: Just to let you know, Diarmuid Connolly will be there this morning. He's one of us, one of the family, and it's good for him and for us that he's back in the fold.

It's quite a shock. I'd half-expected Dermo to come back through the door along with Rory O'Carroll when we returned from the clubs at the start of May but when he didn't I just assumed he was going to be playing in Boston again for the summer. But my initial reaction, which I say to Jim on the call is, 'Look, as you say, Dermo is one of our soldiers. If he wants back and if you feel he can do a job for the team at some point, that's fine with me.'

And that's true. Dermo is a mate and if at some point Jim feels he's the man to do a job to get us over the line, then I'll be singing and dancing with him in September, please God.

But what I can't say on a group call and I shouldn't have to spell out to Jim is: so long as I get my chance too. Last summer while Dermo was in Boston, I was slaving up that hill in Saggart, rehabbing that knee every day. Last December I put in sixteen 6.30am gym sessions hoping to get some game-time in the league only to be left sitting on the bench or sitting at home. I've waited patiently again this summer for my chance.

I thought it might have come last night against Cork. When we had our A versus B a week ago, I was left off at the start again but I came on with ten minutes to go, burned Mick Fitz to kick a point off either foot and set up another two scores for Paddy to help the Bs come back and win again. I got a text from Jayo that evening: Your effort is not going unnoticed. You are doing all you can. It's a credit to your character.

Jim then called me aside before he named the team for Cork. You're not on the bench for this one, he said, but more than likely you will be the next day; it's just that defensively with Cork's powerful running game, we don't think it's the best matchup.

Looking at the game last night though, I think I'd have thrived in an up-and-down game like that. It was man on man, the ball was being kicked in: perfect conditions for me. And physically I'm in the best nick of my life. I'd have been able to track runners, at least some of the way back, coming on as a sub and not having to do it for seventy minutes, so I don't buy that line of Jim's. Towards the end of the league I'd have felt out of my depth if I had been thrown in. But now I feel I'd be dangerous out there.

At times this summer I've felt a bit of a fraud, still being around, not playing, but I've been trying my best to live by what Gary Keegan said in Clontarf: your legacy will be your service to the team. So I've continued giving Mick Fitz feedback. Davy Byrne as well, who is just as voracious about improving and seeking feedback as Mick. I've even been talking to Jack McCaffrey, who I felt before the Leinster final had been overly-cautious this season. It's been good to see him bombing forward again, kicking two points in the Leinster final and then a cracking goal early on against Cork.

But I genuinely now feel I can contribute on the pitch. As I texted Jayo back the other night: I feel like I can add something different and positive out there. And I also said I genuienely appreciated the message – and boost of energy. Which, especially coming from an old friend like him, I do.

Our last night training before playing Roscommon, Jim comes up to me: You're travelling on Saturday evening.

BERNARD BROGAN

That night I'm talking to Flynner. It could be your last time playing for Dublin, he says, so just express yourself. Play like you love it. That's when you play your best.

And while it's no longer quite as easy as it sounds, that's what I'm going to try to do. Play Like A Kid.

If I get to play.

19

Game Time

FINALLY.

Finally I'm going to play. Finally I'm getting my chance.

It didn't happen against Roscommon, even though the lads were ahead by double figures for the whole second half. Jim and I talked about it just there in our midweek meeting in the Westin Hotel and while I wasn't exactly convinced by the reason he gave, I let it go because I got what I wanted from our discussion. He's promised me that I'll be getting 'meaningful game time' in our last Super 8s game up in Omagh against Tyrone as he rests our main men ahead of an All Ireland semi-final only six or seven days later.

Usually I reserve our summit in the Westin until the end of the year but I decided that if I didn't meet with him soon then my year was already over. The morning after the Roscommon game those of us who didn't play were doing our usual catch-up session in St Clare's and I was talking to Paul Clarke, who is the one member of management at these sessions. He's a very genuine guy and he hinted that I should maybe fight my corner a bit more while still letting my football do most of the talking.

So I asked Jim if he could meet me and he did, cancelling some work appointment to accommodate me. He seems up the walls at work at the moment. He was telling me a bit about the implications a no-deal Brexit might have for Irish and European aviation and the war-gaming that involves and it was fascinating; Jim can be personable when he feels he can. I know communicating with everyone can be a challenge for me, he said, so thanks for reaching out.

I told him that I appreciated him making the time before then reminding him of some of our previous meetings here. At the end of 2017 he promised me he'd give me game time in the following year's league and he did. This year the league didn't work out quite as planned – or promised – but after Gary Keegan's talk in Clontarf I parked all that. All that matters is now.

'Jim, the way I've been going the last while in training, I feel I now deserve a meaningful chance to actually show if I have enough to be an option for you.'

I mentioned how I felt it could have come in the Roscommon game and how I felt disappointed at not being brought on at some stage. With ten minutes to go, we were fifteen up yet when Mick Macauley then got a black card, Jim put on Davy Byrne, a defender, who had earlier been told he was being rested that day.

I apologise if you felt that way, said Jim. But you know the way I operate. I'm not into any waving to the fans. I brought Davy on because I wanted to push James McCarthy forward into midfield for a few minutes because he might play there this weekend. So that was the thinking behind it.

I let it go because he soon said the words I wanted to hear: You'll be getting meaningful game time on Sunday. It'll probably be in the second half when the energy slips, but it'll be substantial game time.

That's all I want. While to the outside world it must seem like I'm completely out of the frame, not starting for what will effectively be a second Dublin fifteen, I look at it differently. I'm auditioning to be a Finisher, not a starter. If I were to start, I'd only be either taken off at halftime or spending the second half looking over my shoulder, expecting to be subbed off any minute. So it's fine if other lads start ahead of me, including Dermo. I'm getting my chance too.

The public narrative may be that this game is a dead rubber, academic, irrelevant, with both teams already through to the All Ireland semi-finals. Apparently at some point in the match itself it'll even be dubbed the Coma in Omagh. But that kind of language isn't in my vocabulary or on my radar. This is everything to me. This is an All Ireland final to me. I've waited almost two years for this.

The night before the match, I watch Mayo-Donegal on the couch with Keadán and Donagh, then head over to my parents' house to get a full night's sleep. Mam and Dad are both in Spain so I'm on my own. I pour a glass of water and head straight to bed, sleeping in the same room I used to as a kid, dreaming of one day playing for the Dubs. I sleep like a baby too.

Next morning I head over to St Clare's and get on the bus. There's a lot of fresh faces on it today but towards the back it's all the old crew. I'm sitting with Mick second from the end, across from us are Paddy and Cormac Costello, while in the back row there's O'Gara and Dermo. The usual craic and nonsense, good energy, nice buzz.

We approach Omagh. A lot of Dubs have come up for this one. Kids wave their flags, adults clap and give the thumbs up. The sun is out and it feels like championship. An hour before throw in, the bus pulls up outside Healy Park. We walk past the cameramen trying to get snaps of Dermo on his return, then into the dressing room. Bryan Cullen says above the din, Okay, lads we'll be staying out from 3.38, so we have about thirty-five minutes to go, so take your time. We drop our bags and stroll out to check the pitch and the vibe. It's perfect. Good depth in the grass, but soft. I'm going to wear studs. We stroll up towards the end that Hill 16 on tour has taken over and pick up a blade of grass to see which way the light wind is blowing. It's going into the 'Hill' end. I say to O'Gara beside me, 'I hope we're playing against the wind in the first half so we'll have it in the second.' Which is how it will work out.

We go back in. Slip on our match jerseys. Jim reminds us of the significance of what we've just put on. We want this one. You are the men in the jersey right now so go and do your bit. We'll be getting all six substitutions in early so leave nothing in the tank. Leave it all out there.

At 3.38 on the dot we head out. We warm up by the Dubs' end. There are no nets behind the goals so every ball we kick is bouncing off someone's head in the crowd and the Hill as always finds the humour in it. The atmosphere is bubbling nicely.

I watch the first half alongside O'Gara, as we did in the league back in March, only this time we know we'll both get on. The game is tight but there are one-on-one opportunities in there when we move the ball quickly. At halftime we're up by three and again five minutes into the second half when Bryan Cullen shouts. Berno! EOG! Warm up. Ye're on.

The two of us jog down and limber up along the sideline and give each other some encouragement and pointers. Let's stay close together, let's work for each other. Get a few dunts in on our men.

There's a bond there. We've played a lot of football together. It goes back to 2010. It was against Tyrone actually that we really announced ourselves as a double act: he got that famous goal when the ball came back off the upright while I thrived playing off him. Now, all these years on, here we are again; like he joked during the dog days of this year's league, we come as a package.

We run on for Jonny Cooper and Paddy Small: Robbie McDaid

drops back to centre back, Cormac Costello moves out to the half-forward line and EOG and myself go in to the full-forward line. A nice cheer goes up from our section of the crowd and I stay in close to get some energy from our Hill. This is it. After all that waiting. It feels like my debut back against Meath in Pillar's time. I'm nervous. Excited. Bouncing off the ground. Yet calm. I know I can still play football. I just now need to prove it to Jim and everyone else.

Within seconds, Dermo gets on a ball around the 40. He has the head up and reads the play: EOG and Berno are inside, so let it in.

The ball starts to dip. I slide over and while I can't quite hold it, I break it to the ground, then dive to flick it to Cossie to put him through on goal. It's just like when I palmed those balls to Deano and Fento for their goals in that Kildare game just before the cruciate, only this time the keeper smothers it and the ball is cleared. But I'm in the game now.

There are a couple of times when I feel lads could have popped it back out to me but Philly and Paddy take on the shot themselves that trail wide. I keep moving, working, looking for the ball. I'm involved a couple of times in a move that ends with me shielding Dermo's man, giving him room to swing over a point.

Then Tyrone turn over the ball in our half, giving it straight to Dermo. Right away he picks out Eric Lowndes in midfield who quickly spots that I've ghosted out to the wing, losing my marker. I get the ball around the twenty-metre line, then cut in at a diagonal angle. I take a solo, a hop and then pull the trigger…

I'm aiming for the crossbar. I know a couple of defenders are coming across and if they do get a touch to it, well then it'll either spin in or it should still have enough power to go over the bar.

Sure enough a defender gets his fingers to it but it still goes over for a point to put us up by five.

BERNARD BROGAN

There's a brief break in play and while there is, Jim and Mickey Harte each bring on another sub. Back home Keira is watching on TV where the co-commentator Oisín McConville makes an observation. 'Marty, I know it's only a small thing, but Bernard Brogan's movement since he came on reminds me of Andy Moran. He might have lost a yard or two of pace but he still makes those incisive five-yard, ten-yard runs in there. That's something that Dublin might use later on in the season. We've talked about Diarmuid Connolly a lot before the game, but Bernard Brogan could be a player that may have a part to play in this Dublin setup. I've been impressed with him since he came on. He's looked very lively and very hungry for it.'

I keep looking for ball, I keep looking for work. When Tyrone put a couple of points together to bring it back to three points, I make a run back into our own half to take Evan Comerford's kickout, then turn to play a dink pass down the line to Peadar Ó Cofaigh Byrne. A couple of passes later and Seán Bugler from our club spots O'Gara at the back post and plays it over to him to palm home for the team goal: nine years on and EOG is still scoring goals against Tyrone.

From the kickout I dash out and spot that their number eight is being casual in possession. I blindside him and strip the ball off him to flick it to Peadar.

A few seconds later I can tell by the cheer from the crowd that we've scored a point but I can't see for myself that it was Kevin Mc. While getting in that tackle and touch, I collided head on with one of the Tyrone lads. So I'm lying flat back on the ground, clutching my face, when I suddenly jump to my feet: Christ, if I stay down here they might think I'm concussed and take me off!

Dicey and James Allen run on, grab my face, hold up some fingers for me to count. You okay? Where are we? 'I'm grand!' I tell them.

Three fingers. We're in Omagh. My bloody first game of football for Dublin in two years. Go away from me!

A few minutes later, it's over: Dublin by six points. We've topped the group which means we're out next Saturday against our old friends, Mayo.

There's a nice buzz afterwards in the dressing room. Daniel Davey's eyes meet mine and we salute. Declan Darcy comes over with a big smile: I've been waiting for that turnover from you for a long time! Great tackle. The Colonel nods and winks: Well done. Then Jayo comes over, looks me in the eye and offers a fist bump: Good job.

On the bus home I check my phone. Lots of messages. You still have it. Hopefully now you're there next week. McConville on the telly would have you there anyway.

And then there's the customary call from Dad. He might be over in Spain but certain traditions have to be maintained, especially since it's been so long. He's delighted for me. Felt I could have got a few more passes but that I did something constructive every time I did get the ball. I was involved in most of our scores from the time I came on, set up another goal chance, worked hard, forced turn-overs. A good shift all round.

A few hours later the bus pulls into St Clare's. Only instead of hopping off and heading away in our cars after a long day, we go into the Bunker where Fento, Kilkenny and all the other lads who didn't travel today are already waiting.

While we were playing Game Three of the All Ireland series above in Omagh, they were in here all day prepping for Game Four, dissecting Mayo's game in Castlebar last night as well as ours against Tyrone. Mayo might think they've had a day's extra prep on us but Jim hasn't allowed them that advantage. With him The Process never stops.

He gives a capstone of the day. Well done to all the lads who travelled today. You represented Dublin well. Now it's on to Mayo.

It was always going to be them. To do what we're trying to do this year, we were always going to have to go through them. Before last night's game, most people were fancying Donegal, but I was thinking: No, not with it in Castlebar, not when it's do-or-die. When it comes down to it, the Mayo boys have more dogs of war. They are the ultimate test of your honesty.

So everyone's clued in for the analysis: tonight's five-minute summary on them and then everything we do during the week. We forensically dissect and war-game their kickouts; if they go with Hennelly in goal they'll look to go long; if it's Clarkie, he'll prefer to go short. I'll be in a pod headed by Deano and send him on a breakdown of Chris Barrett and his A game − what he likes to do − and his B game − how you can limit and attack him.

But, for now, next Saturday can wait. Today was a victory in itself. When you sustain the kind of injury that I did, you can become obsessed with trying to get back to where you were. For the last eighteen months that's what I've strived to do: to return to something approximating that player who set up those goals against Kildare, that Jim trusted enough to start that night before I then did my cruciate in Innisfails. For a long time I thought I wouldn't. Then, these past couple of months, I thought that I could. But even then I didn't know.

Today I found out. It wasn't just talk. It wasn't just my imagination. Today I proved to myself that I could still be that player, still do that job, still cut it at this level. And that is hugely satisfying.

Now, did I prove it to Jim?

20

Fathers And Sons

MIDWEEK IN THE CITY, AND AS IT HUSTLES AND bustles with people and traffic, a handful of Dublin footballers are going about their daily routine while knowing there'll be an important call later on from Jim.

Whenever work takes me into town, I try to fit in several meetings to make the most of the time before beating the rush hour gridlock and getting back to our offices in Lucan for an hour or two. This morning I have an 8am breakfast meeting in Carluccio's on Dawson Street with Ruairi Kelleher, son of Robbie who soldiered with my dad for the Dubs. Item number one on the agenda: my old friend, Shane Lowry, who won the British Open two weeks ago. Ruairi is CEO of a company called Immedis who sponsor Shane in a deal that we in Legacy negotiated on their behalf with Shane's agent, Conor Ridge; if you look closely enough, it's their insignia on the right side of Shane's chest. With the Claret Jug now in his possession, he's the hottest property in town. So we're looking at when and how to run some corporate days where Immedis can get some of their key European clients in the same room as Shane to further activate that sponsorship.

Then it's a dash over to the IFSC and the offices of A&L Goodbody down on North Wall. In PepTalk we've identified that with the long hours and stress that's involved in the legal sector, their employees could do with the service we provide, and today's meeting with Aisling from their HR department progresses the negotiations that will lead to a partnership.

After that, it's over to Harcourt Street where my father introduces me to an agent who represents Chinese investors interested in teaming up with a client of ours in Legacy.

I'd like to think I'm fully present at these meetings from years of learning how to compartmentalise, but on my commutes a certain other pending conversation does flash across my mind.

Jim finally calls shortly after three o'clock when I'm back in the car, going along Stephen's Green, down by the Royal College of Surgeons. I let it ring out; this conversation as much as any other today demands my full attention, so I take a little slip road and pull over before calling back.

It's a good thing I've the car parked. He says I won't be travelling on Saturday.

Of course, he tries to cushion it, telling me how I've been exemplary in my application and behaviour around the group and how he has huge respect for me, and so on and so forth. But I'm not having it. I cut him off right there. Three months, six months, TWELVE months of frustration finally bubbles over and the lid comes off.

'Hold on, Jim. That's bullshit, to be honest with you. It shows you have no respect for me! I didn't put a foot wrong the last day: I got on scores, created scores, I tracked back, after waiting ages for the chance to show that I can still do it at this level.

'Why did you bother bringing me back? Why didn't you just have the stones to let me go at the start of the year? You might respect me as a man, but not as a footballer, not now. You should have just had the guts last winter to tell me that there was no place for me. I didn't come back to swan around. I came back to play.

'If you had given me a fifth, a tenth, a *hundredth* of the energy and encouragement you've given Diarmuid, I'd have taken your hand off. You're backing him. That's great, I'm all for empowering players, but if I felt someone was backing me like that, I'd feel bullet-proof. *Bulletproof!* Instead, I haven't gotten an ounce of energy from you or the management. Anything I've got has been on the back of my own resilience and the support of my teammates and some of the backroom.'

While I'm saying this, I don't know for sure if Dermo is on the twenty-six. *But I know.* Everything has been leading up to it: management asking him back in the first place, their interactions with him on the training ground, throwing him right into the first thirty for in-house games, then straight into the first fifteen up in Omagh.

I obviously have no problem with Dermo himself. He's a soldier of ours and a buddy of mine. In the offseason we often go for a round of golf together along with Flynner and Butsy. I join him for pints in his local, Harry Byrne's, just around the corner from Parnell Park. Since he's been back, we've chatted and mixed with one another as normal. And after the Mayo game, he'll be one of the first lads to check in with me, dropping me a text, asking how I am, a gesture which I'll appreciate.

But I have a serious problem with Jim. This is almost like that bleeding story from the Bible about the prodigal son. The one difference is that in that story the older brother seemed to resent his younger brother as much as he did his father for throwing such a huge fanfare for the prodigal boy. I don't resent Dermo. I'm glad he's returned to the family fold. But where I can relate to the older brother is in his disappointment with the father. ('All these years I've

279

been slaving for you and never disobeyed your orders!') I've done some slaving of my own while our brother was away; sixteen mornings in December up at 6am to train on my own or with Lally. I've done some farming, because what was it Gary Keegan said at that workshop after the league? *Farm your culture. Water your values.* And still that can't get me on the bus.

'Jim, six or seven times I've been the thirty-first man in training and gone up to the top pitch on my own. Not once have I said a bad word. I've practised away, played the few minutes you gave me, created scores, finished scores and been positive around the place.

'I had to *drag on my fingernails* just to get the chance to come off the bench against Tyrone. That wasn't my goal! My goal was to add value and play for this team. Instead I've had to sit and watch lads come off the bench and get plenty of game time and still not light it up. And now, after I finally get the chance to show that I'm fit, back to where I was, you're ringing me, saying there's no place for me on the match-day panel?!'

For a moment there's silence.

Then Jim says: I appreciate your honesty, Bernard. I appreciate any feedback. Because I do respect you. As a footballer and as a man.

But again I tell him he can leave it.

'Look, Jim, you don't need to go into any big spiel for me. I'll be at training tonight and I'll give it everything and no one will know how disappointed I am right now. So I'll see you tonight, go now and beat the Mayo boys. But just know that I'm coming for the final and I'm not letting up.'

A FEW hours later and Kevin McManamon is transporting us to a different place and time. We may all be here in our seats in St Clare's on a Thursday evening but his script, narration and use of sound effects take us to Saturday, our biggest day of the year, and the greatest coliseum in the world.

Over the years we've had various people in to work on the mindset. Caroline Currid under Pat; Anne-Marie Kennedy teaching us the benefits of yoga and meditation and the importance of the breath; Gary Keegan's intermittent but brilliant interventions to fine tune The Process. But our environment has evolved to the point now where our psychological prep is yet another aspect that can be mostly player-led and peer-coached. Kevin Mc now works full-time in the field, and Michael Darragh is also fascinated by that whole space, so between them they roll out a guided visualisation exercise with the group before we hit the field for our last training session ahead of any championship game.

Tonight it's Kevin's turn and it's obvious he's put a lot of time and thought into it. He's even managed to track down and play the sounds that'll greet the team as they dash out of that tunnel – the clinking of studs drowned out by that clarion entrance music and the roar of the crowd.

And yet as powerful as his piece is, my mind wanders. I can't stay with it. I'm right there with him at the start, when he suggests we sit back, relax and softly close our eyes, but when he begins painting the pre-match scenes at the Gibson, I tune out. Because it dawns on me: I won't be there. I won't be running out of that tunnel on Saturday. Jesus, I'm going to be at home on the couch with the kids.

But then once we go out onto the field and into our warm-up, I'm locked in, upbeat, sharp. You wouldn't know I'm not on the twenty-six. You'd nearly think that I am starting. I promised Jim earlier today: I'd get out of myself and into the team.

I call the first Three Breaths of the evening. It's something we've adopted from the All Blacks. If you look at when they score or concede a try, they form a huddle and perform a deep breathing exercise together. Stop. Breathe in. Breathe out. And repeat, then once more. It helps them reset on what they need to do next; instead of their thoughts and emotions getting caught up in how much they're ahead or behind, they can simply let them pass and focus their attention on what they need to do from the restart. And so, to help condition us for whenever we experience some turbulence in a game, or in training after we've had a couple of intense drills in succession, someone tends to take the initiative and call Three Breaths. Tonight, that's me.

Near the end of the session then we break up into small groups for ten minutes of skills work. I gravitate to Mick Fitzsimons. 'Do you want me to help you with a few high balls?' Usually I'd strike ten or twelve balls myself but I decide: That's not what the boys need now. It's not like I'll be kicking any scores at the weekend. What will happen at the weekend is Mayo will target some high balls in on top of our full back line. That is our perceived weakness. Last weekend against Donegal, Cillian O'Connor notched a goal from getting his fist to a high ball that dropped short and Mick will be picking him up for periods on Saturday.

Mick asks how I'm fixed. 'No,' I tell him, 'didn't make it.'

He shakes his head. Ah, you're joking?

I make light of it, saying something about maybe the next day, let's just make sure now there is a next day. And so Seán Bugler, another Plunkett's man who hasn't made the twenty-six despite impressing in Omagh, falls in and pings a series of balls inside for Mick to attack with me hanging off him.

It doesn't go unnoticed. As I'm coming off the pitch, I find Jim in my path. He extends his hand, and as I shake it, he looks me in the eye and nods. And though he doesn't say anything, the gesture and his whole demeanour does. It says: Respect. As a footballer and as a man. All the more so after today.

And likewise I look him straight in the eye and nod. 'Best of luck at the weekend.'

SATURDAY evening out in Castleknock and while a few miles away Croker quakes, here in the Brogan living room the television screen is paused, with the white text below the blue-circled pause symbol saying it's been that way for -3 mins. Mayo-Dublin may be the most anticipated match yet of the GAA season, something almost everyone else wants to watch in real-time and would fast-forward if they could save themselves the suspense and agony of not knowing the outcome. But, instead, I'm watching it like most television is viewed these days: on some form of delay, with the use of the Sky Plus remote.

It might seem odd, that one of the select fifty or so people who assembled in St Clare's on Thursday evening in the cause of Dublin football isn't even one of the 82,500 people in Croke Park today. But I just decided that it was too much hassle to go in on my own. I don't need my head wrecked with people spotting me, saying I should be on the match-day panel.

And more than anything, I want to be with Keadán and Donagh. I'm away from them enough as it is. And so I watch this one from the vantage point of the couch, or for considerable periods, the living room floor, playing with and feeding the pair of them.

That means sometimes pressing the pause button. While the rest of the country might be gripped by what's unfolding in Croker, my attention has to occasionally shift to giving Keadán another spoonful of pasta or pick up and comfort a crying Donagh. Colm Boyle may be slicing a point over the bar on the run with the outside of his boot, Brian Howard might be booming one over from over forty yards out, but at the very moment they're executing those acts of brilliance, I'm completely ignorant of them. They exist in the future for me. I only see them once I press play again and fast-forward a bit whenever I come across a stoppage in play. But like everyone else, I don't want to miss a minute's action of this drama.

Before that brilliant point of Howie's on the stroke of half-time, we were trailing Mayo by three points in a very tight, tactical affair. They're being smart and patient with the ball, taking a high proportion of their chances. Our forward unit has yet to click. Even Fento has had a wobble, being stripped of the ball by Aidan O'Shea. I've always felt that this one would go down to the wire, and at halftime I'm even more certain. Although the lads will go in, regroup and reset, Mayo are hardly going to voluntarily go away.

Instead they're simply blown away. Decimated. The lads come out and just steamroll them, blitzing them for 2-6 without reply in twelve minutes.

I watch on in as much awe as anyone. Fenton, Mannion, Con – they've brought this whole project of ours to a whole other stratosphere. They're bringing football to a whole other stratosphere. I know we're all about the collective and some of the team-play today is extraordinary, but those points Mannion clips over at the start of the second half simply come down to individual brilliance. Same with Fenton; another 1-1 from midfield. And then there's Con. Con O'Callaghan is just magic. A beast. Lee Keegan is as magnificent and as streetwise and as tough as any back we've ever encountered. Only last weekend he tied up Michael Murphy. And yet today Con just tosses him aside as if he were a rag doll and leaves him on his arse as if he were a novice skater.

It's actually scary. Mannion is still just twenty-six. So are Ciarán Kilkenny and Fenton. Jack McCaffrey is still just twenty-five. Con is only twenty-three.

It's their world, their team. Everyone else just lives in that world.

And yet this thirty-five-year-old at home with his kids still wants to find his place in it and break back into that team, though his time is running out.

21

Lock Hard

THEY'RE STILL AROUND, THE LOCK-HARD MEN. At least on All Ireland final day they are, when they re-emerge from hibernation and offer a reminder of Dublin in the rare auld times.

Swing it back, he says with his great big cap on his head, and his rolled-up newspaper in hand, ushering me into a spot outside the flats just past Gill's bar, around the corner from Croker.

Now, keep it coming, keep it coming. That's it. Good man.

We get out of the car and I slip him a tenner. 'Thanks very much for that, bud.'

He clocks who he's dealing with. Ah, Jaysus, it's yourself! Would they not have a spot for you in the stadium?! I'll make sure that car is looked after, now.

I love an interaction like that. It reminds me of when I used to go to games with my da, heading in to see the Dubs; finding a spot to leave the car, the bit of banter with some salt-of-the-earth lock-hard, the anticipation in the air. It's a throwback to the past, but also a taste of the future. Now I'm the one bringing the kids to a game, with Keira beside me.

I'm essentially retired as of Friday. Jim rang a few hours before training, saying I wouldn't be travelling with the team. I was in the car and nearly crashed it but this time I didn't fight it; there was no big tirade, no big drama. I'd gone well in training the past couple of weeks – but obviously not well enough to make the twenty-six.

I could tell Jim was genuinely uncomfortable breaking the news. Jayo and Declan are here with me, he said, and we have enormous respect for you. It's very difficult telling you this.

I said that I understood. I had given it everything but I respected that he was doing what he felt was right for the team.

He gave his usual line that there could be another day, that it wasn't necessarily over, and spoke about how I'm still a part of the group. At that point I was driving past Luttrellstown Golf Club and I was welling up. I didn't want to embarrass either of us in case I broke down.

'Listen, I better go here, Jim. I'll see you tonight, sure. Thanks.'

And with that phone call, I've played my last game for Dublin. I've worn the jersey for the last time.

I took a couple of deep breaths, then called Keira. 'Jim rang. I'm not in the mix for Sunday.' She offered words of support, told me that I did my best and could do no more. I got home where Keira's dad, Martin, was helping with the twins but while everyone meant well I was getting emotional and wanted to be by myself. So I grabbed my gear bag for training that night and just legged it. I headed over to Lo-Cal, a café in Castleknock, ordered a flat white and gathered my thoughts. Right, how do I go about tonight's session? How do I go about adding value?

Mick Fitz always welcomes any tips or bit of guidance you have to offer, so I made my way over to him when we were on the pitch in Clare's. 'Do you want me to help you with anything in particular?'

Yeah, great, he said. Can you do a few of those runs like Geaney?

So I started replicating some of the moves Paul Geaney, one of Kerry's key threats, tends to make. I ran at Mick along the endline, then cut back and tried to push off him to get a shot away; then we moved over to the other side and took some shots there too: Geaney is two-footed, just like David Clifford, another outrageous forward who Mick might have to spend some time marking.

Then I checked in with Con. After the Mayo game he was asking me, Have you any advice for me going into the final? You've been dominant in big games like this before. Is there anything I should know?

It shows you the humility of the man, to ask something like that having just burned a player like Lee Keegan, and has already won two All Irelands with us and another two in hurling with his club: Con knows his way around Croke Park. But he's just so open to getting better. I was looking at him earlier this year in the dressing room before one of our league games, sitting there with his notebook, jotting something down, then reading over it again for about ten minutes. I was thinking, What's he after writing in there?! I wasn't doing that when I was twenty-three!

So the week before last I went home and watched a few of his clips: from matches in Croker and training games in St Clare's. There was one recently in which I was playing alongside him and Mannion. He was being marked by Philly but three men wouldn't have been able to hold him. We only played about thirty minutes but he must have finished with 2-4 and set up another two team goals for me. Every time he got the ball he went right at goal. Unbelievable. What stood out was his work rate: the effort he made to get on the ball. Normally I'd make one run and then maybe cut back and offer a second run, but he was actually cutting back three or four times and still had the gas to take on his man. So what I said to him was, 'They're going to put lads in front of you to try to stop you because you're our main goal threat. But your work rate will get you through.'

On Friday night I just asked him had he his triggers, his cue words, when the pressure might come on. And, of course, he had. They were bang on.

I then went over to Jack. Jack is an incredible young man, the kind who always brings a smile to your face because he tends to always have one on his. I don't think I've ever met someone more authentic and more comfortable in their own skin. He's a doctor, yes, he's an incredible footballer, but he's so much more than that. He's obsessed with fantasy and sci-fi literature and unashamedly so. We met for coffee earlier in the year and I was asking him what his triggers were. And he grinned that smile of his and blurted out some line which I hadn't a clue what it meant or even what language it was in: Latin, Elvish, Ewokese? I remember thinking, whatever he just said, the Force is strong with young McCaffrey. But I asked him again: What was that you said? And I typed it out phonetically on my phone.

So on Friday I went over to him and reproduced the phone. 'So your trigger for the weekend is…. "Dove-e Andy See Too-voy-ya see-gain!" Correct?!'

And he burst out laughing. Yeah! And he repeated it again. "Dovie'andi se tovya sagain!" Apparently it's old tongue from the Robert Jordan novel, The Wheel of Time.

And it means? Time To Toss The Dice.

I love it.

The whole group was in a good headspace when I was leaving them on Friday night. Any talk of five in a row is just outside noise. Inside the bubble the only five that matters is winning All Ireland SF Series (Game) Five. We won Game One against Cork. Two against Roscommon. Three against Tyrone. Four against Mayo. Now AI

Series 5 is against Kerry. That's how we approach it. Kevin Mc mentioned a few weeks ago that the talk of the five in a row would crank up after the hurling final and that we'd just have to accept it, understand it and then let it go. He has a great way of phrasing how you should deal with an unnecessary or unhelpful thought, be it in a game or anywhere else: just put it in a balloon and then let it float away. To the lads today isn't about some pinnacle in the history of the game; it's simply about going out and winning the next game.

But now I'm outside that bubble. I'm no longer quite on their wave-length. Last night I watched *Up For The Match*, something which was a no-no in other years, just in case it brought unnecessary emotion into it and threw me a bit. But I enjoyed last night's show. Alan was on, alongside two Kerry lads, my old friend and adversary, Marc Ó Sé, and Aidan O'Mahony. At one stage when Alan was asked how many All Irelands were in our house, he smiled that it'd be fourteen after the Dubs win this one. Marc was in like a shot. So Bernard's on the panel tomorrow?!

I only wish, Marc. While there's speculation out there that I'm on the bench, I'm sadly not.

We walk up Jones's Road: me and Keira, carrying the two lads in their Dublin jerseys. I'm wearing sunglasses. They're important today: the fewer people who notice and stop me, the better. So I keep the head down and keep going, though I notice the odd double-take.

We pop over to the Jury's Croke Park Hotel for a while: Kevin Moore, our managing director in Legacy, is doing MC on a panel with Éamon Fennell and Marc Ó Sé in a room over there. Marc spots me and starts laughing. God, the lengths the Dubs are going to, sending Bernard over here, trying to hide the fact they've slipped him into the twenty-six! Do ye think we're going to fall for that?!

After listening to some of the chat and meeting some of the clients, we cross the road into Croker, up to the Littlewoods' box and watch the match.

When Jack tosses the dice and bangs in the goal, I erupt, giving the two boys such a fright, they nearly cry. Normally when I watch a Dublin game, I'm a model of restraint, either watching from the dugout or at home on the couch as I've done plenty of times the past two years: I'm still in that cold, analytical, performance space. But now I'm back to being a supporter again. A bag of emotions. Up to high doh.

I'm flitting between following the match and keeping an eye on the two lads running around like lunatics. My heart's thumping. Mick Fitz is doing well on Geaney but in the other corner Jonny is shown a second yellow card before halftime for a foul on Clifford so we're down to fourteen men. We're not providing that link in the half-forward line to get enough ball into Mannion and Con. When Killian Spillane comes on and kicks a goal for them midway through the second half, our lead is down to two. Then on sixty-seven minutes he scores a point to put them one up. Christ. We actually could lose here.

The lads keep going, keep going, but each attempt to equalise either keeps dropping short or sailing wide. Paddy Small tries a couple of shots that unfortunately don't come off. Howie, who has been magnificent, has one that just drifts past the upright. Then Dermo comes on for him. Jim is now finally running the bench, Cossie and Kevin are on as well as the board is about to signal seven minutes of added time.

At this stage I'm almost panicking. And yet, I have enough about me to make a calculation: I better stop taking swigs out of this beer here. There could be a replay. There could be a catch-up session tomorrow.

The lads keep going, keep working, keep turning over Kerry even though we're the ones a man down. Cossie comes around on the loop to get a shot off and the umpire reaches for the white flag and waves it. Yes! But no, it goes to Hawkeye. And a big red Níl flashes up on the big screen.

Dermo tries one with the outside of the boot that flashes just wide too.

But again the lads keep going and going and going. Kevin Mc dashes back to chase David Moran, and strip the ball off him to set in motion a move that finishes with Deano putting over the equaliser. Yes! Yes!

I'm on my feet. Let's go for the winner now.

And we nearly get it. Paddy Small wins a free over by the touchline with time almost up. But it's a little too tight and far out even for Deano to convert. And then the final whistle goes. Draw. Replay.

After everyone tries to get their breath, I go over and tell Keira I better make my way down to our dressing room. And so I do, just like several other lads coming from various different parts of the stadium, all in our different civvies, and a few of us with a few beers on board now trying to look completely sober and sensible before we meet Jim and the lads.

The mood in the dressing room is very even keel. I sit down beside a couple of lads who tell us a bit about what it was like out there. Then Jim comes in. We're still alive, men. Some things good there, some things bad, but we dug it out when we needed to. Well done. It's all still to play for. We'll go down now to the Gibson, have our dinner and then get out of there as quick as we can, get home to bed and we'll go back at it tomorrow.

He's right. They dug it out under desperate pressure against a Kerry team with a man advantage for over forty minutes.

And it turns out he was right as well in what he said on the phone to me on Friday. It mightn't be over for me yet.

Hold my beer. I've just come out of retirement.

22

Return Of The Gun

S OMETHING HAS TO BE DIFFERENT THIS TIME.
The previous game plan just won't cut it.

I'm not talking about Jim's game plan. I'm talking about
mine. I've decided to take a leaf again out of *Extreme Ownership* and I
need to be the change that I want to see in the world. Or at least that
I want to see in the twenty-six, maybe even on the pitch.

It's the Saturday between the drawn final and the replay and we're
in St Clare's, playing fifteen-on-fifteen. And in our full forward line
there's Eoghan O'Gara, Dean Rock and Bernard Brogan, only just
not as you've known him recently.

When we had our main internal game down in Doonbeg before
the drawn game, Dermo pinged a lovely crossfield ball to me with
the outside of his boot. I took a bounce past Butsy, shimmied the
next man and was cutting through the middle on the left-hand side
of goal when in the corner of my eye I spotted EOG making a run
to the far post.

If I'd opted to take my point it would have been one hundred
percent a white flag. If I'd chosen to pull the trigger and gone for
goal there was probably a sixty percent chance an umpire would
have been reaching for the green flag. Pass to O'Gara and the

chances of him getting a touch to it for a score were probably about fifty percent. But it might have led to a team goal, this thing that has been rammed down our throats. And it would have looked self-less. I'd have been playing another killer pass, something I've been priding myself on in this pivot man role I've carved out for myself the last couple of years.

So I took another solo and fisted it over to the back post where it took everything for O'Gara to stretch and tip it over the bar.

Running back out the field, and then trooping off it a few minutes later, I was berating myself. Why didn't I just bleedin' drill it?! That's what Con O'Callaghan would have done. He wouldn't have even thought of passing it. He'd have backed himself and simply put the head down and slammed it.

And it's dawned on me: you know who else would have just rattled it? A fella once upon a time ago called Bernard Brogan.

It really came home talking to Lally. I was going on again about how I'd been looking to add value by being that pivot man inside, making the killer pass, creating scores…. You know the rest. I've been like a broken record about it.

And Lally basically said: Well, how about changing the record? They obviously don't like that one. You thought that they would and that maybe they should but they obviously haven't. They haven't bought it anyway!

And you know what, he's right.

In work we always talk about being adaptable, reading the market-place, spotting the gaps, not being afraid to innovate and change. We did it in Legacy, shifting away from the sports marketing space and doubling down on brand, content and digital marketing. In PepTalk, our tech roadmap is grounded in our customers' feedback and users telling us what interests them, not what we think it should be.

BERNARD BROGAN

I'd like to think I've brought a similar mindset to football. After I was left off the starting fifteen for the 2016 final replay, I decided I was going to try to be more of a facilitator instead of a finisher. And though it didn't get me as much game time as I'd have liked in 2017, I doubled down on it that winter and after that opening league game against Kildare in 2018 I was all the more certain it was the way to go. That was the template, that was Plan A. If I could just get back to being that player, I'd get back to being a key man in the rotation; if not starting for us, at least being one of the first men off the bench.

Yet all year I've barely even made that bench. The market, the buyer, Jim, obviously hasn't been sufficiently interested in that kind of product.

It's time to make a change: better late than never. I'm taking off the straitjacket. I'm taking off the leash. I'm putting back on my belt and holster. I'm going back to being a gunner.

That time in Doonbeg, I doubt if any of the management said, Fair play to Bernard, it didn't quite come off but he took the right option, looking for the pass. Instead they were probably saying, He's just lost that killer instinct, hasn't he? He's not what we need against Kerry.

In the drawn game though they needed some strikers on at the end. They left five kicks behind in the closing minutes. There's a gap in the market there. So I'm going after it. And this training game in St Clare's is a chance to go grab it.

O'Gara is up for this one as well. He didn't make the twenty-six the last day either. Let's show them, Berno, he says.

First ball in, EOG is out in front, pops it to me, over the bar.

Next ball, I'm out in front of Davy Byrne and just turn and take him on and shoot straight over the bar.

The same again with the next ball.

The same again with the next.

Another time I spot Deano is through on goal if I just play it over the top and I do and he forces a great save from Clucko. The right option is still the right option. It's just that Plan A has changed now, that's all.

The three of us are moving, talking, feeding off one another. Keep it coming in! Keep moving it quick!

After twenty minutes it's blown up, but I've managed to kick four points. Deano and EOG have scored two apiece.

Cossie, who was playing at the other end of the field and is technically vying for minutes against us, comes up to us afterwards: Jaysus, youse are flying!

O'Gara's buzzing. It's been a frustrating year for him as well but today's been a good day. Bring back the twin towers! he grins. It's 2010 all over again!

And it does feel like a bit of déjà vu. Next week it's unlikely we'll be on the same field as Con, Mannion, Deano. They're the men now, the All Stars, the best that's around, a class of player that at my age I can no longer compete with. But today we belonged with them. I felt like I was the player of four or five years ago. I might not be able to reproduce that kind of performance quite as often as that fella could. But I was able to do it today.

I go home and tell Keira, 'There's actually a good possibility I'll be on the bus the next day.'

THE Tuesday before the replay, we're upstairs in Parnell Park about to go into a quick meditation exercise with Kevin Mc before playing another small match among ourselves.

The mindset is something we always go after, but it's all the more important now ahead of the replay. A couple of days ago we had a mini-camp out in Killiney Castle. Gary Keegan gave another powerful presentation to us. His key message was: Manage Your Energy. A lot of lads felt uptight in the Gibson before the last game and Jim sensed they'd unnecessarily burned up a lot of energy, so himself and Gary honed in on the concept of saving it for when it's needed.

Tonight's mindfulness session is player-led, but just before Kevin takes us through his script, Jim names the respective A and B teams that will start when we go down onto the field. Everyone is fit and available so there are going to be six lads who'll have to sit out at the start but I'll hardly have to worry about that after the way I moved with EOG and Deano the other day.

So Jim reveals the B team: Evan Comerford in goals, Philly, Rory….. Then we get to the full forward line – and there's no Eoghan O'Gara and no Bernard Brogan.

Okay, see ye down below in a few minutes, he says, then heads out the door with the rest of the management, handing the floor over to Kevin.

Alright, says Kevin, just lie back there on the floor, get yourselves nice and comfortable and softly close your eyes…

But I'm not closing my eyes. I'm not lying down. I'm sitting up, my hands behind my head, looking around completely bemused and detached, hoping to catch O'Gara's eye and see if he's also decided to feck all this for a game of soldiers: Can you bleedin' believe this, bud?! I've checked out, sorry! I'm out of here!

I could not have done more our last two nights on the pitch to show that I should be on the pitch. This is a joke. An absolute joke. If I weren't laughing to myself here, I'd be crying.

I'm watching O'Gara. In fairness, he's lying down and trying to shut his eyes. But eventually he opens them. His mind must be a million miles away from where Kevin's trying to take it.

A few minutes later we shuffle down the stairs and onto the pitch and go into our warm-up. I don't think I've ever been so distant or disengaged on a training ground in all my time with Dublin. Give me back that beer, I've just been retired again.

And then, no sooner have I it back in my hand, I've to give it back again in exchange for a bib. James McCarthy's hammer is at him a bit so he has to sit out. Bernard, says Jim, you're corner forward.

I don't know if I'm coming or going and it shows. I'm a waste of space in that game. I go home to Keira. 'You can cancel those plans we had for the weekend. I'm not going to be on that bus now.'

I DON'T sleep well that night. And I sleep even worse the following night. Because that's the eve of our last training session before the final and Jim will once again be giving me bad news.

I'm not going to be as passive this time as I was before the drawn game so I'm here tossing and turning because of all the points I want to get across to him and how I want to make them.

For one, he's not retiring me for a second time over the phone. If he calls, I'm going to let it run out and text him back after the missed call: Sorry, Jim, caught in work here. Would prefer to see you face to face this evening.

In the morning, after getting some bit of sleep, I go through it with Keira and make use of her expertise. It's all about tone, she advises. You want to be calm, cool, collected but assertive.

O'Gara's in a similar boat. After being left out for that short A-versus-B game, he texted Jim that night in keeping with his honest, no-bullshit way: I don't want your call on Thursday! If you want to meet for a chat, I'll meet ya.

So, just after I let Jim's call ring out around midday, I text O'Gara: Wanna meet up for a coffee before training this evening?

At four o'clock we meet in McMahon's, a café on Botanic Avenue in Glasnevin. EOG shakes his head. Berno, how could he not put us on the other night after how well we went at the weekend?!

He's a fantastic, genuine fella, O'Gara. He can be fiery, passionate, aggressive, sarcastic, and yet soft, thoughtful, loveable, loyal: a great big grizzly bear disguising the teddy bear within.

I have so much admiration for him. He comes from a family of ten in Terenure, as he puts it, a 'real either-eat-or-be-eaten', blue-collar environment. As a kid he was desperately shy and introverted, and really struggled with low self-esteem. When the economy crashed in 2008 he lost his job as a bricklayer. The following year he was no sooner called up to the senior squad than he was let go again; Pat Gilroy told him that he was all over the place and too lazy.

Plenty of guys would have just given up then. Instead it lit a fire under Eoghan's arse. He got back onto the panel for 2010. And he went back to college and got himself a degree.

Mick Bohan, who'd have coached both of us in DCU and then again with the Dubs in Jim's first two years, often tells the story about the Shooting Challenge he used to have us do in 2013. Back then you'd have had Dermo, me, Alan and Flynner in and around our peak. Mannion, Kilkenny, Dean and Cossie were also coming through around then. A lot of sharpshooters, a lot of blue-chip talent there vying to be the top dog in the pack. And yet the season best score in Mick's shooting challenge that year was EOG going for thirty-three out of thirty-six the last night before the All Ireland final. It was testament to the work he put in on his game and it showed in the final when he came on and kicked two points in a one-point match. That night in the Gibson, Eoghan's mother told Mick that it had been the first season she had been able to go to games without hearing some of the crowd abusing her son's skill level.

I always knew and appreciated though what we had in Eoghan back in 2010: a fearless battering ram with a nose for goal and someone who had a great understanding with me of each other's movement. Even now any time he's called on he'll do the business for Dublin. In his one and only start last year he scored 2-2 against Roscommon. In his only cameo this year he got that goal up in Omagh. And yet, like me, it wasn't even enough to get on the twenty-six the last day against Kerry.

I suppose we've been fighting for the same spot on the matchday panel. Earlier in the year he'd have been ahead of me; now maybe I've crept a little ahead of him. But yet while it would mean one less body in the way of me making the team bus, I'd hate if he had left. A few times this year I've had to talk him down from the ledge. And in fairness, he's stuck with it and hung on and never shown his disappointment to the group. He's always attacked the next session. It can't have been easy. He has the biggest commute of anyone on the panel. He now lives in Wexford where Elaine is from and they're building a house for themselves and their two kids. He has a lot on. We don't say it here, but we both know this will be our last training session together with Dublin.

So we talk about our plans then for Saturday. I'm going to get him and his family up to our Littlewoods box, we'll watch the game there, have a few pints, make a good day of it.

We rise from our table, settle the bill, then head to our cars and on to St Clare's.

I drop my bag in the dressing room, then knock on the door of Jim's office. I'll just be another minute here, Bernard, Jim says. He's talking to James McCarthy, who is going to midfield on Saturday.

My heart is thumping. Right, stay cool, calm, composed. Be assertive. I rehearse in my head the points I'm going to make. Then Jim pops the head out. Okay, Bernard. Declan Darcy is here as well. We all sit down. Jim begins. Talks about the massive respect he has for me, what a great leader I've been around the group, how he's seen me talking to and helping a lot of lads. That I've really stepped it up the last few weeks in training…

I'm just waiting for the BUT. I'm nodding along but I'm only half-listening because I've heard it all before and I'm just waiting for that word: BUT.

But there is no BUT. It's an AND instead.

…And so, says Jim, you're travelling on Saturday.

I nearly fall off the chair. 'What?!'

You're on the bus for the weekend, Jim repeats. You're on the match-day panel.

I lean back in my chair, resting my head in my hands, and exhale. 'God, I wasn't expecting that, to be honest!' There goes that speech I'd prepared!

'Thank you. I appreciate you giving me my shot. I said at the start of the year to you that there would be a war coming and that if you needed me, I'm there if you want me. So if you need me, I'll be ready.'

Then Declan says something that will stay with me forever. He doesn't really talk a lot, Declan, but when he does, everyone listens because of the respect he commands within the group. And he says: In all my years involved with Dublin, you're probably the best player I've ever seen run onto that field. And I'm so delighted that you'll be running out onto Croke Park next Saturday.

Wow. So Declan Darcy does do sentiment after all.

And it leaves me speechless. Humbled. Moved.

I bite my lip, rise from my chair, and nod. 'Thank you very much.' Then I shake both of their hands and close the door behind me.

And outside, what's the first thing that crosses my mind?

Eoghan O'Gara.

There we were, making plans to watch the game together, and now we won't. The two of us have hardly squeezed onto the bus. And I feel awful for him.

I look over in the corner of the dressing room and there he is. He spots me. Walks over. Well, what's the story?

'I'm in,' I say, shaking my head.

And he can see that I'm conflicted about it. 'God, bud…'

Will you stop! he says, hitting me on the shoulder. I'm delighted for you! At least one of us is there!

Eoghan O'Gara. What a teammate. What a friend. What a man.

A few hours later I'm back in the car and ring Keira. 'We're going to have to change our plans again for Saturday…'

TODAY there won't be need for any lock-hard going into Croker.

With it being a Saturday evening replay, Shep swings over to the house at around 1pm on his way to collecting Paddy Andrews and bringing us into the Gibson, but of course there still has to be some bit of drama. Don't I bloody well fail to close the boot properly and next thing we spot that my gear bag is in the middle of the road fifty yards back! All the kids on the estate are out in their Dublin jerseys, gawking at me jumping out of the car and racing back to get my stuff. 'Don't worry, guys,' I smile, 'everything's under control!' Then, at the second time of asking, I slam the door shut. A bit like what we're hoping to do with Kerry today.

At the hotel there's the usual good vibes and banter.

Mannion and Kevin Mc slag me when we're sitting down for our pre-match meal: Hi, Bernard, welcome to the Gibson, this is where we meet before games!

After the food, I go up to Dicey to get strapped and get the legs loosened by our match-day masseur, Paul. James McCarthy is on the table across from me, getting a rubdown, oil for the Machine. He nods: Good to see you here.

Well, Maccer, you told me twelve months ago to come with you on the journey. So here I am.

I know what I'm here for; I know what my role is tonight, though no one else, including Jim, has spoken to me about it. I've war-gamed this over and over and the only scenario where I'll be called upon is with five minutes to go and it's level or we're a point or two behind. Then Jim will bring me on. I'm the insurance policy, the break-glass-in-case-of-emergency option, the sniper. One shot. Maybe a second, that's it. That's all I have, that's what I'm here for, that's what I've visualised. Coming around on the loop from the corner forward spot. Head down. Pure strike. Not looking up until the ball is gone from my foot. Follow through. Ball sailing between the posts. A roar rises. Target hit.

We continue to go about our routine. Foam rolls. Table tennis. Stretch bands. Headphones. Outside the bubble the rest of the world might be fixated on whether or not we will pull off an immortal and unprecedented Five In A Row, but here in the Gibson, The Process just goes on as normal, as if it were a league game in February.

Then we get the word: okay, lads, Jim wants ye in now for the team meeting. And again we stick to the usual routine. Lads standing up and walking through the kickouts, for and against.

We've done a pile of work on them over the last couple of weeks, just as we do for every game. War-gaming. Posing questions and coming up with solutions. Jim, Declan, Jayo are all excellent coaches but they've the humility and the cop-on to hand some of the coaching over to the players. Especially when it comes to kickouts. Clucko is as much a coach as he is a goalie when we're working on them. If this were American football, he'd be our kickout special teams co-ordinator.

Shortly after that walkthrough and some final words from Jayo and Jim, it's onto the bus. Four Garda bikes are waiting and as they lead us out and their sirens start to wail, the sound of beeping cars stopped in the traffic begins as well. Random passersby stop and stare at the bus in their midst.

We drive round by Fairview, coming onto the Coast Road. In the park, kids point and wave and adults clap and cheer. Outside Gaffney's at the corner, there are hundreds of punters outside, waiting for us, and as usual, they raise their glasses and give us a big cheer: C'mon The Dubs!

All the time Croker is looming closer, larger. Inside the bus the mood is deliberately casual. When you treat games in March like they were September, you come to treat games in September as if it's March. And yet there is a simmering buzz that can only come from championship, do or die. The gun is loaded. All our soldiers are here. Managing our energy right now but ready for war.

We come onto the Clonliffe Road. Nearly there now. As we squeeze through the narrow terraced lane, some young fellas bang the side of the bus. Security guards then usher us through the stadium gates on the Cusack side and the bus snakes its way through the bowels of the stadium to right outside our dressing room door.

Inside, our jerseys are on their hangers, waiting for us. And this year there's no drama looking for a No.27 and stressing out Davy Boylan. There is no sense of being an impostor. For the first time in a long time I feel I'm exactly where I should be. Here in Croker on the big day. Here on merit. Here to do a job.

Then out we go. I jog slowly from the corridor to the tunnel, No.18

on my back, but once we turn the corner, I dash out into the light and onto the grass, the roar from the crowd again sending a current of electricity right through me. As we turn and run away after the team picture, I clip a ball towards a Hill in full voice and have never felt more alive.

Back when I was starting in All Ireland finals, I actually liked to miss a few shots in the warm-up. It wasn't like I deliberately missed any but if they happened not to go over, I'd say to myself, Well, that's almost my quota of missed shots for today, that's the crap out of the system! But tonight, I'm nailing nearly everything. Off my left, off my right, shots on the run and even a few frees, if something were to happen to Deano. The sniper's eye is in.

So is Con's. Kilkenny's. Mannion's. The three of them were quiet by their standards the first day but this evening they've each kicked a point inside the opening three minutes. By fifteen minutes it's two each. We're getting them much more involved, much more on the ball. The same with Scully. A big thing we've talked about over the last two weeks is having more link options; basically to move the ball quicker and get it up to someone in the half-forward line who can then feed it inside before Kerry can get back to set up their engagement line and force us to go sideways. Midway through the half, we're four up, playing brilliant football.

But Kerry will not go away. They're kicking some amazing scores themselves and by halftime it's level again, ten points apiece. And while as a player you don't think in these terms, especially in real-time, it's probably as perfect a half of Gaelic football as there's ever been. We've yet to kick a wide. All our scores have been from play. All but two of theirs have been as well.

I'm a bit anxious going down the tunnel. God, we're in a game here, we need to step up. But we'll reset now, manage our energy and work it out. And so, while the lads who've been playing refuel and cool down, those of us who haven't get the blood up in the green-carpeted warm-up area, passing by foot and hand to one another. Then we come back into the dressing room and join our respective conclaves. In the forwards, I try to radiate some positivity instead of that anxiety I had a few minutes ago. Tell Kilkenny he's flying it, keep looking for it. We talk about getting back to linking the play better. 'Once we get it inside the 45, we'll do damage. They can't keep up with us. We just need to get it up there quicker. We need to work together to get the ball to the link zone and then move it forward.'

There's also one change at halftime. Jack has pulled a hamstring so Dermo is in for him. But Jack – or at least his spirit – will still be out there for that second half. A play is mentioned that we usually try to run for Jack straight off the throw-in. We're going to try run it for Murch now. Just in case something comes from it. Toss the dice, as the man once said. Or as Jack himself would say, "Dovie'andi se tovya sagain!"

And amazingly it does come off. Kerry's David Moran 'wins' the throw-in, but only to knock it down to Murch. And then the lads create the space for him to run through the centre. And run. And run. And then goal. It's his first-ever for Dublin in competitive football but it's been seen a couple of times before in St Clare's.

We keep the lead. Occasionally Kerry narrow it, then several times our lads stretch it. With three minutes of normal time left, Jim brings on Kevin Mc and with his first possession he sets up Dean who curls it over to put us up by five. The Hill can feel that history is in the air and strikes up a chant. The whole stadium can sense it. We're into injury-time now. A bit of me is thinking Jim might bring me in now. A nod to an old servant on his last day in the jersey. But no, he wants to make a change around the middle so it's Mick that comes on for Howie. It'll take a blood sub for me or someone else to come on now.

It would have been nice to have got on there. I don't think anyone would have held it against me if I had, but I'm not surprised. And I'm not going to complain or argue. Jim is about to lead his county to a fifth All Ireland in a row. Something no one in the history of the GAA has ever done before.

So I'm going to soak up this moment. Bask in it. I gesture to Paddy Andrews beside me. 'Will we go down for one last run? There might be a blood sub yet!'

We head down. The floodlights are now on, the pitch is gleaming and the Hill is now chanting that old, familiar refrain: 'COME… ON…YOU…BOYS IN BLUE, COME ON YOU BOYS IN BLUE…!' I used to sing it myself when I stood there and now while I stretch a bit of me is singing it to myself again.

It's a glorious sound, and a glorious sight too: the flags and banners, the hand-claps in unison, the ocean of blue.

I make one last dash down the sideline in front of the Hogan and can hear the shouts above the din of the Hill. Good man yourself, Berno! Thanks for everything, Bernard! Ah, you're coming on!

And moments later I am on the pitch. Only the final whistle has sounded and I'm going around congratulating and embracing the men who got us over the line and made Irish sporting history. We're joined by other lads who ran earlier legs in the relay – like Butsy, who unfortunately picked up an injury last week, and Bugsy and O'Gara who've all made their way down.

I seek out and find Keira and the two lads, second row from the front towards the Hill end. Keira and I hug and then I take the twins back down towards the group.

We go up the steps. Clucko first. Then the rest of us. I head up with Butsy and we each take one of my young fellas and an ear of Sam and raise it up together.

We go round on a lap of honour at our own pace. I'm lagging happily behind the group as the twins explore the pitch and play with the fallen confetti. Jim meets me halfway round, clasps and shakes my hand with a smile, then crouches down: Hello, Keadán! Hello, Donagh! We get a pic taken together. And then he offers to keep an eye on the lads to let me catch up with the lads. And I tell him I'll gratefully accept: if he could just give me thirty seconds to go over and say goodbye and thanks to an old friend.

I remember the first time I looked up on Hill 16 from pitchside. I was ten or eleven, playing for Scoil Thomáis in a Cumann na mBunscol final alongside Ross McConnell. When we won the semi-final out in Artane we did a big pile-on, the Klinsmann slide was in fashion at the time, and then we all launched into a sing-song: We're On Our Way to Croker! The whole school went along to see us there in our huge red jerseys that were hanging off us and our old cardboard O'Neill's white shorts. Darndale ended up hammering us but we got over it quickly enough. We all had pizza back at the school – and we'd played in Croker! We'd gone up the steps of the Hogan to collect our runners-up medals. When we came back down, I high-clapped all 'our fans', imaginary and real, just as I'd seen my sporting heroes do on TV, all the way until I was going down the tunnel back to our dressing room. And then I copped: Wait, all the rest of the lads are still out there! Can I go back out now?! Will I look an eejit if I do after already saluting the fans?

I turned around, went back out, and saw all the lads talking with family and friends in the stand, getting photos, just soaking it all up. So I did the same, and then decided to go one better. I turned towards the Hill. Of course it was completely empty, but still, I couldn't resist. In my head it was packed. So I saluted the concrete terracing with another round of high-claps.

Now, twenty-five years later, that boy goes back up to the Hill again. Only this time it's packed and his county has just won five All Irelands in a row to bring his tally to seven in all. He's scored goals in front of it, like the time he got his first, back in the Leinster final of 2007 and was so overcome by the shockwaves it sent through his body, he bloody collapsed! Some of his toughest days were played out right in front of it. Tyrone in the poxy rain. Kerry making startled earwigs of him and his buddies. The Miss in 2012. But all the time it was there. And there was nowhere else he ever wanted to be.

So he races up to it to get one more blast of electricity from it and waves to acknowledge his gratitude. The Hill responds in style and it's a wonderful shared moment between us.

And then as it starts chanting BERN-O! BERN-O!, that Boy In Blue high-claps it once more before eventually heading down the tunnel with his twin sons, only this time never to return.

23

After The Ball

A MONTH LATER AND ON A DULL OCTOBER morning I'm going along Westmoreland Street, on my way to a familiar location.

I'm meeting with Jim and though I know he's not a romantic, I am, so I've chosen our usual place, the Westin Hotel, to tell him that I'm hanging them up, I'm handing back in the gun and badge.

I've sought the counsel of a number of people I really trust the last few days about how to go about this. Kiera, obviously. Flynner. O'Gara, who'll be having a similar conversation with Jim the following week. Alan Clancy, who I own a few bars with, Brogan's in Kilkenny and Lilly's in Portlaoise. And Dad.

It hurt Dad for some time how he finished up with Dublin. After he was hospitalised playing against Kildare, the only time he ever heard from either the management or the county board again was when the latter rang asking for his jersey back. He bumped into Donal Colfer, one of the selectors, one day and said, Will ye just tell me I've been bloody dropped?! Just have the balls to ring me and say, Look, we don't want you back, we're happy with what we have now, thanks very much for your time.

He never got to broach it with Heffo and he sometimes wishes he had. In time that wound would heal and he'd get along fine with all the management when they'd invariably meet each other at matches and on the reunion circuit, but he doesn't want me to feel like he did for those few years. Don't let it linger, he's advised me. Say what you've to say so ye can look each other in the eye and shake hands and move on.

Alan Clancy said much the same. Be grateful. Ye've had an amazing journey together. Just because the last twelve months of it was rocky at times, don't let it sully in any way the whole seven years. Flynner said it will all fade and be forgotten who played in which final: all that will matter is what we achieved together and the relationships we have with one another. Keira reinforced the message. Be honest but be tactful and grateful.

I get there before Jim does but he still arrives early. He apologises for not being able to meet last week – he was in Brussels for more discussions about the ramifications of Brexit for European aviation – but I soon get to the point of why I wanted to meet up. I'm handing in the gun and the badge.

He's not exactly shocked but he talks me through it anyway.

Okay, he says. Why do you feel like that?

'It's just time. I got back to a level I'm proud of but I've always said when there are enough people around who can do it better than me, it's time to go. I've had a great run. Fifteen summers. I just wanted as a courtesy to tell you first and to thank you for all you've done for me and Dublin football over the past seven years. For almost all of that you backed me and allowed me to live my dream for so long.'

Well, he says, I'm sorry to hear that you're handing in that gun but it's one that's been well used. You've had a magnificent career. And I want to thank you. When I came in you were one of the senior players. I've seen it before from my own playing days that the transition from one manager to another isn't always smooth but you made it easier for me. You bought into my philosophy and really helped things settle for me. And to score 2-3 then in the final to get us over the line: whenever I think of Bernard Brogan, what you did for me in 2013 will stay with me and I'll be eternally grateful to you for that.

I'm honest and I tell him that I'd love if he had brought me on in the final, but I proved to myself that I could get back to the highest level at thirty-five and after a cruciate injury and that I was proud of that. I was there to call on if he needed me. That was enough for me. I learned more about myself in 2019 – and 2018 – than I did when I was one of the first names on his sheet; that getting onto the bus for the replay meant more than playing in some All Irelands after how challenging the past year or two had been.

Well, he said, we had no choice but to bring you on the bus after how you played the Saturday before the replay. I'd love to have seen that six weeks earlier: that's what we were looking for and waiting for. You know we don't bring people along on the bus for the ride but you were there that day on merit and I was delighted to see you earn your way back onto the match-day panel. And just seeing you in the circle in the Gibson that afternoon, it gave confidence to the group. The leadership you showed all year was immense.

I give him some more honest feedback, about how I felt through the year and how it might help his management going forward, assuming he's staying on. Let players know where they stand, let them know what they need to work on to move up the grid. And I tell him he needs to get back to empowering the bench a bit more. Bring them in earlier. We slipped a bit on that in 2019.

Of course, much of this will prove to be academic. Six weeks later Jim will hand in his own badge and gun. I have no idea talking to him here in the Westin that he might be leaning that way. But he accepts my points are valid. This season was a squeeze, he admits, with the year that was in it. He just had to throw everything at it. He didn't want to be looking back saying we should have done this and we should have done that.

After a while, he asks about work. He's genuinely interested – and often proud – in how lads are developing their careers. I often say to friends that Pat triggered me to found Legacy and that Jim's emphasis on the holistic person helped inspire me to found PepTalk. And he says to me, how you've established and expanded your own businesses at your age is a credit to you.

As I finish my club sandwich and he's on his last bite of his croque monsieur, I gesture to the waiter for the bill please. 'This one is on me,' I say to him. 'You always get it!' But Jim insists: no, of all days he has to get this one.

We rise to our feet, talk about the team holiday to Bali on the way out, and then outside the door, we face each other. I look him in the eye. 'Thanks a million for everything. I appreciate everything.'

No he says, shaking my hand. Thank you, Bernard.

And then after sharing so much of a journey together, we go our separate ways, him back to the aviation authority office and me towards the car park on Fleet Street.

I'M at peace with my decision. For one, while football has been a way for me to express myself, it is not how I define myself. Besides, I still have football. I can still play the game because I still have the club.

One of my favourite days of the whole year was a sunny evening in July when Plunkett's played Brigid's just down the road in a league game. Only a few weeks earlier we were pointless and obviously in real danger of losing our Division One status so we had to scramble for bodies anywhere we could find them. Alan hadn't played or trained with us since the previous year's championship but we persuaded him to give us a dig out. I put out an SOS to our brother Paulie as well. He'd been happy out playing with the intermediates where the pace wasn't as taxing on his knees which have suffered numerous cruciate injuries but I begged him in a text: Come on, there's twenty minutes in you!

So Paulie was there in the dressing room, applying some tiger balm on those battered knees. Our cousin Darragh, who'd fancy himself as the most stylish man in the dressing room now that Paul Galvin has left the building, was beside him, unable to open his eyes from the burning smell. And of course everyone was cackling at Darragh's discomfort, especially the alpha of our pack, Gareth 'Nesty' Smith.

Before I broke onto Dublin teams, Nesty was someone I looked up to, studying in particular his kicking action. But he's even more of a hero to me now. He's Alan's age, two years older than me, yet he's at every training session; lads reckon it must be fifteen years since he last missed one. Deep down he probably knows that our window to win a championship has probably closed, but still he plugs away. Obviously, he just loves it but the club loves him just as much back. He is Mr Plunkett's.

That particular night Brigid's would reel off seven straight points after halftime to go five ahead. But then Paulie came on, looking like the tank he is from all the body-building he's been doing, and juggernauted a fella to win a free for Nesty to point. Then Alan bombed one over from forty yards out. I got going. Everyone did. We ended up winning by three.

As we were walking off, Mam called us over to get a picture: God knows the next time we'll see the three of ye on the same pitch again, she said. And it became a photo of all the family. Mam and Dad were there. So too five or six of our uncles. And that night really gave me some perspective on it all. It was around the time I was frustrated with Dublin, not getting on matchday panels, sometimes not even starting for the B team in St Clare's. But the club sustained me by reminding me how much it's still about simply playing the game that you love. Playing Like A Kid. All the clichés are true. Club is family. You start with the club and you end with the club. The club will always be there for you.

ONLY weeks after I hand in the gun and badge to Jim, I get to experience some pretty cool and prestigious gigs in my work in the corporate space. At the Web Summit in Lisbon it is my pleasure and honour to introduce to the stage a few superstars of world soccer: the original Ronaldo, Ronaldinho and my childhood idol, Eric Cantona. I also give a talk on high performance, culture and entrepreneurship based on my experiences with PepTalk, Legacy and the Dubs.

Then a few months later grim reality hits us with a bang. It will stress-test to the max whether all that talk about high performance and culture and entrepreneurship has just been corporate waffle: Covid-19.

If you're not adaptable, if your culture and values have not been farmed and watered, then the pandemic will emotionally hijack you and devastate your business.

In sport it's much easier to have a collective purpose than it is in business. You want to go the extra mile to win something, to bail out your teammates, to represent where you're from. Covid-19 will be a lightbulb moment as to why we do what we do. Are we really a team? Do we really practise and value humility? Do we really practise Extreme Ownership? In Legacy that's what we'll strive to do. Our staff have to take a bit of a cut in salary, but only four percent, while we in management will take a fifteen percent hit.

A bit like Dublin became a different team after the startled earwigs episode or after Donegal ambushed us in 2014, Legacy becomes a different company, a new type of agency. 2030 arrives in 2020. The way people purchase products is fast-forwarded ten years. People become increasingly more accustomed to using the net to help survive the pandemic and they're not going to revert to how things once were. So in Legacy we recognise that. Traditionally when you worked in marketing or PR it was about using age-old strategy and making the brand famous. We would build brilliant campaigns centered in creativity and media coverage and hope it resulted in sales. Truthfully, like many marketeers, we often wouldn't be sure. With the world speeding into a new digital age we now have the ability to really measure this final piece of the puzzle which is so powerful and really exciting. Legacy will work on closing the circle between brand fame and sales. We are already at the top of our game when it comes to creating brand fame and are now focused on enhancing that while also growing businesses through SEO (Search Engine Optimisation) and digital growth marketing. By marrying what we know with what we know is coming we are giving brands a competitive edge.

Meanwhile, PepTalk will actually be more in demand as the importance of digital well-being and the changing nature of the workplace hits home for employers.

We'll raise substantial venture capital to allow for international expansion and to capitalise on the movement towards a digital employee experience to help get the best out of staff wherever they may be located.

As I've learned from people like Pat Gilroy, Jim Gavin and Pillar, a crisis can actually be an opportunity to change and get better.

The lessons of the Bunker will stay with me for life.

THIS is the toughest part.

A few days after my last meeting with Jim, and a few hours before issuing the press release announcing my retirement, I've to send a message to the players' WhatsApp group and then immediately opt out: Bernard Brogan left.

I'm actually in the UK on business with PepTalk, in a Crossways service station, when I press the send button, a little video message that I'd prepared earlier.

And then, after inhaling a deep breath, I opt out.

Within minutes the phone is buzzing with messages. And it continues like that for hours and days, lads having wanted a bit of time to process what they've to say.

Some don't even try. Kevin Mc, as deep and as sincere as ever: I'll do my talking when I see you. It's not for WhatsApp.

But those who do manage to nail it.

Mannion's is the first one: Man, I'm gonna miss ya! Been a dream come true to play with ya after growing up watching ya for so long. What an epic career. Holy moly. Legend forever. I love ya. Blue Heart emoji.

Then there's one from a fellow old-timer. Dermo's one makes me bite the lip. As he alludes to, we both got our first starts in the team way back in 2007 yet, as he says: Only seems like yesterday – two young pups battling it out for the jersey. Who'd have thought we'd go from the bare-foot runs in St David's to Seven of the best. Was so lucky to be your teammate. True gent. Love ya. DC.

Cian O'Sullivan's is characteristically thoughtful. In ways Cian is the opposite of me: while I've tended to breeze over the homework piece and opposition analysis, Cian is very analytical. This season he'd have made numerous presentations to the group and it became a bit of a running joke: Only ten minutes now, Cian, and we're out of here! But Cian, with that calm, measured speaking way of his could sometimes push the half-hour mark!

As always, his message is eloquent and considered: It was an absolute privilege playing alongside you the past eleven years, man. You were capable of doing things no other player could and it always gave me great confidence taking to the pitch with you. You probably don't remember but back in 2011 you gave me a few words of encouragement before the Tyrone game and I couldn't begin to tell you the lift and encouragement that it gave me. What you've done off the pitch is just as equally impressive and it makes me very proud to see the strides you're taking in the business world. Next chapter beckons. Please God we'll enjoy a few pints along the way.

That we will, Cian.

Someone else who left the group also makes contact – Paul Flynn. It's one of the most powerful messages I'll get.

PF: I don't know if you're aware of the impact you've had on people, including me, to start reaching higher. And that wasn't just on the field but off it. You were the catalyst, for how you approached it and being ballsy and going for it and leveraging your career on the pitch into your career off it. If you look around that Dublin dressing room, they're all doing that now. And that's as big a legacy as something like those two goals in that All Ireland in 2013. I know I've changed my career because of you and I'd say there are many other people in that dressing room that have done the same.

I'll treasure that, just as I will a message from Ciarán Kilkenny. On the Drive for Five, he has been the conductor, the fulcrum, the constant of our attack. Over the last few years I maybe haven't been on the field with him as much as I'd have liked but what he says about that period in my career makes it all worthwhile that I stayed on.

CK: You have inspired me with your words and actions through the years, but I've especially admired you over the last two or three for how driven you were to get back and into the shape you are now – and how you inspired and motivated us as a group with your attitude, honesty and insight. The biggest thing of all is how genuine and much of a gentleman you are. You will go down as the greatest and most influential Dublin forward of all time.

Don't know about that, Ciarán. But thank you. Especially the bit you mentioned about influence and legacy.

That's what I wanted. Back when Pat was trying to break us to make us and mould us, we had that session with Caroline Currid and I said that I'd love to be part of a team that had the bond and the legacy that my father's team had. We didn't quite have it back then at that stage on the journey but we have it now.

We'll have it forever.